# 2013 SUPPLEMENT

## HART AND WECHSLER'S

# THE FEDERAL COURTS
## AND
# THE FEDERAL SYSTEM

### SIXTH EDITION

*by*

**RICHARD H. FALLON, JR.**

Ralph S. Tyler, Jr. Professor of Constitutional Law
Harvard Law School

**JOHN F. MANNING**

Bruce Bromley Professor of Law
Harvard Law School

**DANIEL J. MELTZER**

Story Professor of Law
Harvard Law School

**DAVID L. SHAPIRO**

William Nelson Cromwell Professor of Law, Emeritus
Harvard Law School

FOUNDATION PRESS

© 2010, 2011, 2012 By THOMSON REUTERS/FOUNDATION PRESS
© 2013 LEG, Inc. d/b/a West Academic Publishing

      610 Opperman Drive

      St. Paul, MN 55123

      1–800–313–9378

Printed in the United States of America

**ISBN** 978–1–60930–320–4

Mat #41405742

# PREFACE

This cumulative supplement includes discussion of important decision-al law, legislation, and secondary literature that postdate publication of the Sixth Edition in 2009.

Following are summaries of decisions rendered since publication of the 2012 supplement that are of particular interest:

- In Windsor v. United States, the Supreme Court held that the United States may appeal from a judgment holding a federal statute unconstitutional, even if the Executive Branch agrees with the constitutional determination, as long as the Executive Branch continues to enforce the law against the plaintiff and the appellate courts are assured that there will be adversary presentation of the issues (Chapter II).

- In Hollingsworth v. Perry, the Supreme Court ruled that the sponsor of a state ballot initiative lacks standing to defend the constitutional-ity of the initiative, even if the state executive declines to defend the initiative and even if state law authorizes the sponsor to do so instead, if the sponsor is not an "agent" of the state (Chapter II).

- In Clapper v. Amnesty International USA, the Supreme Court concluded that various lawyers, journalists, and advocacy organizations who work with individuals abroad lacked standing to challenge surveillance activities under the Foreign Intelligence Surveillance Act of 1978 because the probability of their own surveillance was too speculative to give rise to injury in fact (Chapter II).

- In Kiobel v. Royal Dutch Petroleum Co., the Supreme Court, after invoking the canon of construction that statutes have no extraterritorial application unless circumstances indicate a contrary legislative intent, determined that the Alien Tort Statute does not apply to conduct occurring abroad (Chapter VII).

- In Gunn v. Minton, the Supreme Court, applying the Grable decision to a state law case alleging legal malpractice in federal court patent litigation, unanimously rejected the argument that the case arose under federal law because the state law claim depended upon an issue of federal patent law and claims arising under the patent laws fall within the exclusive jurisdiction of the federal courts (Chapter VIII).

As in the past, material in footnotes is intended primarily for scholars and researchers, and our expectation, which we announce to our classes, is that students need not read the footnotes in the editorial Notes unless specifically assigned. (We do caution students that they are expected to read the selected footnotes included in principal cases.)

Various of us have had involvement of one sort or another in matters that relate to material in this supplement. Beginning in 2011–12, those of us who are active members of the Harvard Law School faculty have detailed the matters whose reporting is required under Harvard Law School's conflict of interest policy on a website linked to the faculty member's individual web pages on the Harvard Law School website.

We are grateful to Amanda Frye, Charlie Griffin, Sam Harbourt, Jason Neal, Matthew Rowen, and Rachel Siegel for their able research assistance. We thank our faculty assistants Carol Bateson, Peggie Flynn, and Kimberly O'Hagan for their valuable help in bringing this manuscript to completion.

RHF
JFM
DJM
DLS

July 2013

# TABLE OF CONTENTS

# TABLE OF CASES

# 2013 SUPPLEMENT

### HART AND WECHSLER'S

# THE FEDERAL COURTS
## AND
# THE FEDERAL SYSTEM

# CHAPTER I

# THE DEVELOPMENT AND STRUCTURE OF THE FEDERAL JUDICIAL SYSTEM

**Page 20.  Add at the beginning of footnote 119:**

For a comprehensive and illuminating examination of the ratification debates, see Pauline Maier, Ratification: The People Debate The Constitution, 1787–1788 (2010).

**Page 35.  Add to footnote 106:**

For commentary on a variety of issues involving the Federal Circuit and its performance, see *Symposium: The Federal Circuit as an Institution*, 43 Loy.L.A.L.Rev. 749 (2010). Gugliuzza, *Rethinking Federal Circuit Jurisdiction*, 100 Geo.L.J. 1437 (2012), maintains that the narrowness of the Federal Circuit's non-patent jurisdiction adversely affects both its development of patent law and its performance in non-patent-law cases and calls for a major reshaping of the court's non-patent jurisdiction.

**Page 44.  Add to footnote 170:**

For a study of the case management systems through which different circuits determine which cases will receive oral argument, which dispositions will initially be drafted by staff attorneys rather than judges, and which opinions will be unpublished, see Levy, *The Mechanics of Federal Appeals: Uniformity and Case Management in the Circuit Courts*, 61 Duke L.J. 315 (2011). The author, who finds a nearly pervasive lack of formal transparency, reports on the basis of extensive interviews that considerable variation exists among the circuits. For example, of the five circuits surveyed, one (D.C.) holds oral hearings in more than 44% of cases terminated on the merits, compared with 13% in the Fourth.

**Page 47.  Add to footnote 182:**

*Cf.* George & Guthrie, *"The Threes": Re–Imagining Supreme Court Decisionmaking*, 61 Vand.L.Rev. 1825 (2008) (advocating statutory reform to allow the Supreme Court to sit in panels of three (with or without *en banc* review) and thereby expand the number of cases that the Court can hear).

# CHAPTER II

# THE NATURE OF THE FEDERAL JUDICIAL FUNCTION: CASES AND CONTROVERSIES

## SECTION 1. INTRODUCTION AND HISTORICAL CONTEXT

**Page 56. Add a new footnote 6a at the end of the second paragraph of Paragraph (3):**

**6a.** For a consequentialist analysis of declaratory judgment actions, see Bray, *Preventive Adjudication*, 77 U.Chi.L.Rev. 1275 (2010), which contends that such actions are appropriate when the administrative and error costs of anticipatory litigation are outweighed by the benefits of legal clarification, as he concludes is true in cases involving legal status (such as citizenship) and clouds on title. Is this use of cost-benefit analysis judicially manageable? Is it consistent with the text and history of the Declaratory Judgment Act?

**Page 71. Add a new footnote 9a at the end of the penultimate sentence of the second paragraph:**

**9a.** For a sweeping historical account of both the Court's role as a catalyst of political debate and the influence of public opinion on the development of constitutional doctrine, see Friedman, The Will of the People: How Public Opinion Has Influenced the Supreme Court and Shaped the Meaning of the Constitution (2009).

**Page 72. Add the following at the end of footnote 11:**

Whittington & Rinderle, *Making a Mountain out of a Molehill? Marbury and the Construction of the Constitutional Canon*, 39 Hastings Const.L.Q. 823 (2012) (arguing that while courts and commentators cited Marbury for various purposes in the nineteenth century, the case attained its status as the cornerstone of judicial review near the turn of the twentieth century).

**Page 75. Add a new footnote 4a at the end of the last sentence of Paragraph (4):**

**4a.** Recent scholarship suggests that rules concerning the parties' right to frame their cases also reveal a great deal about the nature of the judicial function. The conventional wisdom is that "[i]n our adversary system, * * * we rely on the parties to frame the issues for decision and assign to courts the role of neutral arbiter of matters the parties present." Greenlaw v. United States, 554 U.S. 237, 243 (2008). Professor Frost argues, however, that in practice, the federal courts frequently address issues not raised by the parties—for example, when federal jurisdiction is at stake, when the court finds plain error, or when the Supreme Court reformulates the question presented in a petition for a writ of certiorari. See Frost, *The Limits of Advocacy*, 59 Duke L.J. 447 (2009). Doing so, Frost contends, pragmatically accommodates the federal courts' dual roles as dispute resolvers and law declarers. It ensures, moreover, that the parties' framing of issues will not distort the law, foist inappropriate interpretive methods on courts, or negate the effect of relevant legislative enactments. For a contrasting view, see Lawson, *Stipulating the Law*, 109 Mich.L.Rev. 1191 (2011), which argues that giving the parties substantial discretion to structure the issues in their own cases promotes judicial restraint and decisional minimalism.

**Page 75. Add the following in lieu of the second paragraph of Paragraph (5):**

Professor Monaghan has argued that the Supreme Court now substantially embraces the law declaration model as the dominant approach to its own jurisdiction. Although litigants and the lower federal courts generally hold litigation to the restrictive premises of the dispute resolution model, the Supreme Court is not so restricted. It can, within wide though not unlimited bounds, act entirely on the law declaration model. First, in addition to noting some of the examples cited in the previous paragraph, Professor Monaghan argues that the Court's special rules governing review of official immunity decisions (see Sixth Edition pp. 100–06; pp. 13–14, 102–03, 115–118, *infra*) and its qualification of the statutory "final judgment" rule of 28 U.S.C. § 1257 (see Sixth Edition pp. 518–31) show that the Court will often find a way around jurisdictional constraints that would otherwise limit its ability to review important propositions of law decided by other judicial actors. Second, he catalogues a broad array of what he characterizes as "agenda control" devices—making limited grants of certiorari, reformulating questions presented, injecting new questions into cases, appointing amici to defend positions abandoned by the litigants, and strategically accepting or rejecting party stipulations, waivers, or concessions. Based on these phenomena, he concludes that the Court has defined "its current place in our constitutional order" in a way that establishes "a 'final say' default position." See Monaghan, *On Avoiding Avoidance, Agenda Control, and Related Matters*, 112 Colum. L. Rev. 665 (2012). To the extent that these innovations deviate from the assumptions about justiciability that govern the lower courts, does the Court have an obligation to specify some basis in the text or history of Article III for treating its own jurisdiction differently? Do the practices identified by Professor Monaghan raise concerns about judicial self-aggrandizement? Cf. Vermeule, *The Judicial Power in the State (and Federal) Courts*, 2000 Sup. Ct. Rev. 357, 361 (discussing "cognitive pressures that cause judges to press judicial prerogatives to implausible extremes").

---

# SECTION 2.  ISSUES OF PARTIES, THE REQUIREMENT OF FINALITY, AND THE PROHIBITION AGAINST FEIGNED AND COLLUSIVE SUITS

**Page 92. Add a new footnote 7a at the end of the last sentence of Paragraph (3)(b)(i):**

**7a.** Historical scholarship on private bills has identified an early Supreme Court case in which the federal courts exercised jurisdiction over a claim against a defendant naval officer for the unlawful seizure of a ship, even though (a) the naval officer was never served and did not appear and (b) it was plain that the plaintiff's recovery depended entirely on congressional willingness to appropriate funds to pay any judgment. See Pfander & Hunt, *Public Wrongs and Private Bills: Indemnification and Government Accountability in the Early Republic*, 85 N.Y.U.L.Rev. 1862, 1920–22 (2010) (discussing Maley v. Shattuck, 7 U.S. (3 Cranch) 458 (1806)(Marshall, C.J.)). Assuming that Pfander and Hunt's account is correct, does such a precedent settle the meaning of Article III with respect to the justiciability of claims against the United States? Does the fact that there was a nominal individual defendant, even though he was never served and never appeared, differentiate this case from those solely involving claims against the United States?

---

# SECTION 3.   SOME PROBLEMS OF STANDING TO SUE

---

**Page 100.   Substitute the following for the last paragraph of Paragraph (5)(b):**

(c) What are the justiciability implications of the executive's decision to enforce a statute whose constitutionality it will not defend? In United States v. Windsor, 133 S.Ct. 2675 (2013), the plaintiff, who had entered a lawful same-sex marriage, challenged the constitutionality of § 3 of the Defense of Marriage Act (DOMA), 110 Stat. 2419, which excluded partners in a same-sex marriage from the definition of "spouse" for federal law purposes. This provision rendered Windsor ineligible for the "surviving spouse" exclusion from the federal estate tax. Windsor paid $363,053 in federal estate taxes under protest and filed suit in federal district court challenging DOMA and seeking a refund.

While the case was pending, the President instructed the Department of Justice not to defend the constitutionality of § 3 of DOMA. He simultaneously directed the executive branch to continue to enforce § 3 and thus to refuse to provide the refund. The President's directive made clear that this approach was designed to "recogniz[e] the judiciary as the final arbiter" of constitutionality. The House committee that advises the Speaker on legal matters—the Bipartisan Legal Advisory Group (BLAG)—intervened in the district court to defend the statute's constitutionality.

The district court found § 3 unconstitutional and ordered the Treasury to refund the plaintiff's estate tax payments. Although the United States agreed with the merits of the district court's decision, it refused to comply with the judgment and appealed to the Second Circuit from a judgment with which it agreed. After the Second Circuit affirmed, the United States sought review in the Supreme Court. After granting the petition, the Court designated Professor Vicki Jackson as an amica curiae and asked her to argue that the petitioners lacked standing.

In an opinion by Justice Kennedy (joined by Justices Ginsburg, Breyer, Sotomayor, and Kagan), Justice Kennedy found that a justiciable controversy existed between Windsor and the United States both in the district court (a position that the dissenters did not contest) and on appeal (a position that the dissenters disputed). The Court reasoned that whatever commonality the parties had concerning the law, the government's continued enforcement meant that Windsor's "injury (failure to obtain a refund allegedly required by law) was concrete, persisting, and unredressed." The United States continued to have a justiciable interest in the suit as well; however much the government might welcome a ruling that § 3 is unconstitutional, such a ruling would inflict injury upon it by requiring a refund of several hundred thousand dollars in taxes. As long as the United States refused to satisfy the judgment below, the Court reasoned, the litigation presented "a controversy sufficient for Article III jurisdiction."

In the Court's view, the parties' agreement that DOMA was unconstitutional implicated only the "prudential limits" that the judiciary has traditionally placed on the exercise of its own power. See Sixth Edition pp. 75–76. Thus, the Court needed only to assure itself that the case presented the concrete adverseness necessary to ensure sharp presentation of the issues. Here, the fact that the attorneys for BLAG presented "a substantial argument" for DOMA's constitutionality fully addressed the "prudential concerns" that might otherwise counsel against hearing a case in this unusual posture. The Court added that a failure to address the question presented would leave the district courts in "94 districts throughout the Nation * * * without precedential guidance not only in tax refund suits but also in cases involving the whole of DOMA's sweep involving over 1,000 federal statutes and a myriad of federal regulations."[a] Finally, Justice Kennedy's opinion emphasized that "if the Executive's agreement with a plaintiff that a law is unconstitutional is enough to preclude judicial review, then the Supreme Court's primary role in determining the constitutionality of a law that has inflicted real injury on a plaintiff * * * would become only secondary to the President's."

In dissent, Justice Scalia, joined by Chief Justice Roberts and Justice Thomas, argued that the case was nonjusticiable on appeal: "Windsor's injury was cured by the judgment in her favor," and "[w]hatever injury the United States has suffered will surely not be redressed by the action that it, as a litigant, asks us to take." Rejecting the proposition that the Court's role is to declare legal propositions in the absence of disagreement among the parties, Justice Scalia wrote that "[i]n the more than two centuries that this Court has existed * * *, we have never suggested that we have the power to decide a question when every party agrees with both its nominal opponent *and the court below* on that question's answer." In Justice Scalia's view, the matter should not have come before the judiciary in this posture, and the proper course for the government was to decline to enforce a statute that it regarded as unconstitutional. He concluded by stressing that Justice Kennedy's concern about preserving the Court's law declaration function conflicted with the founders' vision of the Court as a dispute resolver and reflected an ahistorical "desire to place this Court at the center of the Nation's life."

Should the Court have confronted more directly the question of "departmentalism"—whether and to what extent each branch has its own obligation to say what the law is in conjunction with the exercise of its constitutionally assigned functions?[b]

———

**a.** Having determined that the suit between Windsor and the United States satisfied constitutional and prudential requirements for standings, the Court found it unnecessary to determine whether BLAG would have standing in its own right. Because they found that there was no justiciable controversy between Windsor and the United States, both Justice Scalia and Justice Alito found it necessary to address the question whether BLAG had standing to oppose Windsor on appeal. For discussion, see pp. 12–13, *infra*.

**b.** For a variety of perspectives on departmentalism, see, *e.g.*, Barron, *Constitutionalism in the Shadow of Doctrine: The President's Non-enforcement Power*, 63 Law & Contemp.Probs. 61 (2000) Calabresi, *Caesarism, Departmentalism, and Professor Paulsen*, 83 Minn. L. Rev. 1421 (1999); Devins & Prakash, *The Indefensible Duty to Defend*, 112 Colum.L.Rev. 507 (2012); Greene, *Interpretive Schizophrenia: How Congressional Standing Can Solve the Enforce–But–Not–Defend Problem*, 81 Fordham L.Rev. 577 (2012); Huq, *Enforcing (But Not*

## SUBSECTION A:  PLAINTIFFS' STANDING

---

### Page 114.   Add at the end of footnote 2:

For the intriguing suggestion that the legal system's earlier focus on common law causes of action and prerogative writs would provide a more workable framework than contemporary standing law's emphasis on injury in fact, see Mashaw, *Rethinking Judicial Review of Administrative Action: A Nineteenth Century Perspective*, 32 Cardozo L.Rev. 2241 (2011). Professor Mashaw adds that Congress should have the authority to supplement these nineteenth century sources with fresh statutory causes of action. For further discussion of this possibility, see Sixth Edition pp. 129–53.

### Page 114.   Add at the end of footnote 3:

Based on an empirical study of more than 1500 standing cases decided between 1921 and 2006, Professor Daniel Ho and Erica Ross conclude that attributing the rise of standing doctrine to the progressive goals of Justices Brandeis and Frankfurter misstates the history. See Ho & Ross, *Did Liberal Justices Invent the Standing Doctrine? An Empirical Study of the Evolution of Standing*, 1921–2006, 62 Stan.L.Rev. 591 (2010). In particular, they argue that the early standing cases (1921–1930) had no political valence; many were unanimous or at least included some of the conservative Justices associated with the Lochner era and, later, with the Court's resistance to the New Deal. During the New Deal, however, Ho and Ross's study finds that the doctrine shifted, and that voting blocs substantiate the liberal reliance on standing to insulate administrative agencies from judicial review. After 1950, the valence of standing doctrine shifted again, as it became more associated with conservative efforts to insulate government action from public interest challenges. Assuming that Ho and Ross have correctly determined the political valence of standing doctrine during the periods they studied, what conclusions should we draw from their findings? How is your answer affected by their further observation that our evidence shows that standing preferences are distinguishable from merits preferences? For discussion of the current political valence of standing doctrine, see Elliott, *Standing Lessons: What We Can Learn When Conservative Plaintiffs Lose Under Article III Standing Doctrine*, 87 Ind.L.J. 551 (2012), which argues that standing limitations increasingly filter out not merely progressive interest group litigation, but also litigation by conservative interest groups seeking to challenge laws dealing with same-sex marriage, health care reform, and stem cell research.

### Page 118.   Add the following at the end of footnote 16:

If a party, or a court sua sponte, raises a jurisdictional defect late in the trial court proceedings or on appeal, what measures should the court take to ensure the development of an adequate record? See Pidot, *Jurisdictional Procedure*, 54 Wm. & Mary L.Rev. 1 (2012).

### Page 118.   Substitute following for Paragraph (3)(e):

(e) The Court has taken varying positions on whether and when a plaintiff can predicate Article III standing on the objective probability of sustaining harm and the reasonable concerns flowing from such a probability.

*Defending) 'Unconstitutional' Laws*, 98 Va. L.Rev. 1001 (2012); Johnsen, *Presidential Non-enforcement of Constitutionally Objectionable Statutes*, 63 Law & Contemp.Probs. 7 (2000); Lawson & Moore, *The Executive Power of Constitutional Interpretation*, 81 Iowa L.Rev. 1267 (1996); Meltzer, *Executive Defense of Congressional Acts*, 61 Duke L.J. 1183, 1228 (2012); Miller, *The President's Power of Interpretation: Implications of a Unified Theory of Constitutional Law*, 56 Law & Contemp.Probs. 35, 37–38 (1993); Paulsen, *The Most Dangerous Branch: Executive Power to Say What the Law Is*, 83 Geo. L.J. 217 (1995); Strauss, *The President and Choices Not to Enforce*, 63 Law & Contemp. Probs. 107 (2000); Strauss, *Presidential Interpretation of the Constitution*, 15 Cardozo L.Rev. 113, 113 (1993); see also May, Presidential Defiance of "Unconstitutional" Laws: Reviving the Royal Prerogative (1998).

(i) In Summers v. Earth Island Institute, Inc., 555 U.S. 488 (2009), the Court (5–4) rejected efforts by environmental organizations to secure Article III standing based on the statistical probability that some of their members would suffer harms by virtue of the U.S. Forest Service's pervasive application of challenged regulations to sites throughout a park system frequented by the organizations' members. The Forest Service Decision Making and Appeals Reform Act, 16 U.S.C. § 1612, afforded interested parties the right to notice and comment and to an appellate process concerning certain land and resource management plans implemented by the Forest Service. The plaintiffs sought to enjoin the enforcement of Forest Service regulations excluding fire-rehabilitation activities and salvage-timber sales of a certain size from those procedures. Consistent with the requirements of Sierra Club v. Morton, Sixth Edition pp. 115–16, a member of one of the plaintiff groups had filed an affidavit stating that he had visited and intended again to visit the site of a particular salvage-timber sale that the challenged regulations exempted from the Act's procedures. Because the litigation concerning that site had been settled, however, the plaintiff groups could not rely on that injury to sustain injunctive relief. Compare City of Los Angeles v. Lyons, Sixth Edition pp. 217–18. Nor, said the Court, could the plaintiff organizations establish the requisite concrete, particularized injury by relying on the affidavit of another member who simply averred that he has visited many National Forests and plans to visit several unnamed National Forests in the future.

In a dissent joined by Justices Stevens, Souter, and Ginsburg, Justice Breyer argued that given the sweep of the Forest Service's policy and the vast membership of the plaintiff organizations, establishing the requisite injury in this case should not necessarily depend on whether any identifiable individual member of the plaintiff organizations had alleged a sufficiently concrete injury. In particular, he contended that the government's application of the challenged regulations to thousands of projects in the future sufficed to establish a realistic threat of injury to the plaintiffs' many thousands of members who, according to uncontested allegations in the complaint, have used and intend to use the national forests to which the regulations apply.

Invoking the organizational standing rules established in Morton, the majority responded that "[t]his novel approach to the law of organizational standing would make a mockery of our prior cases, which have required plaintiff-organizations to make specific allegations establishing that at least one identified member had suffered or would suffer harm." Justice Breyer's dissent, in turn, emphasized that in contrast with the single, infrequently visited development site at issue in Morton, the challenge here addresses "procedures affecting 'thousands' of sites, involving hundreds of times as much acreage, where the precise location of each may not yet be known," making it unreasonable not to infer that at least some of plaintiff groups' members would sustain the requisite injury in fact. How convincing is the majority's rejoinder that if the dissent was correct about the scope of the members' injuries, it should not be "a difficult task" for the plaintiff organizations to identify particular members who suffered the requisite harm?

(ii) In contrast, in Monsanto Co. v. Geertson Seed Farms, 130 S.Ct. 2743 (2010), the Court held that conventional alfalfa growers had standing to challenge the Secretary of Agriculture's deregulation of genetically-engineered alfalfa, given the "reasonable probability" that such action would result in cross-contamination of conventional and organic alfalfa with the altered gene.

This risk of cross-contamination concretely injured the conventional growers in at least two ways. First, in order to continue marketing their product to consumers "who wish to buy non-genetically-engineered alfalfa, [the growers] would have to conduct testing to find out whether and to what extent their crops have been contaminated." Second, "the risk of gene flow [from genetically altered to conventional alfalfa] will cause them to take certain measures to minimize the likelihood of potential contamination and to ensure an adequate supply of non-genetically-engineered alfalfa" for customers who insist on such crops. The Court found these harms sufficed to confer standing, even if the growers crops were not actually infected.

Why does the reasonable probability of an injury suffice to confer standing here if it did not in the Summers case? Does the difference flow from the reasonable concern that consumers would have about cross-contamination? From the costly precautions that the plaintiffs in Monsanto had to take to avoid those concerns?

(iii) In Clapper v. Amnesty International USA, 133 S.Ct. 1138 (2013), the Court signaled a renewed caution about finding injury in fact based on probabilistic injury and the reasonable concerns that flow from it. Pursuant to the Foreign Intelligence Surveillance Act of 1978, as amended, 50 U.S.C. § 1881a, the Attorney General and the Director of National Intelligence may seek an order from the Foreign Intelligence Surveillance Court (FISC) that enables them to "authorize jointly, for a period of up to 1 year * * *, the targeting [for surveillance] of persons reasonably believed to be located outside the United States to acquire foreign intelligence information." The statute prescribes safeguards to prevent surveillance of persons in the United States or U.S. persons abroad. It also specifies that acquisitions of data must comply with Fourth Amendment requirements.

The plaintiffs—who alleged that § 1881a violates the First and Fourth Amendments and the constitutional separation of powers—were attorneys and human rights, labor, legal and media organizations who work with clients and sources abroad. The plaintiffs' declarations averred that their work requires them to communicate by telephone or email with individuals abroad whom the government believes to be affiliated with terrorist groups, who live in areas that are the "special focus" of U.S. counterterrorism efforts, or who actively oppose U.S.-supported governments. These circumstances, they claimed, created an objectively reasonable likelihood that their communications would be intercepted pursuant to § 1881a. The declarants also stated that their apprehension of being monitoring compelled them to incur costly and burdensome measures to maintain confidentiality, in some cases traveling abroad to communicate with individuals rather than using email or telephone communication.

Reasoning that the declarations did not show a "substantial risk" that the identified harms would come about, Justice Alito's opinion for a closely divided(5–4) Court concluded that the plaintiffs lacked standing. The Court found it "speculative" (a) that the government would target parties with whom the plaintiffs communicated, (b) that it would rely on § 1881a rather than some other source of authority, (c) that FISC would authorize the surveillance, (d) that the surveillance would successfully intercept the intended communications, and (e) that the interceptions would include the plaintiffs' communications. This "speculative chain of possibilities," in the Court's view, did not establish that injury based on potential future surveillance is "certainly impending." Rebuffing the plaintiffs' assertions that they felt compelled to take costly measures in order to preserve confidentiality, the Court admonished that plaintiffs cannot "manufacture" standing through their responses to "fears of hypothetical future harm."[c] Finally, the Court added that "we have often found a lack of standing in cases in which the Judiciary has been requested to review actions of the political branches in the fields of intelligence gathering and foreign affairs."

Justice Breyer's dissent, joined by Justices Ginsburg, Sotomayor, and Kagan, argued that the probability that the plaintiffs' communications would be intercepted was hardly speculative. At least two plaintiffs were attorneys who represented high profile detainees at Guantánamo Bay and whose work required communications with the detainees' family, friends, acquaintances, and other associates abroad. Justice Breyer argued that the government would have a strong motive to intercept such communications, which might lead to information about crimes or terrorist plots, and that past governmental behavior showed the government's propensity and capacity to intercept such communications. Justice Breyer also disputed the majority's suggestion that a future harm must be "certainly impending" before it could sustain standing. "Would federal courts," he asked, "deny standing to a plaintiff who seeks to enjoin as a nuisance the building of a nearby pond which, the plaintiff believes, will very likely, but not inevitably, overflow his land?"

The majority conceded that it was not insisting that the plaintiffs show that interception of their communications pursuant to § 1881a "is literally certain", but rather that a "substantial risk" of interception would suffice. In

**c.** In so holding, the Court in Clapper distinguished Friends of the Earth Inc. v. Laidlaw Environmental Services (TOC) Inc., 528 U.S. 167 (2000), in which the Court—over a dissent by Justice Scalia (joined by Justice Thomas)—held that plaintiffs had standing to challenge the defendant's alleged violation of the Clean Water Act, even though the district court had found that the defendant's actions had not "result[ed] in any health risk or environmental harm". The plaintiffs alleged that the defendants' actions concretely harmed their recreational and aesthetic interests, and Justice Ginsburg explained for the Court that "[t]he relevant showing for Article III standing is not injury to the environment but injury to the plaintiff", which existed because of the plaintiffs' "reasonable concern" that pollution damaged land that they otherwise would have used. The Court in Clapper distinguished Laidlaw on the ground that, in the earlier case, the defendant's environmental discharges into the waterway were ongoing, and the only question was whether the plaintiffs, who were nearby residents, "acted reasonably in refraining from using the polluted area." Is that distinction convincing, or does Clapper evince a new skepticism toward standing based on a plaintiff's "reasonable concerns"?

Does Already, LLC v. Nike, Inc., 133 S.Ct. 721 (2013), shed further light on the question? Nike brought suit against Already, a rival footwear producer, for trademark infringement arising out of two new shoe lines that Already was marketing. Already, in turn, counterclaimed against Nike, alleging that the particular trademark on which Nike relied in its suit was invalid. During the litigation, Nike gave Already a comprehensive "Covenant Not to Sue" it or its distributors or retailers for infringing Nike's trademark for the relevant lines of footwear or future ones derived from them. The Court found the covenant comprehensive enough to moot Already's trademark invalidity counterclaim. Significantly, the Court also rejected Already's claim that it had a continuing injury because some investors indicated that they would invest in Already only if Nike's trademark were invalidated, and that the "mere existence" of Nike's trademark "hamper[ed] [Already's] ability to attract capital." The Court answered, in effect, that the covenant took care of the investor concerns and that Already could not predicate standing on "the fact that some individuals may base decisions on conjectural or hypothetical speculation" that Nike would not honor that covenant. Do Monsanto, Clapper, and Nike suggest that the Court makes case-by-case determinations about probabilistic standing that are not generalizable?

light of that concession, does the disagreement in Clapper reduce mainly to one about either the actual likelihood that the harms alleged by plaintiffs will in fact occur or the threshold likelihood that Article III demands? What probability should the Court insist upon before finding standing based on the threat of a future harm? What is the significance of the fact that the classified nature of the program in Clapper limited the plaintiffs' ability and the government's willingness to present evidence bearing on likelihood?[d] For perspectives on the challenges posed by such litigation, see, *e.g.*, Michelman, *Who Can Sue over Government Surveillance?*, 57 UCLA L.Rev. 71 (2009); Rubenfeld, *The End of Privacy*, 61 Stan.L.Rev. 101, 138 (2008). * * *

**Page 122.   Substitute the following for Paragraph (4)(a)(iv):**

(iv) The Roberts Court has divided over the continuing reach of Flast v. Cohen and over whether it remains—or should remain—good law. In Hein v. Freedom from Religion Foundation, Inc., 127 S.Ct. 2553 (2007), a plurality read Flast narrowly. The President, by executive order, had created a White House office and several centers within federal agencies to ensure that faith-based community groups would be eligible to apply for federal funding for activities that were not inherently religious. Suing as taxpayers, the respondents challenged a number of executive actions that, they said, violated the Establishment Clause by expending public funds to promote religious community groups over secular ones. The plurality opinion by Justice Alito, joined by Chief Justice Roberts and Justice Kennedy, held Flast distinguishable on the ground that the expenditures at issue were not made pursuant to any specific Act of Congress, as in Flast, but rather occurred under general appropriations to the Executive Branch.

Concurring in the judgment, Justice Scalia (joined by Justice Thomas) argued that Flast ultimately rested on the principle, indefensible in his view, that Psychic Injury, rather than Wallet Injury, sufficed to establish standing. Arguing that efforts to distinguish Flast had been arbitrary and unconvincing, he maintained that the precedent's lack of a logical theoretical underpinning has rendered our taxpayer standing doctrine such a jurisprudential disaster that it ought to be overruled. Justice Souter's dissent (joined by Justices Stevens, Ginsburg, and Breyer) agreed that efforts to distinguish Flast were unconvincing, and contended that the respondents sought not to 'extend' Flast, but merely to apply it. When executive agencies spend identifiable sums of tax money for religious purposes, no less than when Congress authorizes the same thing, taxpayers suffer injury.

(v) In Arizona Christian School Tuition Org. v. Winn, 131 S.Ct. 1436 (2011), the Court again divided over Flast's meaning. Under Arizona law, taxpayers earn tax credits for money they contribute to "school tuition organizations" (STOs) that fund scholarships for children attending private schools, including sectarian ones. Arizona taxpayers challenged the state statute, arguing that it violates the Establishment Clause. In an opinion by Justice Kennedy, a closely divided Court held that the plaintiffs could not "take advantage of Flast's narrow exception to the general rule against taxpayer standing." In

---

**d.** Nash, *Standing's Expected Value*, 111 Mich.L.Rev. 1283 (2013), suggests that it makes little sense for standing analysis to focus merely on the probability of a threatened injury. The expected value of a harm, after all, is a product of both the probability and cost of its occurrence. Should the Court recognize standing for low probability events if their realization would produce catastrophic consequences?

particular, the Court noted that Flast had relied on James Madison's influential Memorial and Remonstrance Against Religious Assessments (1785), which had objected to public funding for religion on the ground that it "would coerce [taxpayers into] a form of religious devotion in violation of conscience." Since the STO program consisted entirely of voluntary contributions by taxpayers, the Court reasoned that, in contrast with the expenditures challenged in Flast, the program did not forcibly extract money from religious dissenters.

In dissent, Justice Kagan, joined by Justices Ginsburg, Breyer, and Sotomayor, argued that the Court's position was unsupported by precedent or fiscal reality. In particular, she emphasized that the Court had resolved five cases involving state tax expenditures (the use of tax relief rather than direct expenditures to achieve public purposes) but had not once questioned Flast's applicability. In addition, she maintained that "targeted tax breaks" are economically no different from a direct appropriation because each requires the diversion of tax revenues to support religion. As Justice Kagan elaborated, "Suppose a State desires to reward Jews—by, say, $500 per year—for their religious devotion. Should the nature of the taxpayers' concern vary if the State allows Jews to claim the aid on their tax returns in lieu of receiving an annual stipend?" Justice Kagan would have reaffirmed Flast and upheld standing in Winn. In an opinion concurring in the Court's opinion, Justices Scalia and Thomas again urged that Flast be overruled.

(vi) Do the taxpayer standing cases support Professor Fletcher's theory that standing reflects a judgment about the availability of a right of action under particular constitutional provisions? Don't the economic realities of Winn confirm that the Court's efforts to distinguish Flast have led it to draw essentially arbitrary lines in its standing jurisprudence? Has the Court engaged in a "stealth" overruling of Flast by drawing thin distinctions that essentially limit Flast to its facts? See, *e.g.*, Friedman, *The Wages of Stealth Overruling (With Particular Attention to Miranda v. Arizona)*, 99 Geo.L.J. 1, 9–11, 34–36, 47–49 (2010); Sherry, *The Four Pillars of Constitutional Doctrine*, 32 Cardozo L.Rev. 969, 977–81 (2011).

**Page 123.   Add a new Paragraph (4)(b)(iii):**

(iii) The issue of congressional standing arose again in United States v. Windsor, 133 S.Ct. 2675 (2013), which considered the constitutionality of the Defense of Marriage Act's exclusion of same-sex married couples from the definition of "spouses" for purposes of federal law. As discussed at pp. 5–6, *supra*, the President directed the Attorney General not to defend the Act's constitutionality but also directed the executive branch to continue to enforce the Act in order to give Congress an opportunity to defend its validity. Pursuant to the rules of the House, the Speaker consulted with the Bipartisan Legal Advisory Group (BLAG) to discuss the proper course of action. By a 3–2 party line vote, BLAG in 2011 recommended that the Speaker direct the House General Counsel to intervene in Windsor to defend DOMA's constitutionality. After the Supreme Court granted certiorari, the House itself passed a resolution "authoriz[ing] [BLAG] * * * to defend [DOMA's] constitutionality * * * including in the case of Windsor v. United States."

Because the Court found that there remained a justiciable controversy between Windsor and the United States, it declined to reach the question whether BLAG had standing. The dissenting Justices, however, not only reached the question but also disagreed about its resolution. Justice Alito concluded that BLAG had standing because the House, which authorized BLAG to represent it, suffered a concrete, justiciable injury. Justice Alito noted that when the executive declined to defend the legislative veto in INS v. Chadha, 462 U.S. 919 (1983), the Court held that the House and Senate had standing to defend the statute authorizing such a veto. Justice Alito reasoned that just as invalidation of the legislative veto injured Congress's institutional power, so too did the refusal to defend DOMA. "[B]ecause legislating is Congress' central function," he wrote, "any impairment of that function is a more grievous injury than the impairment of a procedural add-on." Justice Alito added that in Coleman v. Miller, Sixth Edition pp. 122–23, the Court recognized standing for 20 Kansas State Senators who claimed that their votes against ratification of a constitutional amendment were sufficient to block it but had been nullified by Kansas's illegal certification of the amendment's ratification. Justice Alito reasoned that because the House was a necessary party to DOMA's passage, judicial "repeal" of the statute effectively nullified the House's vote in favor of its passage.[e]

In an opinion joined by Chief Justice Roberts and Justice Thomas, Justice Scalia rejected Justice Alito's analysis of congressional standing. Because DOMA, unlike the legislative veto, did not regulate Congress's institutional authority as such, he argued that Justice Alito's position would permit Congress to "hale the Executive before the courts not only to vindicate its own institutional powers to act, but to correct a perceived inadequacy in the execution of its laws." This approach, he added, would permit Congress to "pop immediately into Court" not only when "the President refuses to implement a statute he believes to be unconstitutional," but also when he or she "implements a law in a manner that is not to Congress's liking." Such matters, in Justice Scalia's view, have long been properly "left for political resolution" between Congress and the President.

### Page 125.   Add the following at the end of the third paragraph:

One commentator suggests that one can make sense of at least some of these cases by analogizing the causation prong of standing to the tort doctrine of proximate cause, which asks whether the plaintiff's alleged injuries were the foreseeable consequence of the very type of conduct that the law sought to prevent. See Meier, *Using Tort Law to Understand the Causation Prong of Standing*, 80 Fordham L.Rev. 1241 (2011). But is the tort doctrine of proximate cause any easier to administer than standing law? Compare Prosser, *Palsgraf Revisited*, 52 Mich.L.Rev. 1 (1953)

### Page 127.   Add the following at the end of footnote 26:

See also Hall, *Asymmetrical Jurisdiction*, 58 UCLA L.Rev. 1257 (2011), which argues that the Court should develop distinctive rules of justiciability that treat its own appellate jurisdiction as coextensive with state court jurisdiction to hear federal questions.

### Page 129.   Add a new Paragraph (8):

**(8) Appellate Standing for a Prevailing Party.** In Camreta v. Greene, 131 S.Ct. 2020 (2011), the Court held that a government official who has prevailed

---

**e.**  Justice Alito distinguished Raines v. Byrd, Sixth Edition p. 123, in part, on the ground that the six individual Members of Congress who sought to challenge the Item Veto Act neither had the institutional back- ing of the House nor the status of pivotal actors whose votes would have altered legislative outcomes absent the challenged procedure.

in a lawsuit on qualified immunity grounds may nonetheless take an appeal to contest a merits ruling made by the lower court in conjunction with finding qualified immunity. In an action for damages brought pursuant to 42 U.S.C. § 1983, Greene (as next friend) alleged that the petitioners—a state child protective services worker and a deputy sheriff—had violated her minor daughter's Fourth Amendment rights by going to the child's elementary school and, without a warrant or parental consent, interviewing her about a third-party's allegations of paternal abuse. Pursuant to the two-step framework established in Pearson v. Callahan, Sixth Edition pp. 78, 1005–06, the court of appeals first ruled that the petitioners' conduct had violated the Fourth Amendment, but then held that petitioners were entitled to qualified immunity because their action did not violate "clearly established" law. See Sixth Edition pp. 1002–06 (discussing qualified immunity). The court of appeals explained that it opined on the merits in order to "provide guidance to those charged with the difficult task of protecting child welfare within the confines of the Fourth Amendment."

Although the court of appeals had entered judgment in their favor, the public officer defendants petitioned the Supreme Court for review of the court of appeals' merits ruling on the ground that it would limit their freedom of action in future investigations. In an opinion for the Court joined by Chief Justice Roberts and Justices Scalia, Ginsburg, and Alito, Justice Kagan concluded that, although the petitioners had prevailed below, they nonetheless had standing to seek further review.[f] The Court emphasized that by reaching the merits of the Fourth Amendment claim, the court of appeals established case law that could negate qualified immunity in future cases if the defendants engaged in similar conduct again. Justice Kagan thus wrote: "If the official regularly engages in that conduct as part of his job * * *, he suffers injury caused by the adverse constitutional ruling. So long as it continues in effect, he must either change the way he performs his duties or risk a meritorious damages action."

In a dissenting opinion joined by Justice Thomas, Justice Kennedy argued that by accepting a petition for certiorari by a prevailing party, the Court was, in effect, issuing an advisory opinion. Drawing an analogy to the adequate-and-independent-state-ground doctrine (see Sixth Edition pp. 460–65), Justice Kennedy quoted Herb v. Pitcairn, Sixth Edition pp. 461–62, for the proposition that " '[o]ur power is to correct wrong judgments, not to revise opinions.' "

Who has the better of the argument? Isn't the injury recognized in Camreta just a predictable byproduct of Pearson's granting lower courts discretion to reach (unnecessarily) the merits of a constitutional claim in a case that could be resolved entirely on qualified immunity grounds? Is the injury identified by the Court in Camreta conceptually any different from the injury sustained by a regulated party seeking to bring a pre-enforcement challenge to a regulation with which that party must comply at the risk of incurring liability? Compare Abbott Laboratories v. Gardner, Sixth Edition pp. 202–05. From the injury suffered by a non-party when a lower court declares some conduct in which that non-party regularly engages to be unconstitutional? For further discussion of Camreta v. Greene, see pp. 27, 54–55, 113, 115–117, *infra*.

**f.** Justice Kagan also noted that the relevant jurisdictional statute authorized the Court to grant certiorari "upon the petition of any party" (28 U.S.C. § 1254(1))—language broad enough "to cover petitions brought by litigants who have prevailed as well as those who have lost, in the court below."

**Page 141.   Add at the end of Paragraph (1)(a):**

For a thoughtful historical analysis suggesting that the competitor standing cases reflected—and, at the time, were generally understood by the legal community to reflect—the Court's view that Congress could authorize those without *any* private legal interest to sue on the public's behalf, see Magill, *Standing for the Public: A Lost History*, 95 Va.L.Rev. 1131 (2009).

**Page 144.   Add a new footnote 2a at the end of Paragraph (2)(a):**

**2a.** Citing the Court's invalidation of congressional efforts to redefine the (judicially settled) scope of individual rights under Section 5 of the Fourteenth Amendment (see City of Boerne v. Flores, Sixth Edition p. 179), one commentator deems it "almost inconceivable * * * that the Court would accept congressional efforts to redefine the constitutional limits of standing." Elliott, *Congress's Inability to Solve Standing Problems*, 91 B.U.L.Rev. 159, 192 (2011). Does Congress' identification of a novel injury "redefine" standing law or merely establish a right of action where none existed before? Might the scope of Congress's authority depend on the context in which it has acted to create standing? See Lee & Ellis, *The Standing Doctrine's Dirty Little Secret*, 107 Nw.U.L.Rev. 169 (2012)(arguing that the Court has properly applied more relaxed standing requirements in contexts in which Congress exercises its Article I powers to confer new procedural rights on the public, as in the National Environmental Protection Act or the Freedom of Information Act).

**Page 146.   Add a new Paragraph (2)(c):**

   (c) Recall that in Summers v. Earth Island Institute, Inc., 555 U.S. 488 (2009), discussed at p. 8, *supra*, a 5–4 Court rebuffed efforts by environmental organizations to base standing on the statistical probability that at least some of their members would suffer harms from the U.S. Forest Service's application of challenged regulations to parklands frequented by the organizations' members. Five Justices, however, hinted that the case might come out differently if Congress were to create a right of action for such probabilistic harms to the enjoyment of the national parks. In a concurring opinion, Justice Kennedy wrote that "[t]his case would present different considerations if Congress had sought to provide redress for a concrete injury 'giv[ing] rise to a case or controversy where none existed before' " (quoting Lujan v. Defenders of Wildlife, Sixth Edition p. 135 (Kennedy, J., concurring in part and concurring in the judgment)). Similarly, in dissent, Justice Breyer (joined by Justices Stevens, Souter, and Ginsburg) posited a hypothetical statute that "expressly permitted environmental groups * * * to bring cases just like the present one, provided (1) that the group has members who have used salvage-timber parcels in the past and are likely to do so in the future, and (2) that the group's members have opposed Forest Service timber sales in the past (using notice, comment, and appeal procedures to do so) and will likely use those procedures to oppose salvage-timber sales in the future." Citing both Massachusetts v. EPA and Sierra Club v. Morton, the dissent then observed that "[t]he majority cannot, and does not, claim that such a statute would be unconstitutional."[g] Would

**g.** Quite apart from the creation of a new right of action based on the statistical probability of harm, could Congress create standing in a case such as Summers by recognizing new forms of property interests? Professor Farber, for example, argues that Congress "might transfer a conservation easement over certain federal lands to a non-profit in order to ensure that an outside monitor would have standing to sue over future violations of laws protecting those lands." Farber, *Owning up to the Environment*, 40 Envtl.L.Rep. 10994, 10998 (2010). Once Congress vested such a property right in a group such as the Sierra Club, then government action interfering with the easement would presumably give rise to standing by invading that property right. If Congress such a framework deal with the intractable problems of degree that now characterize the Court's treatment of probabilistic standing?

**Page 151: Add a new Paragraph (5a):**

**(5a) State Law Authority to Sue.** In Hollingsworth v. Perry, 133 S.Ct. 2652 (2013), the Court held that state law cannot authorize the official proponents of a state ballot initiative to defend its constitutionality when the state's executive declines to do so. Pursuant to the initiative process set forth in the California Constitution, voters enacted Proposition 8, which limited marriage to opposite-sex couples. Respondents, same-sex couples who wished to marry, filed suit in district court challenging Proposition 8's constitutionality and seeking to enjoin the governor and other state officials from enforcing it. After the district court held the initiative unconstitutional, state officials refused to defend the law further, and the initiative's proponents—those who got it on the ballot and shepherded it through the election process—successfully moved to intervene. When they sought to appeal, the Ninth Circuit certified to the California Supreme Court a question about the proponents' state law status; the state court replied that as a matter of California statutory and constitutional law, proponents of a ballot initiative have authority to defend the initiative's constitutionality when state officials do not do so. The Ninth Circuit accordingly held that the proponents had standing to appeal.

In an opinion by Chief Justice Roberts, joined by Justices Scalia, Breyer, Ginsburg, and Kagan, the Supreme Court reversed. The Court noted that because the proponents' involvement with the initiative ended with its adoption, "[t]heir only interest in having the District Court order reversed was to vindicate the constitutional validity of a generally applicable California law." Such a "generalized grievance" could not support standing. Nor could the premise that the proponents were authorized by state law to sue on the state's behalf. The Court acknowledged that the state has a "cognizable interest" in defending Proposition 8 and that it may vindicate that interest by "designat[ing] agents to represent it in federal court." The Court found, however, that despite the California Supreme Court's ruling, the proponents were not acting as agents of the state. The Court stressed that under the Restatement of Agency, an agent owes a fiduciary duty to a principal, and the principal must be able to control the agent—elements wholly lacking in the proponents' relationship to the California government. Nor did the proponents take an oath of office or receive attorney's fees from the state. The Court stressed that whatever state law might say, "standing in federal court is a question of federal law," and "the fact that a State thinks a private party should have standing to seek relief for a generalized grievance cannot override this Court's settled law to the contrary."

Justice Kennedy, joined by Justices Thomas, Alito, and Sotomayor, dissented. The dissent stressed that California law gave the proponent of an initiative "authority to appear in court and assert the State's interest in defending an enacted initiative," at least when public officials would not do so. He added that nothing in Article III requires a state "to comply with the Restatement of Agency or with this Court's view of how a state should * * * structure its government." He further reasoned that because the purpose of ballot initiatives

could properly create standing in that way, why shouldn't it be able to confer a statutory right of action upon such groups without the added formality of establishing property interests?

was to establish a lawmaking process that "does not depend upon state officials," the Court's insistence upon the presence of state officials or others answerable to them would undermine the initiative process. "A prime purpose of justiciability is to ensure vigorous advocacy," the dissent concluded, "yet the Court insists upon litigation conducted by state officials whose preference is to lose the case."

Other than the Guarantee Clause, U.S. Const. Art. IV, § 4, the Constitution contains no explicit limitation on the way states structure their governments. And the Court has recognized that a state may designate the state Speaker of the House or President of the Senate to defend a statute if the state Attorney General will not. See Karcher v. May, 484 U.S. 72 (1987). In that light, what Article III principle or tradition precludes the state from designating official proponents of a ballot initiative as the initiative's official defenders? On the other hand, if Justice Kennedy is correct, what limiting principle should apply to a state's designation of legal representatives? What if state law authorized "any interested citizen" to defend a state law on its behalf if the state executive would not?

---

## SUBSECTION B: STANDING TO ASSERT THE RIGHTS OF OTHERS AND RELATED ISSUES INVOLVING "FACIAL CHALLENGES" TO STATUTES

---

**Page 160.   Add at the end of the first paragraph of footnote 6:**

Bond v. United States, 131 S.Ct. 2355 (2011), ruled that a criminal defendant could challenge the constitutionality of the law being enforced against her on the ground that it exceeded congressional authority under Article I and the Tenth Amendment. Limits on third-party standing had no applicability, the Court held, because "[s]tates are not the sole intended beneficiaries of federalism": Federalism principles, which protect individual liberty, gave the petitioner rights that "do not belong to a State."

Justice Ginsburg (joined by Justice Breyer) joined Justice Kennedy's opinion for a unanimous Court but wrote separately to assert a more categorical position: "Bond, like any other defendant, has a personal right not to be convicted under a constitutionally invalid law." With the majority having accepted that defendants can challenge laws on separation-of-powers and federalism grounds, is there any good reason to stop short of Justice Ginsburg's more general conclusion?

**Page 163.   Add to Paragraph (2):**

*But cf.* Fallon, *Fact and Fiction About Facial Challenges,* 99 Cal.L.Rev. 915 (2011), arguing that the ascription to Yazoo of a presumption of severability "leaves open the question of how Yazoo related to such cases as the nearly contemporaneous Lochner v. New York, [198 U.S. 45 (1905),] which upheld a facial challenge to a law regulating the hours of employment of baker workers under the same Due Process Clause that was involved in Yazoo. In Lochner, the Court made no suggestion that the possibility of statutory severing limited the challenger to asserting as-applied claims." According to Fallon, a general presumption of severability would make it impossible for courts ever to hold a statute irrational because excessively broadly written, but "Yazoo is easily distinguishable from cases that have held statutes irrationally overinclusive * * * because in Yazoo, unlike those cases, there was an obvious surgical cure [that would remove the problem of irrational overbreadth] if severing turned out to be necessary in a future case. Even if the challenged statute was invalid as applied to cases involving frivolous, excessive, or disputable claims for damages, it could have been so severed as to remain enforceable in cases involving admittedly valid claims, such as the one before the Court.'' If a truly general presumption of severability applied, what would be the point of asking whether a *statute* was rationally related to a legitimate state interest or narrowly tailored to a compelling state interest?

### Page 164.   Add a new footnote 1a at the end of Paragraph (3):

**1a.**   Scoville, *The New General Common Law of Severability,* 91 Tex.L.Rev. 543 (2013), reads Ayotte v. Planned Parenthood of New England, Sixth Edition p. 176, which held that federal courts should prefer partial to facial invalidations of state statutes, as having rejected the rule that the severability of state statutes is a matter of state law. According to Scoville, the result is a new general common law of severability that is difficult to square with Erie R. Co. v. Tompkins, Sixth Edition p. 558. Even if Ayotte is read more cautiously, Professor Scoville seems correct that there may be a tension in some cases among the Supreme Court's asserted preference for as-applied over facial challenges, its insistence that federal courts must not re-write statutes in order to save them, and its long-held stance that state law governs the separability of state statutes.

### Page 165.   Add new Paragraphs (4)(e)–(g):

(e) A separability issue arose in Free Enterprise Fund v. Public Company Accounting Oversight Board, 130 S.Ct. 3138 (2010), after the Justices, 5–4, held that the Sarbanes–Oxley Act imposed unconstitutional limitations on the president's power to remove the board's members. In an opinion by Chief Justice Roberts, the Court held that the language unduly limiting the president's removal power could be severed: The remaining provisions were capable of operating independently, "and nothing in the statute's text or historical context makes it 'evident' that Congress, faced with the limitations imposed by the Constitution, would have preferred no Board to a Board whose members are removable at will.'' Justice Breyer, joined by Justices Stevens, Ginsburg, and Sotomayor, dissented on the merits and did not reach the separability issue.

(f) In National Federation of Independent Business v. Sebelius, 132 S.Ct. 2566 (2012), the Court held that a provision of Patient Protection and Affordable Care Act violated principles of constitutional federalism by coercively requiring states to dramatically expand their Medicaid coverage or potentially forfeit all Medicaid funds. But that problem could be adequately remedied, Chief Justice Roberts held (in an opinion for a plurality only on this point), by barring any cut-offs of pre-existing funds that were unconnected with the challenged expansion mandate. This limitation was supported, he argued, by a separability clause in the chapter of the U.S. Code in which the provision authorizing funds cutoffs was codified.

In a joint dissenting opinion, Justices Scalia, Kennedy, Thomas, and Alito concluded that two major provisions of the Act—the Medicaid extension and a mandate to otherwise uninsured individuals to purchase health insurance— were both unconstitutional. (The majority had found the latter to be valid under the Taxing and Spending Clause.) Having so determined, the joint opinion would have held the Act inseverable and therefore invalid in toto.

According to the dissent, severability is improper unless "Congress would have enacted" the otherwise valid provisions of a partially invalidated law "standing alone". A number of the Act's otherwise unchallenged "major provisions" were inseparable because they could not "operate as Congress intended without the Individual Mandate and Medicaid Expansion." With respect to a number of "minor provisions"—including such matters as break times at work for nursing mothers and taxes on tanning booths and some medical devices—the dissenting Justices quoted a statement by the Senate majority leader in support of the conclusion that "Often, a minor provision will be the price paid for support of a major provision. So, if the major provision were unconstitutional, Congress would not have passed the minor one."

Is the inquiry into which provisions Congress would have passed "standing alone" a judicially manageable one?

Is a willingness to invalidate statutory provisions at the behest of parties who are unaffected by them consistent with the Court's often-expressed aversion to "facial challenges"? According to the four dissenting Justices, "[a]n automatic or too cursory severance of statutory provisions risks 'rewrit[ing] a statute'" and "impos[ing] on the Nation, by the Court's decree, its own new statutory regime" in contravention of the separation of powers. Do cases in which the Court holds statutes unconstitutional as applied but declines to entertain facial challenges pose comparable risks?

(g) In thinking about the large separability issues framed by the dissent in National Federation of Independent Business v. Sebelius, one might begin by considering the respective attractions of two polar alternatives: (i) never sever and (i) always sever.

For a close approximation of (i), see Campbell, *Severability of Statutes*, 62 Hastings L.J. 1495 (2011), arguing that severability doctrine should be abolished, with the effect that any statute with even a single invalid application would be deemed invalid in toto. If Dean Campbell's proposal were adopted, would there be any way of avoiding constitutional litigation based on bizarre hypotheticals involving potentially invalid statutory applications?

In an approximation of (ii), Walsh, *Partial Unconstitutionality*, 85 N.Y.U.L.Rev. 738 (2010), argues that early courts declined to enforce statutory provisions insofar as they were "repugnant" to the Constitution, but did not frame the further "severability" question of whether a partially unconstitutional statute could survive. Professor Walsh argues for a return to the earlier approach, under which courts would enforce all partially (un)constitutional federal statutes to the extent of their constitutional validity unless Congress had enacted a non-severability clause. In comparison with the older model, he argues, the function of modern severability doctrine is not to "save" statutes from invalidity, but instead to authorize judicial invalidation of statutes in toto based on judicial ascriptions of counterfactual congressional intent.

Between these polar alternatives, is there any possible middle position that would not require some kind of inquiry into what Congress intended or whether it would have enacted particular provisions if it had known that others would be invalidated? Aren't such inquiries hard to square with the textualist theories of statutory interpretation, see Sixth Edition pp. 624–25, that at least some of the dissenting Justices in National Federation of Independent Business v. Sebelius normally favor?

**Page 171.  Add to Paragraph (4):**

The Court again entertained and upheld a First Amendment overbreadth challenge without first conducting an as-applied assessment in United States v. Stevens, 559 U.S. 460 (2010), which invalidated a statute criminalizing the commercially motivated creation, sale, or possession of depictions of animal cruelty.

**Page 173.  Add a footnote 11a at the end of Paragraph (6):**

**11a.**  Alexander, *There Is No First Amendment Overbreadth (But There Are Vague First Amendment Doctrines); Prior Restraints Aren't "Prior"; and "As Applied" Challenges Seek Judicial Statutory Amendments*, 27 Const.Comm. 439 (2011), argues that the idea of "overbreadth" doctrine is nonsensical because "Article VI of the Constitution, which declares the Constitution to be the supreme law of the land," of its own force establishes that the purportedly "overbroad" extensions of statutes cannot be "law" at all. Is Professor Alexander's "entirely analytical" point, as he terms it, of any practical consequence? If not, doesn't its very lack of consequence raise questions about whether it accurately analyzes "First Amendment overbreadth doctrine" as that term is generally understood?

**Page 174.  Add a new Subparagraph (8)(d):**

(d) With United States v. Williams, in which the Court said that it had "relaxed the requirement" that a plaintiff whose own conduct is clearly proscribed "cannot complain of the vagueness of the law as applied to the conduct of others", compare Holder v. Humanitarian Law Project, 130 S.Ct. 2705 (2010). There, as a prelude to rejecting an as-applied First Amendment challenge to a statute that makes it a federal crime to "knowingly provid[e] material support or resources to a foreign terrorist organization", Chief Justice Roberts' opinion for the Court flatly asserted that "even to the extent a heightened vagueness standard applies" to expressive conduct, "a plaintiff whose speech is clearly proscribed cannot raise a successful vagueness claim under the Due Process Clause of the Fifth Amendment * * * [a]nd he certainly cannot do so based on the speech of others." Although dissenting on the merits, Justice Breyer, joined by Justices Ginsburg and Sotomayor, agreed with regard to vagueness, saying that, "[l]ike the Court, and substantially for the reasons it gives, I do not think this statute is unconstitutionally vague."

If the Court will allow facial challenges to overbroad statutes that threaten to chill third-party speech, does it make sense not to allow vagueness challenges predicated on the possible chilling of third-party speech? In Holder v. Humanitarian Law Project, Chief Justice Roberts suggested that if the Court were to adopt a different stance in First Amendment cases involving vague statutes, the First Amendment overbreadth and Fifth Amendment vagueness doctrines "would be substantially redundant." Do you agree? If an interest in avoiding the chilling of speech provides a sound basis for First Amendment overbreadth doctrine, why would some redundancy with regard to vagueness doctrine be improper?

**Page 174.  Add a new Paragraph (9):**

**(9) Other First Amendment Facial Challenges Not Involving Overbreadth.** In Citizens United v. Federal Election Commission, 558 U.S. 310 (2010), the Court sustained a facial challenge to a statutory provision that barred corporations and unions from expending funds on "electioneering communications" relating to candidates for federal office within 30 days of a primary or 60 days of a general election. The challenger, a not-for-profit corporation that wished to fund cable on-demand viewings of a 90–minute film about a presidential candidate (Hillary Clinton), had challenged the statute only "as applied" to its case. But the Court, in an opinion by Justice Kennedy, held the applicable provision invalid on its face. Justice Kennedy's reasoning included three strands. First, the Court could not "resolve this case on a narrower ground without chilling political speech". Second, a party's pleadings could not "prevent[] the Court from considering certain remedies if those remedies are necessary to resolve a claim [of unconstitutionality] that has been preserved". Third, "we cannot easily address [the issue of whether the statute would be unconstitutional as applied] without assuming a premise—the permissibility of restricting corporate political speech—that is itself in doubt." In a dissenting opinion, Justice Stevens—who would have upheld the statute both on its face and as applied—also objected to the majority's sustaining a facial challenge when it could have found the state unconstitutional as applied to a feature-length video-on-demand film or to a not-for-profit corporation.

If facial invalidation is a "remedy", how does the Court determine when that remedy is appropriate? Does it gauge "chilling" effect on a case-by-case basis? And why couldn't the Court "assum[e]", arguendo, the "premise"—however questionable—that the statute could be applied to for-profit corporations showing 30–second electioneering advertisements? When the Court insists in other cases that statutes can only be challenged as applied, doesn't it always assume that those statutes have valid applications while leaving open the possibility that it might actually conclude otherwise in response to subsequent as-applied challenges?

Neither the majority nor the dissenting opinion characterized Citizens United as an overbreadth case. Is there any way in which such a characterization would have been inapt?

### Page 176.    Add to Paragraph (2):

Fallon, *Fact and Fiction About Facial Challenges,* 99 Cal.L.Rev. 915 (2011), maintains that "facial challenges to statutes are common, not anomalous," based on an examination of "every case decided by the Supreme Court in the 2009, 2004, 1999, 1994, 1989, and 1984 Terms": "In all of those Terms, the Court adjudicated more facial challenges on the merits than it did as-applied challenges". In the sample as a whole, moreover, facial challenges had a 44% success rate compared with 38% for as-applied challenges. According to Fallon, another "convincing measure of the frequency of facial challenges emerges from an informal survey of leading Supreme Court cases establishing and applying doctrinal tests, many if not most of which direct attention to a statute on its face, not as applied." These include the familiar strict scrutiny, intermediate scrutiny, and rational basis tests, tests of validity under the First Amendments's Free Speech and Religion Clauses, and tests of congressional authority under Article I and the separation of powers. The real puzzle, Fallon argues, is to explain how the rhetoric in a few leading cases has either generated or supported the conventional but mistaken understanding that facial challenges are disfavored.

### Page 181.    Add a new footnote 3a at the end of Paragraph (6):

**3a.**    For a range of perspectives on doctrines governing facial and as-applied challenges and emerging trends in their application, see Symposium, *The Roberts Court: Distinguishing As–Applied Versus Facial Challenges,* 36 Hastings Const.L.Q. 563 (2009) (including articles by

Professors Borgmann, Faigman, Franklin, Manian, and Walsh). See also O'Grady, *The Role of Speculation in Facial Challenges*, 53 Ariz.L.Rev. 867 (2011) (concluding that the Roberts Court is especially reluctant to uphold facial challenges predicated on speculative claims about the behavior that untested statutes are likely to trigger).

In Persily & Rosenberg, *Defacing Democracy?: The Changing Nature and Rising Importance of As–Applied Challenges in the Supreme Court's Recent Election Law Decisions*, 93 Minn.L.Rev. 1644, 1674 (2009), the authors argue that the importance of having clear election rules specified in advance suggests that "the courts ought to relax the burdens on facial challenges that exist in the ordinary case" when "characteristically election-related concerns are present." To what extent, if any, is this argument different from contending that the substantive tests of constitutional validity applied to election-related rules should be unusually difficult to satisfy?

Metzger, *Facial and As–Applied Challenges Under the Roberts Court*, 36 Fordham Urb.L.J. 773, 798 (2009), asserts that Chief Justice Roberts and Justices Kennedy and Alito have a "greater affinity for as-applied challenges" than the other Justices but that, even for them, "substantive constitutional law drives the Court's approach to facial and as-applied challenges" and determines which statutes are constitutional or unconstitutional in whole and which in part.

### Page 181.  Add a new Paragraph (6)(d):

(d) In *Shelby County v. Holder,* 133 S.Ct. ___ (2013), the Court, by 5 to 4, sustained a facial challenge to the coverage provision of the Voting Rights Act of 1965 (VRA), which identified jurisdictions, mostly in the south, that could not change their voting procedures without seeking prior clearance from the Department of Justice. Chief Justice Roberts' majority opinion reasoned that the coverage formula, which remained unchanged from the 1960s and 1970s when Congress most recently re-enacted the VRA in 2006, did not bear sufficient relation to current conditions to pass muster under Section 2 of the Fifteenth Amendment. In one of just two paragraphs explaining why facial invalidation was appropriate, the Chief Justice concluded that "[w]e cannot * * * try our hand at updating the statute ourselves, based on the new record compiled by Congress." Although the dissenting Justices would have upheld the coverage formula in toto, they also argued that facial invalidation would be inappropriate even if the coverage formula had invalid applications. According to Justice Ginsburg, a number of relatively recent episodes of discrimination by Alabama and its subdivisions demonstrated that "as applied to Shelby County, the VRA's preclearance requirement is hardly contestable." Justice Ginsburg also emphasized that the VRA includes a severability provision, which directs that "[i]f any provision of [this Act] or the application thereof * * * is held invalid, the remainder of [the Act] and the application of the provision to other persons not similarly situated or to other circumstances shall not be affected thereby."

Did the Court impliedly hold the VRA's severability clause unconstitutional, at least as applied to the case before it?

### Page 181.  Add to Paragraph (7)(a):

In Doe v. Reed, 130 S.Ct. 2811 (2010), the Court acknowledged that the line between facial and as-applied challenges is not always sharp. Nevertheless, in an opinion joined by five other Justices, Chief Justice Roberts entertained one challenge to a statute under the test applicable to facial challenges, while leaving an as-applied challenge to be considered in further proceedings in the lower courts. The Washington Public Records Act ("PRA") makes all "public records" available for public inspection and copying. As interpreted by the state, the PRA applies to the signatures on petitions to have referenda placed on the ballot. The plaintiffs in Doe v. Reed were the sponsor and some of the signers of a petition seeking a popular vote on Referendum 71, a proposal to reject legislation enacted by the Washington legislature that expanded the rights of registered domestic partners, including same-sex partners. The plaintiffs maintained in Count I of their complaint that the PRA was unconstitutional as applied to referendum petitions generally. Count II claimed that the PRA was unconstitutional as applied to signatories of the Referendum 71 petition in particular, due to a "reasonable probability" that they "will be subjected to threats, harassment, and reprisals."

Chief Justice Roberts held that Count I could not succeed without satisfying the standards applicable to facial challenges. Noting that the Count I attack was " 'as applied' in the sense that it does not seek to strike the PRA in all applications" but " 'facial' in that it is not limited to the plaintiffs' particular case", the Chief Justice concluded that "[t]he label is not what matters": "The important point is that plaintiffs' claim and the relief that would follow * * * reach beyond the particular circumstances of these plaintiffs. They must therefore satisfy our standards for a facial challenge to the extent of that reach."

On the merits, the Chief Justice ruled that the plaintiffs' Count I challenge failed, because the PRA's general demand for disclosure of petition signatures satisfied the "exacting scrutiny" applicable to First Amendment challenges "in the electoral context" in light of "the State's interest in preserving the integrity of the electoral process." The Count II claim remained available for consideration by the District Court.

Justices Stevens and Scalia concurred in the judgment. Justice Thomas would have upheld the plaintiffs' challenge as applied to all disclosures of referendum petitions.

Consider whether the majority opinion exemplifies the view advanced in the text of the Sixth Edition that (a) all constitutional challenges are "as applied" insofar as those advancing them necessarily assert that a statute cannot constitutionally be applied to them and (b) the extent of any resulting invalidation will depend on the nature of the constitutional test under which a statute's application might be held invalid. How else could the "exacting scrutiny" applied to "First Amendment challenges in the electoral context" have raised the possibility that the PRA might be invalid as applied to referendum petitions, but not to other disclosures that the PRA mandates?

**Page 182.   Add a new Subparagraph 7(c):**

(c) Rosenkranz, *The Subjects of the Constitution*, 62 Stan.L.Rev. 1209 (2010), argues that some of the Constitution's language inherently calls for facial challenges by designating Congress as the relevant actor and thus making any constitutional violation one that can be committed only by Congress at the time when it enacts a challenged a law. This is true, Professor Rosenkranz maintains, of all provisions of the First Amendment, of the Commerce Clause, and of Section 5 of the Fourteenth Amendment. When Congress violates one of these provisions, he thus concludes, its attempted lawmaking is void, and a court should invalidate the failed effort it by deeming it no law it all. See also Meier, *Facial Challenges and the Separation of Powers,* 83 Ind.L.J. 1557 (2010) (similarly maintaining that challenges to Congress' power to enact a law under the Constitution's power-conferring provisions, such as the Commerce Clause or Section 5 of the Fourteenth Amendment, are inherently facial).

If a court were to adopt Professor Rosenkranz's framework, what should count as a "law" that was inherently and necessarily open to facial attack? Suppose a multi-page revenue bill provides in one section for a special tax on the press. Should a court invalidate the entire bill (on the assumption that it is all one "law"), or should it treat the offending provision as the "law" that violates the First Amendment? Suppose Congress enacts a statute forbidding the interstate shipment of any material that is "(a) obscene or (b) lewd." Should a court invalidate both (a) and (b), or is (b) alone the relevant "law"? Should it make a difference if instead Congress enacts a single provision forbidding the shipment of "any material that is obscene or lewd"? Might it be said that Congress violated the First Amendment insofar, but only insofar, as the law that it enacted abridges constitutionally protected expression? Although Professor Rosenkranz does not address such questions in his article, he reports in a footnote that he intends to do so in future work. Professor Meier would permit the severance of linguistically distinct bits of statutory text—so that each provision of a multi-part enactment could stand or fall separately from the rest—but not of statutory "applications".

In *The Objects of the Constitution,* 63 Stan.L.Rev. 1005 (2011), Professor Rosenkranz extends the analysis of his earlier article by arguing that the Constitution's grammar and structure sometimes mark either the President or the judicial branch as the object of a prohibition and that in such cases a constitutional challenge is necessarily as-applied (because rights against those branches are not rights against the enactment of "laws"). As an example, he cites the Jury Trial Clause of the Sixth Amendment: "In all criminal prosecutions, the accused shall enjoy the right to a speedy and public trial, by an impartial jury of the State and district wherein the crime shall have been committed * * *." After concluding that this provision cannot be understood as binding Congress (because, among other things, "it does not"—like the First Amendment—"say, 'Congress shall make no law authorizing bench trials' "), Rosenkranz infers that it applies only to the federal courts and thus concludes that the Supreme Court erred in entertaining and upholding a facial challenge to the congressionally authorized federal Sentencing Guidelines in United States v. Booker, Sixth Edition p. 164. Are you persuaded? Acting pursuant to powers that include Article I's Necessary and Proper Clause, Congress had passed something that looked like a law making the Guidelines mandatory in every case to which they applied. In order to determine whether the federal courts were bound by that attempted mandate in the case before it, the Court had to reach conclusions about the nature of the Sixth Amendment guarantee; and its reasoning established that the Guidelines could not be validly applied to any case (unless the statute mandating application of the Guidelines were somehow severed). If a challenger's attack on the application of a statute implies that a statute could have no valid applications, is any useful purpose served by insisting that "[a] challenge under the Jury Trial Clause * * * is inherently an 'as-applied' challenge"?[h]

**h.**  Keller & Tseytlin, *Applying Constitutional Decision Rules Versus Invalidating in Toto,* 98 Va.L.Rev. 301 (2012), argue that Professor Rosenkranz—along with other commentators—errs by failing to distinguish "constitutional decision rules", which deter-mine whether statutes are constitutionally valid or invalid, from "invalidation rules", which determine whether the appropriate remedy for an invalid statute is severance or total nullification.

**Page 183.  Add a new Paragraph (9):**

**(9) Facial Challenges and Narrowing Constructions.** The Court propounded a saving construction of a federal statute that had been subjected to a facial challenge on vagueness grounds in Skilling v. United States, 130 S.Ct. 2896 (2010). That statute, 18 U.S.C. § 1346, makes it a crime to fraudulently "deprive another of the intangible right of honest services." In an opinion by Justice Ginsburg, the Court acknowledged that Skilling's argument that the statute was unconstitutionally vague "has force" in light of the "disarray" among prior judicial opinions that Congress, in enacting § 1346, had "meant to reinstate" (following a decision by the Supreme Court that the mail fraud statute as previously written did not support liability based on the deprivation of honest services). "To preserve the statute" under the doctrine that calls for courts to consider "limiting constructions" that might avert holdings of constitutional invalidity, see Sixth Edition pp. 77–80, the Court held that "§ 1346 criminalizes *only*" the bribery and kickbacks that constituted the "core of the * * * caselaw" that Congress had meant to restore. "Apprised that a broader reading of § 1346 could render the statute impermissibly vague, Congress, we believe, would have drawn the honest-services line, as we do now, at bribery and kickback schemes", Justice Ginsburg wrote.

In an opinion concurring in part and concurring in the judgment, Justice Scalia, joined by Justice Thomas and in part by Justice Kennedy, argued that the majority's "paring down" of the statute was "clearly beyond judicial power." In his view, the Court had not chosen between "fair alternative[]" interpretations of § 1346—as would have been proper under the doctrine of constitutional avoidance—but simply rewritten it.

The majority appears to have advanced its saving construction in response to Skilling's argument that § 1346 was so vague as to be facially invalid. Was that argument well-founded? Suppose that neither Skilling nor any other defendant could challenge § 1346 on its face, but only as applied. Would the statutory prohibition against fraudulently "depriv[ing] another of the intangible right of honest services" be unconstitutionally vague as applied to an employee who accepted bribes and kickbacks? If not, is the net effect of Skilling possibly to achieve in one step via a "saving construction" the same result that might have emerged from a series of cases adjudicating claims that § 1346 was unconstitutional as applied—namely, a situation in which § 1346 can be applied to cases involving bribes and kickbacks but not those predicated on other conduct?

---

# SECTION 4.  MOOTNESS

———

**Page 188.  Add a new footnote 2a at the end of the first sentence in the last paragraph in Paragraph (1):**

**2a.** In Pacific Bell Telephone Co. v. Linkline Communications, Inc., 129 S.Ct. 1109 (2009), the plaintiffs in an antitrust action conceded in the Supreme Court that they could not prevail on the theory of the case upon which they had predicated their complaint and upon which they had prevailed in the court of appeals. On that basis, the plaintiffs asked the Court to vacate the court of appeals' decision in their favor and to remand the case to the district court for them to amend their complaint based on an alternative antitrust theory first articulated by the dissent in the court of appeals. Rejecting the suggestion that the newfound lack of adversariness on the question presented in the Supreme Court made the case moot, Chief Justice Roberts' opinion for the Court concluded that the case was not moot because the parties still sought different forms of relief and because ambiguity in the plaintiffs' new position preserved a live dispute for the Court's resolution.

In so holding, the Court articulated some prudential concerns about finding mootness in the Supreme Court despite the lack of adversariness on the question presented:

Plaintiffs defended the Court of Appeals' decision at the certiorari stage, and the parties have invested a substantial amount of time, effort, and resources in briefing and arguing the merits of this case. In the absence of a decision from this Court on the merits, the Court of Appeals' decision would presumably remain binding precedent in the Ninth Circuit, and the Circuit conflict we granted certiorari to resolve would persist. Two amici have submitted briefs defending the Court of Appeals' decision on the merits, and we granted the motion of one of those amici to participate in oral argument. We think it appropriate to proceed to address the question presented.

Should continued adversity with respect to the requested relief keep the case alive when the parties agree on the *only* question before the Court? Given that agreement, does the Court's decision in Linkline Communications—relying on amici to present the plaintiffs' case on the merits—suggest that the Court regards mootness, at least when the question first arises on appeal, as grounded in prudential rather than constitutional concerns?

## Page 189.   Replace the last paragraph in Paragraph (2) with the following:

Whoever had the better of the argument, should historical practice be dispositive of the constitutional authority of Article III courts to decide moot cases? See, *e.g.*, Hall, *The Partially Prudential Doctrine of Mootness*, 77 Geo. Wash.L.Rev. 562 (2009) (arguing that the Court's longstanding practice has treated post-filing events that moot the issue underlying the claim as a jurisdictional bar negating a case or controversy, while treating events that merely moot the plaintiff's personal stake in the matter as a prudential limitation on the exercise of judicial power); Lee, *Deconstitutionalizing Justiciability: The Example of Mootness,* 105 Harv.L.Rev. 603 (1992)(suggesting that though there might be statutory, doctrinal, or prudential impediments to the adjudication of moot cases, they remain cases within the meaning of Article III).

## Page 193.   Add new Paragraphs 6(d) and (e):

(d) In Alvarez v. Smith, 130 S. Ct. 576 (2009), the Court made clear that the Bancorp exception to vacatur would not apply if the circumstances demonstrated that the parties had not arranged their affairs to render the case moot. In Alvarez, the plaintiffs (six individuals) had brought a due process challenge to the procedures used under Illinois law to seize property used to facilitate a drug crime and had prevailed on their claims in the Seventh Circuit. The Supreme Court, however, found that the case was moot: the plaintiffs had sought only injunctive and declaratory relief, and, by the time the case reached the Supreme Court, the state had returned the forfeited property to three of the plaintiffs; two had conceded that the state could keep the forfeited property; and the final plaintiff and the state had come to an agreement pursuant to which the state kept some but not all of his forfeited property. In an opinion by Justice Breyer, the Court held that the case was moot because the dispute over the validity of the Illinois law was no longer embedded in any actual controversy about the plaintiffs' particular legal rights.

Although the case had been mooted by the settlement of the state proceedings that underlay the federal challenge, the Court concluded that Bancorp did not govern. First, the Court found it significant that the parties did not settle the federal case itself; rather, [t]he six individual cases proceeded through a different court system without any procedural link to the federal case before us. Second, the plaintiffs had not raised their federal claims in the state forfeiture cases themselves. Third, [t]he disparate dates at which plaintiffs' forfeiture proceedings terminated—11, 14, 27, and 40 months after the seizures—indicate that the [state] did not coordinate the resolution of plaintiffs' state court cases, either with each other or with plaintiffs' federal civil rights case. Fourth, at oral argument in the Supreme Court, both parties resisted the suggestion of mootness, and neither argued that the federal case had been a factor in role in the termination of the proceedings. Accordingly, the Court concluded that the presence of this federal case played no role at all in producing the state court terminations and followed its ordinary practice of vacating the judgment of the court of appeals. Justice Stevens dissented.

Does the Court's approach reaffirm the idea that the equitable remedy of vacatur invites consideration of all the circumstances and that settlement alone should not automatically preclude the availability of vacatur? Should the Court have done more to determine whether the timing of *any* of the underlying state settlements seemed consistent with the state's desire to moot the case and then to obtain vacation of an adverse Seventh Circuit precedent? Given the difficulty of identifying the motives underlying the settlement of a case, does a bright-line rule precluding vacatur in cases of settlement make more sense than the apparent standard the Court adopted—one that invites a fact-specific inquiry into whether the settlement appeared to be motivated by such an objective?

(e) In Camreta v. Greene, 131 S.Ct. 2020 (2011), which is further discussed at pp. 13–14, *supra*, and pp. 54–55, 113, 115–117, *infra*, the Court addressed the appropriateness of a Munsingwear order in a qualified immunity case in which the lower court had ruled both on the merits and on grounds of qualified immunity. As discussed, Pearson v. Callahan, Sixth Edition pp. 78, 1004–05, had held that in order to "promote[] the development of constitutional precedent", federal courts in constitutional tort actions have discretion to reach the merits of a constitutional claim before deciding whether the defendants are entitled to qualified immunity on the ground that the asserted rights were not "clearly established". In Camreta, the Court held that when a lower court applying Pearson ruled against a state official on the merits but for him or her on qualified immunity grounds, the official could seek certiorari despite having prevailed in the court below. Of interest here, because Camreta became moot while the defendants' case was pending before the Supreme Court, the Court issued a Munsingwear order vacating the court of appeals' adverse merits decision. In so doing, the Court rejected the argument that vacatur was inappropriate in this context because it would undermine Pearson's goal of giving the court of appeals discretion to resolve constitutional questions for future cases. The Court reasoned that because "a constitutional ruling in a qualified immunity case is a legally consequential decision" that entitles even a prevailing defendant to Supreme Court review, the normal rule of vacatur should apply when "happenstance prevents that review from occurring". Is it obvious that the Court properly reconciled the competing impulses of Pearson and Munsingwear? What criteria should inform that assessment?

**Page 194.   Add a new Paragraph (8):**

**(8) Mootness and the Merits.** In Chafin v. Chafin, 133 S.Ct. 1017 (2013), Chief Justice Roberts' opinion for the Court admonished lower courts not to hold a case moot because the claim at issue reflected a low probability of success on the merits, or because the judgment was unlikely to be executed if the plaintiff prevailed. The case involved an international child custody battle. Lynn Chafin, a citizen of the United Kingdom, filed an action in the U.S. District Court for the Northern District of Alabama seeking the return of her daughter to Scotland under the Hague Convention on the Civil Aspects of International Child Abduction and implementing U.S. legislation. After the district court ordered the child's return to Scotland, Lynn Chafin returned to Scotland with the child. Jeffrey Chafin appealed to the Eleventh Circuit, which held that an appeal under the Convention is moot once the child has been returned to a foreign country.

The Supreme Court reversed. Lynn Chafin argued that the case was moot because the district court lacked authority under the Convention, and had no inherent equitable powers, to order the re-return of the child if the court of appeals reversed. The Court held that this argument's dependence on the proper interpretation of the Convention confused the question of mootness with that of the merits, adding that Jeffrey Chafin's claim "cannot be dismissed as so implausible that it is insufficient to preserve jurisdiction." The Court also rejected the contention that the case was moot because Scottish courts would "ignore" any district court order to return the child to the United States. "A re-return order," said the Court, "may not result in the return of [the child] to the United States, just as an order that an insolvent defendant pay $100 million may not make the plaintiff rich." Whatever the "potential difficulties in enforcement," the Court found that Jeffrey Chafin retained a sufficiently "concrete" interest in the case to defeat mootness.

**Page 197.   Substitute the following for Paragraph 2(d):**

(d) Genesis Healthcare Corp. v. Symczyk, 133 S.Ct. 1523 (2013), held that a plaintiff cannot maintain a collective action if her individual claim becomes moot before she has moved for certification. The plaintiff sued under the Fair Labor Standards Act (FLSA), 29 U.S.C. § 201 *et seq.*, on the ground that the employer illegally deducted 30 minutes for an unpaid lunch break each day, even when the employee performed compensable work during that time. Under the FLSA, a plaintiff may file an action on behalf of him- or herself and "other employees similarly situated." 29 U.S.C. § 216(b). Before Symczyk moved for "conditional certification," Genesis Healthcare tendered a settlement offer that purported to satisfy the full amount of the plaintiff's individual claim. Because the lower courts had held that this tender mooted the plaintiff's individual claim (even though she did not accept the offer), and a majority of the Justices thought the plaintiff had failed to preserve a challenge to that finding, the Court, in an opinion by Justice Thomas, accepted the premise that her claim was moot.[i] Given that premise, the Court held that the plaintiff could not maintain the collective action on behalf of other similarly situated employees under the FLSA. The Court emphasized that Geraghty had "explicitly limited

---

**i.** In dissent, Justice Kagan (joined by Justices Ginsburg, Breyer, and Sotomayor) argued that the mootness of the individual claim was properly before the Court, and that the employer's tender of a settlement offer could not moot the individual claim if the plaintiff did not accept it.

its holding to cases in which the named plaintiff's claim remains live at the time the district court denies class certification." The plaintiff in Genesis Healthcare, however, had not even moved for conditional certification under § 216(b) when her claim became moot.[j]

(e) Geraghty and Genesis Healthcare make clear that filing a motion for certification defines the moment after which a plaintiff may maintain a putative class action even though his or her individual claim has become moot. Did the Court draw the proper line? What constitutional or prudential interests would have been served by holding, as Justice Powell would have in Geraghty, that the named plaintiff may continue to represent the class only if formal certification has taken place before the individual claim has become moot? After all, a class may be certified without any real contest between the parties, since certification may be to the advantage of both sides, and even after certification, other members of the class may be able to opt out (see Fed. R.Civ.P. 23(c)(2)), or to challenge the adequacy of representation and thus the binding effect of the judgment in a collateral proceeding (see Hansberry v. Lee, 311 U.S. 32 (1940)). Conversely, what interests, if any, are served by insisting, as Genesis Healthcare seems to, that the motion for certification be filed before the individual claim becomes moot? Will the Court's position prevent strategic litigation behavior or merely ensure that plaintiffs move for class certification when they file their complaints?

# SECTION 5. RIPENESS

**Page 212. Add the following before the penultimate paragraph of Paragraph (5):**

In Holder v. Humanitarian Law Project, 130 S.Ct. 2705 (2010), plaintiffs challenged on due process vagueness and First Amendment grounds a statute making it a crime knowingly [to] provid[e] material support or resources to a foreign terrorist organization. 18 U.S.C. § 2339B(a)(1). The plaintiffs alleged that they were seeking to provide support for the nonviolent and lawful activities of two groups that had been designated as foreign terrorist organizations by the Secretary of State, and that the material-support statute prevented them from doing so. The Court found the case to be ripe because the plaintiffs faced "a credible threat of prosecution" (quoting Babbitt v. United Farm Workers National Union, Sixth Edition p. 210). In particular, the Court explained that (a) the plaintiffs alleged that they provided support to [the relevant groups] before the enactment of § 2339B and that they would provide similar support again if the statute's allegedly unconstitutional bar was lifted, and (b) the government informed the Court that it has charged about 150

**j.** The Court also emphasized that the premise of cases such as Geraghty and Sosna was that "a putative class acquires an independent legal status once it is certified under [Fed. R. Civ. P.] 23." In contrast, certification under the FLSA procedure merely resulted in sending notice to employees, who could then become parties by filing written consent with the court. Does this alternative ground of decision dilute the importance of the Court's holding concerning timing?

persons with violating § 2339B, and that several of those prosecutions involved the enforcement of the statutory terms at issue here.

**Page 219.   Add a new footnote 1a at the end of Paragraph (2):**

**1a.**  Looking at the other side of the coin, may the entry of an injunction, once the judgment has become final, provide a basis for standing even if the plaintiff seeking to enforce the injunction would not have had standing in the first instance? Salazar v. Buono, 130 S. Ct. 1803 (2010), involved an Establishment Clause challenge to a Latin cross erected in 1934 in a federal preserve by citizens seeking to honor soldiers who died in World War I. Buono, who visits the site regularly, brought an Establishment Clause challenge alleging that he was offended by the cross's placement on public lands. In Buono I, the district court found that Buono had standing and ruled for him on the merits, entering an injunction that required the cross's removal. In Buono II, the Ninth Circuit affirmed, and the government did not seek review.

Subsequently, Congress enacted legislation that authorized the transfer of the parcel containing the cross to the Veterans of Foreign Wars, in exchange for which a private citizen would transfer a parcel of equal value to the federal government. Buono returned to the district court, seeking to enforce the injunction and arguing that the transfer of property was merely a way of evading the order in Buono I and II. In Buono III, the district court granted Buono's motion, and the Ninth Circuit affirmed. In the Supreme Court, the government argued that Buono lacked standing to challenge the transfer because he was not offended by the cross itself, just by its presence on federal land.

The Court held that whether or not Buono had standing in Buono I and II, he now had a judicially cognizable interest in enforcing the injunction once the matter had gone to final judgment. In his opinion for the Court, Justice Kennedy wrote: Buono's entitlement to an injunction having been established in Buono I and II, he sought in Buono III to prevent the Government from frustrating or evading that injunction. Based on the rights he obtained under the earlier decree—against the same party, regarding the same cross and the same land—his interests in doing so were sufficiently personal and concrete to support his standing. In an opinion concurring in the judgment, Justice Scalia (joined by Justice Thomas) argued that Buono was, in fact, seeking new relief for which he had to establish an independent basis for standing. Should the standing inquiry turn on whether a plaintiff's request can be characterized as seeking to enforce an existing injunction or as a request for new relief? Why should characterizing an action as enforcement of an injunction give rise to standing if the plaintiff would not suffer injury-in-fact from the action against which enforcement is sought?

# SECTION 6.   POLITICAL QUESTIONS

**Page 234.   Add the following at the end of footnote 3:**

For a broad-ranging critique of the political question doctrine, see Paulsen, *The Constitutional Power to Interpret International Law*, 118 Yale L.J. 1762, 1817–1823 (2009) (arguing that some aspects of the political question doctrine—the textual-commitment and lack-of-judicially-manageable standards inquiries—constitute hidden merits determinations, and that other aspects relating to the appropriateness of judicial decision involve an invented judicial discretion to decline to decide a case within its jurisdiction for ad hoc policy reasons of the Court's own choosing). If Paulsen's analysis is sound, does that mean that Court should abandon the approach? That it should retain it but be candid about its discretionary nature?

**Page 236.   Add a new footnote 5a at the end of the first paragraph of Paragraph (3):**

**5a.**  Bradley & Morrison, *Historical Gloss and the Separation of Powers*, 126 Harv.L.Rev. 411, 429–430 (2012), argue that finding "a textually demonstrable constitutional commitment of [an] issue to a coordinate political department" often depends on an assessment of historical practice. For example, they explain, historical practice largely accounts for the constitutional principle that the Article II power to "receive Ambassadors" (U.S. Const. Art. II, § 3) also confers upon the President exclusive power to recognize foreign governments.

### Page 237.   Add a new footnote 7a to the end of the first paragraph of Paragraph (4):

**7a.**   Might the Court lack judicially manageable standards if there is law to apply but it is articulated at too high a level of abstraction? Huq, *Removal as a Political Question*, 65 Stan.L.Rev. 1 (2013), argues that "democratic accountability"—one of the Court's main criteria for assessing the validity of statutory restrictions on presidential power to remove executive officials—fails the judicially manageable standards test for that reason. He argues that the mechanisms of democratic accountability are complex and multifaceted, that it is unclear to what extent presidential removal power makes bureaucrats accountable to the people, and that a one-dimensional focus on removal ignores the diverse mechanisms for securing accountability. If Professor Huq's assessment is correct, does it suggest that the Court should try to avoid, where possible, taking constitutional analysis to high levels of abstraction such as democracy, accountability, and the like? Would that concern also apply to organizing concepts such as federalism? For the argument that the Court often deals with such indeterminacy not by finding a claim nonjusticiable but rather by adopting a posture of deference to the political branches, see Young, *Popular Constitutionalism and the Underenforcement Problem: The Case of the National Healthcare Law*, 75 Law & Contemp.Probs. 157, 179 (2012).

### Page 240.   Add a new Paragraph (7):

**(7) Constitutional Challenges to Statutes.** Zivotofsky v. Clinton, 132 S.Ct. 1421 (2012), suggests that the Court may be especially reluctant to find a political question where the question at issue is whether an Act of Congress impinges on authority asserted by the government to be exclusively executive. Zivitofsky presented a question involving the constitutionality of Section 214(d) of the Foreign Relations Authorization Act, Fiscal Year 2003, 116 Stat. 1350, which provides that an American citizen born in Jerusalem may list Israel as his or her place of birth on a U.S. Passport. Given the contested status of that city, State Department policy had long provided that American citizens born in Jerusalem could list Jerusalem, but not Israel or Jordan, as their place of birth. Born in Jerusalem to American parents, Zivotofsky (through his parents) sued the Secretary of State under the statute, seeking to enjoin her to designate Israel as the place of birth on his passport. The court of appeals held that Zivotofsky's complaint presented a political question because the Constitution assigns the executive unreviewable discretion to recognize foreign sovereigns and because the State Department's determination fell within that power.

After describing the political question doctrine as a "narrow exception" to its presumptive duty to hear cases within its jurisdiction, the Supreme Court reversed. The Court focused only on the first two Baker factors—textual commitment of the question to a coordinate branch and the absence of judicially manageable standards. The Court reasoned that Zivotofsky's invocation of an Act of Congress made both of those criteria harder to establish. First, the Court argued that whether or not the President has exclusive authority to recognize foreign governments and thus to make appropriate designations on U.S. Passports, "there is, of course, no exclusive commitment to the Executive of the power to determine the constitutionality of a statute." The judiciary, the Court made clear, must properly resolve any conflicts between Congress and the President over the contested allocation of power over passports.

Second, the Court suggested that if it had been asked to determine the political status of Jerusalem in the absence of a statute, it would have lacked judicially manageable standards to do so. But the problem "dissipate[d] * * * when the issue is recognized to be the more focused one of the [statute's] constitutionality.'' In arguing that the contested power lay exclusively with the executive, the government relied on the constitutional text, longstanding executive practice, congressional acquiescence in that practice, and judicial precedent. Zivotofsky, by contrast, contended that the power to designate a citizen's place of birth fell squarely within Congress's authority over immigration and foreign commerce, and that Congress had traditionally exercised extensive control over the form and content of passports. Relying on passages from the Federalist Papers, moreover, Zivotofsky argued that the recognition power is not exclusively executive and that, even if it were, designating a citizen's place of birth does not intrude on that power. After cataloguing (but not resolving) these competing arguments, the Court concluded that Zivotofsky's claims ''sound in familiar principles of constitutional interpretation'' and, while difficult, did not leave the Court without manageable standards.

Justice Sotomayor, joined in part by Justice Breyer, concurred in the judgment. She criticized the Court for failing to consider whether its assertion of jurisdiction would impinge on Baker's prudential factors, such as the need for the government to speak with one voice. She added that, in her view, the political question doctrine could, under proper circumstances, apply to a constitutional challenge to a statute. Finally, she noted that the Court should not have held that the case presented judicially manageable standards simply because the parties made textual, structural, and historical arguments—something that the parties in Nixon v. United States, Sixth Edition p. 222, had also done. She argued that when ''parties' textual, structural, and historical evidence is inapposite or wholly unilluminating, rendering judicial decision no more than guesswork, a case relying on the ordinary kinds of arguments offered to courts might well still present justiciability concerns.''[k] Justice Breyer dissented. Invoking the prudential Baker factors, he concluded that ''this case is unusual both in its minimal need for judicial intervention and in its more serious risk that intervention will bring about 'embarrassment,' show lack of 'respect' for the other branches, and potentially disrupt sound foreign policy decisionmaking.''

By framing the political question inquiry wholly in terms of the first two Baker factors—textual commitment and absence of judicially manageable standards—did Zivotofsky signal the Roberts Court's endorsement of Professor Wechsler's ''classical'' position over Professor Bickel's ''prudential'' one? Justice Sotomayor also accurately notes that the Court's test for a judicially manageable standard seems more forgiving in Zivotofsky than in Nixon, where the Court found a political question despite the availability of conventional textual, structural, and historical evidence about the nature of the Impeachment Power. Does Zivotofsky establish a stricter standard for finding a political question for challenges to an Act of Congress generally, or only when the Act of Congress requires the Court to umpire competing claims of constitutional authority made by Congress and the executive?

### Page 243.   Add the following at the end of footnote 4:

For a thoughtful critique of recent lower court cases invoking the political question doctrine to justify judicial deference to the executive in the foreign relations context, see Note, *Developments in the Law—Access to Courts*, 122 Harv.L.Rev. 1151, 1193–1204 (2009).

---

**k.**   Justice Alito also wrote separately to make clear that ''determining the constitutionality of an Act of Congress may present a political question, but I do not think that the narrow question presented here falls within that category.''

**Page 248.   Add a new footnote 15a at the end of Paragraph (5)(c):**

**15a.**  In determining whether to apply the political question doctrine (or, indeed, Judge Posner's "reverse political question doctrine") to contested elections, should the Court consider what roles courts of other countries play in the creation and maintenance of functioning democratic processes? See, *e.g.*, Ginsburg & Elkins, *Designing a Judiciary: Ancillary Powers of Constitutional Courts*, 87 Tex. L. Rev. 1431, 1452–53 (2009); Issacharoff, *Constitutional Courts and Democratic Hedging*, 99 Geo.L.J. 961, 977–79 (2011). By what metric should the Court determine whether judicial refereeing of election disputes abroad has been successful?

# CHAPTER III

# THE ORIGINAL JURISDICTION OF THE SUPREME COURT

**Page 252.  Add to the end of Paragraph (3)(b):**

For discussion of whether statutory restrictions on the exercise of federal habeas corpus jurisdiction apply to the Supreme Court when entertaining "original" writs of habeas corpus, see p. 37, *infra*.[6]

**Page 259.  Add a new Paragraph (6):**

**(6) Intervention by Nonstate Parties.** In South Carolina v. North Carolina, 558 U.S. 256 (2010), the Court clarified its standard for intervention by nonstate parties in an original action. South Carolina sued North Carolina, seeking an equitable apportionment of a river's waters. Three nonstate entities—the Catawba River Water Supply Project (CRWSP), Duke Energy Carolinas, and the city of Charlotte, North Carolina—all moved to intervene. In considering that motion, the Supreme Court, although noting that Article III posed no absolute impediment, emphasized that it had traditionally applied a high bar for permitting such intervention. In particular, the Court noted that " '[a]n intervenor whose state is already a party should have the burden of showing some compelling interest in his own right, apart from his interest in a class with all other citizens and creatures of the state, which interest is not properly represented by the state' " (quoting New Jersey v. New York, 345 U.S. 369, 373 (1953) (per curiam)). This strict standard, the Court explained,

---

**6.**  The Court recently sidestepped the question of congressional authority to regulate the procedures applicable to a case within the Court's original jurisdiction. In Kansas v. Colorado, 556 U.S. 98 (2009), the Special Master filed a report recommending the assessment of witness attendance fees against Colorado pursuant to 28 U.S.C. § 1821, which authorizes the award of such fees at a rate of $40 per day for proceedings in "any court of the United States". Kansas, the prevailing party in a dispute over Colorado's alleged depletion of the Arkansas River, sought a higher fee for the costs it had incurred in retaining expert witnesses, contending that § 1821 does not apply to an original action. More important, it argued that Congress could not limit the Court's ultimate authority to set its own procedures for original actions, whose origins lie directly in Article III, § 2, of the Constitution, rather than in a statutory grant of jurisdiction.

In an opinion by Justice Alito, the Court found it unnecessary to address either issue. "[A]ssuming for the sake of argument that the matter is left entirely to [its] discretion," the Court decided to apply the limitations found in § 1821 on the ground that "the best approach is to have a uniform rule that applies in all federal cases."

Chief Justice Roberts, joined by Justice Souter, wrote a concurrence to address the constitutional question. Noting that Article III, § 2, authorizes Congress to make "Exceptions" and "Regulations" concerning the Court's appellate jurisdiction but says no such thing about its original jurisdiction, the Chief Justice wrote that "[i]t is accordingly our responsibility to determine matters related to our original jurisdiction, including the availability and amount of witness fees." On the merits, he agreed that the $40 rate set by statute was reasonable, but stressed that "the choice is ours."

properly acknowledged that original actions "tax" the Court's limited resources by requiring it to play the role of factfinder and by diverting its attention from its " 'primary responsibility' " as an appellate court. The Court added that respect for state sovereignty reinforced these limits on nonstate intervention because the Court's original jurisdiction under 28 U.S.C. § 1251 was intended to resolve controversies that, had they arisen among separate sovereigns, would have been resolved by treaty or force. Applying the "compelling" circumstances test, the Court concluded that the CRWSP—an "unusual municipal entity" established as a joint venture between two separate counties in the two states— and Duke Energy Carolinas had compelling interests in the litigation that neither state would sufficiently represent. Chief Justice Roberts, joined by Justices Thomas, Ginsburg, and Sotomayor, dissented, reasoning that original jurisdiction was meant to resolve "sovereign" disputes and noting that "this Court has never before granted intervention in such a case to an entity other than a State, the United States, or an Indian Tribe."

Since 28 U.S.C. § 1251 provides that "[t]he Supreme Court shall have original and exclusive jurisdiction of all controversies between two or more States," what is the source of the Court's authority to permit (and, if it has such authority, to limit) intervention by nonstate entities? Is this a form of supplemental jurisdiction, exercised without following the "complete diversity" approach generally followed in 28 U.S.C. § 1332? Cf. Sixth Edition, p. 258, Paragraph (4); UMW v. Gibbs, Sixth Edition p. 825, and the Note following the Gibbs decision.[6] Why does the Court treat its appellate jurisdiction as its "primary responsibility"?

### Page 263.   Add to Paragraph (4):

For a critical examination of aggregate litigation brought by state attorneys general on behalf of their citizens, see Lemos, *Aggregate Litigation Goes Public: Representative Suits by State Attorneys* General, 126 Harv.L.Rev. 486 (2012). She notes that such litigation resembles private class actions but is not governed by provisions, like those in Fed.R.Civ.Proc. 23, that are designed to protect the interests of the class members. The absence of such safeguards is particularly troublesome, she argues, given the reasons to believe that state attorneys general will often not be good representatives of private claimants. Those reasons include conflicts of interest arising from the attorneys general's responsibility to represent the distinct interests of state agencies, their concern about the effect of litigation on the public interest, and their electoral ambitions, as well as their inclination to accept inadequate but quick settlements in

---

**6.** On a related note, the Court in Alabama v. North Carolina, 560 U.S. 330 (2010), held that sovereign immunity does not bar suit by a nonstate plaintiff (in this case, an interstate compact commission), provided that the nonstate plaintiff "assert[s] the same claims and request[s] the same relief" as a plaintiff state whose claims are not barred by sovereign immunity under existing case law. See p. 102, *infra.* Chief Justice Roberts, joined by Justice Thomas, dissented, reasoning that the commission's ability as a party to "object to settlement, seek taxation of costs, advance arguments we are obliged to

consider, and plead the judgment as res judicata in future litigation" violated the defendant state's immunity.

In view of the Court's strict posture toward intervention in South Carolina v. North Carolina, does its forgiving view of sovereign immunity in this case make sense? Quite apart from sovereign immunity, if the Court is reluctant to permit nonstate parties to intervene under 28 U.S.C. § 1251, why should a compact commission be able to join the action as a plaintiff simply because its claims and interests are aligned with those of a plaintiff state?

view of their lack of personal financial incentive to obtain larger recoveries and the limited resources most offices possess. And the problem of inadequate representation is of special concern given that a judgment in a suit brought by a state on behalf of its citizens is often held to preclude the citizens from suing on their own behalf.

**Page 266.   Add a new Paragraph (5):**

**(5) State Standing to Challenge the Affordable Care Act.** In Virginia ex rel. Cuccinelli v. Sebelius, 656 F.3d 253 (4th Cir.2011), the court of appeals ruled that Virginia lacked standing to pursue a constitutional challenge to the "individual mandate" provision of the federal Patient Protection and Affordable Care Act (PPACA). With some exceptions, the PPACA requires individual taxpayers to either maintain adequate health insurance coverage or pay a penalty. The day after the PPACA was enacted, the Governor of Virginia signed into law a state statute that declared that "[n]o resident of [Virginia] ... shall be required to obtain or maintain a policy of individual insurance coverage." Virginia contended that the PPACA injured the state's sovereign interest in "creat[ing] and enforc[ing] a legal code", as recognized in Alfred L. Snapp & Son, Inc. v. Puerto Rico, Sixth Edition p. 262. In finding no standing, the Fourth Circuit ruled that insofar as the state law barred localities and private employers from requiring insurance, the PPACA did not conflict with it. And insofar as the state law purported to bind the United States, it was simply an attempt "to immunize Virginia citizens from federal law"; citing Massachusetts v. Mellon, Sixth Edition p. 263, the court concluded that Virginia lacked a legitimate sovereign interest in providing such protection. For reaction to the Fourth Circuit's holding, compare Cuccinelli, Getchell & Russell, *State Sovereign Standing: Often Overlooked, But Not Forgotten*, 64 Stan.L.Rev. 89 (2012) (a critical reaction by the architects of Virginia's challenge) with Vladeck, *States' Rights and State Standing*, 46 U.Rich.L.Rev. 845 (2012) (supporting the court's ruling).

**Page 271.   Add to Paragraph (7):**

For the first time since 1962, the Supreme Court, in In re Davis, 130 S.Ct. 1 (2009), transferred a petition for an original writ of habeas jurisdiction, filed in the Supreme Court, to a district court. Separate opinions accompanying the Court's order raised issues about the scope of congressional power to regulate the Supreme Court when entertaining such petitions.

The Court's order transferring the habeas petition, which had been filed by a state prisoner under a death sentence for murder, directed the district court to receive testimony and determine whether evidence not obtainable at trial clearly establishes the prisoner's innocence. Dissenting from the order, Justice Scalia (joined by Justice Thomas) noted that the Court had not transferred such a petition for nearly 50 years,[7] and objected that there was no showing that "exceptional circumstances warrant the exercise of the Court's discretionary power" given that the petition "is a sure loser."

Had Davis filed his habeas petition in the district court, various statutory rules would have limited that court's exercise of habeas jurisdiction. Among those rules are: (1) a ban, found in 28 U.S.C. § 2254(d)(1), on the award of

---

**7.**   See Byrnes v. Walker, 371 U.S. 937 (1962); Chaapel v. Cochran, 369 U.S. 869 (1962).

relief unless the state court decision was contrary to, or an unreasonable application of, clearly established federal law as determined by the Supreme Court; and (2) sharp limits on consideration of successive petitions (Davis already had filed one habeas petition that was denied and had been rebuffed under those statutory rules when he tried to file a second petition). See Sixth Edition pp. 1249–66, 1293–96. Justice Scalia focused on the former of these limits in characterizing the petition as a "sure loser".

In response, Justice Stevens (joined by Justices Ginsburg and Breyer) suggested that § 2254(d)(1) might not apply, or might not apply "with the same rigidity", to an original habeas petition, or that if it did apply, it might be unconstitutional insofar as it purported to bar relief for a death row inmate who has established his innocence.

There may be questions about Congress' power to eliminate altogether the Supreme Court's jurisdiction over a case that falls within the original jurisdiction. See Sixth Edition p. 251. But recall that the so-called "original writ" of habeas corpus in the Supreme Court is not an exercise of the original jurisdiction under Article III, but instead is an exercise of appellate jurisdiction. (The Court in Davis did not specify from what decision an appeal was being taken, but presumably it was from either a state court decision affirming the judgment of conviction or denying postconviction relief or from the lower federal courts' denial of his earlier petition for a writ of habeas corpus, filed in the district court.) What constitutional problems, if any, would arise from application to an original petition of the same limits that govern the district courts, given that the Supreme Court has held that it exercises *appellate* jurisdiction when entertaining an original writ of habeas corpus?

If the Suspension Clause or another constitutional provision gives Davis a right of access to a court (or more specifically to a federal court) on his habeas claim, then presumably Congress could not foreclose that right altogether. But would it be sensible to provide that any such constitutional right may be exercised only in the Supreme Court and not in the district court? (And if statutory limits apply to the district courts but not to original writs sought from the Supreme Court, do they apply when, as in Davis, a district court entertains a case transferred to it by the Supreme Court?)[8] On the other hand, if Davis had no constitutional right of access to a court, is it sensible to interpret congressional limitations on habeas jurisdiction as inapplicable to the original writs sought in the Supreme Court?

For discussion of some of these issues and a more general review of the original writ of habeas corpus, see Kovarsky, *Original Habeas Redux*, 97 Va.L.Rev. 61 (2011).

---

**8.** Section 2241(b) authorizes the Supreme Court to transfer a petition to the district court. Since Davis' petition fell within the Supreme Court's appellate jurisdiction, is the district court exercising appellate jurisdiction when adjudicating the transferred petition?

# CHAPTER IV

# CONGRESSIONAL CONTROL OF THE DISTRIBUTION OF JUDICIAL POWER AMONG FEDERAL AND STATE COURTS

## SECTION 1. CONGRESSIONAL REGULATION OF FEDERAL JURISDICTION

**Page 278.  Add to Paragraph (3):**

The Sixth Edition notes that jurisdiction-stripping proposals are almost never enacted. Professor Grove argues that the bicameralism and presentment requirements of Article I explain this pattern of failure. See Grove, *The Structural Safeguards of Federal Jurisdiction*, 124 Harv.L.Rev. 869 (2011). Relying on history and social science scholarship, Grove argues that all political actors in a competitive political system have long-term incentives to maintain an independent judiciary that can check the opposition party when it becomes dominant, and that the hurdles erected by Article I generally allow the minority faction to block attempts by the majority to strip jurisdiction. In a subsequent article, she further contends that the President and the Department of Justice have strong incentives to oppose jurisdiction stripping bills and to adopt narrow interpretations of any that do survive the legislative process. See Grove, *The Article II Safeguards of Federal Jurisdiction*, 112 Colum.L.Rev. 250 (2012).

**Page 281.  Add a new footnote 21a at the end of Subparagraph (5)(a)(ii):**

**21a.**  Frost & Lindquist, *Countering the Majoritarian Difficulty*, 96 Va.L.Rev. 719 (2010), consider a potential role for the federal courts in alleviating the "majoritarian difficulty" created by state judicial elections, which, they contend, threaten the rule of law by effectively allowing popular review of state court decisions. To counter this difficulty by deterring state judges from failing to adequately enforce federal law and by providing political cover for state judges in close cases, the authors urge heightened review of elected (rather than appointed) state judges by the Supreme Court, as well as by lower federal courts when exercising habeas corpus jurisdiction to review custody under state criminal convictions.

Professor Shugerman's work on the rise of judicial elections in the nineteenth century shows a different picture of their relationship to judicial review. See Shugerman, *Economic Crisis and the Rise of Judicial Elections and Judicial Review*, 123 Harv.L.Rev.1063 (2010). He contends that when elections swept the country in the 1840s and 1850s, they replaced a system in which appointments had become a tool of political cronyism. Elections were designed to strengthen the exercise of the power of judicial review, notably with regard to legislative overspending and corruption, and the shift in selection mechanisms proved to have that effect.

## Page 291.   Add a new footnote 6a at the end of the last full paragraph:

**6a.**   Professor Fitzpatrick contends that the debate on jurisdiction stripping has been dominated by two views that are in tension: first, that constitutional decisionmaking requires the kind of independence that federal judges possess and state judges lack; and second, that the text and original understanding of Article III permit leaving federal constitutional claims exclusively to the state courts. He seeks to resolve this tension by focusing on the extent to which state court judges have been insulated from control by state political branches or state electorates. In the Founding era, state judges possessed a degree of independence comparable to federal judges. But beginning in the nineteenth century, appointment and life tenure gave way, generally, to limited terms and service depending in some way on popular elections. In light of this change, he suggests that the original understanding needs to be "translated" to the present circumstances: because state court judges lack the independence they possessed in 1789, leaving constitutional claims to the state courts should now be deemed impermissible. See Fitzpatrick, *The Constitutionality of Federal Jurisdiction–Stripping Legislation and the History of State Judicial Selection and Tenure*, 98 Va.L.Rev. 839 (2012).

Those commentators who find in the original understanding not simply a recognition of broad congressional power but also a concern about judicial independence might take issue with Fitzpatrick's view that state courts were constitutionally adequate in 1789. Their objection would be that a guarantee of independence in state law at any given time is no guarantee at all, since it can always be eliminated by the state government. By contrast, more traditionalist commentators, who view the Constitution as leaving to Congress the choice between state and federal courts, might respond to Fitzpatrick by contending that changes in state court selection processes are precisely the kind of circumstance that Congress was to consider in allocating jurisdiction, but do not, in themselves, take the choice out of congressional hands.

## Page 295.   Add to footnote 13:

Pfander & Birk, *Article III and the Scottish Judiciary*, 124 Harv.L.Rev. 1613 (2011), find historical support in the example of the Scottish judiciary for the view that the Constitution requires a single Supreme Court with supervisory authority over inferior courts. The Scottish Court of Session exercised supervisory authority over all inferior courts in civil cases, and the authors contend that the Scottish system furnished a model available to the Framers when drafting Article III. The claim that that model had influence in America rests not on specific evidence from the Convention or Ratification debates adverting to Scotland but instead on the more general observation that the Scottish model was well-known in America—and, notably, known to James Wilson, who, as a member of the Committee of Detail at the Convention, drafted the provision that became the Exceptions Clause. Pfander and Birk point particularly to Article XIX of the 1707 Acts of Union between England and Scotland, which subjected the Court of Session "to such Regulations for the better Administration of Justice, as shall be made by the *Parliament* of *Great-Britain*", while providing that "all Inferior Courts" in Scotland would "remain Subordinate, as they are now to the Supream Courts of Justice" of Scotland "in all time coming." The authors view the exceptions clause as remarkably similar to Article XIX, and contend that the Exceptions Clause, like Article XIX, insulates the judicial system "from the threat that ordinary legislation could pose to its independence, structure, or jurisdiction."

## Pages 296–97.   Add to footnote 15:

See also Glashausser, *A Return to Form for the Exceptions Clause*, 51 B.C.L.Rev. 1383 (2010) (arguing that the first draft of what became the Exceptions Clause was intended only to permit Congress to transfer cases from the Court's appellate jurisdiction to its original jurisdiction, but that this meaning was obscured by revisions that culminated in the current language).

## Page 302.   Add a new footnote 21a at the end of the first, carryover paragraph:

**21a.**   Fletcher, *Congressional Power Over the Jurisdiction of Federal Courts: The Meaning of The Word "All" in Article III*, 59 Duke L.J. 929, 934 (2010), argues on textual and historical grounds that the import of the word "all" in Article III is to "authorize[ ], but * * * not require, Congress to confer exclusive jurisdiction on the federal courts".

## Page 302.  Add a new footnote 21b at the end of the first full paragraph:

**21b.**  Professor Amar argued that in fact Section 25 covered all federal questions, because whenever one party claimed a federal right, the other party could claim a federal immunity (*e.g.*, that the other party lacked a federal right). In response, Professor Meltzer acknowledged that some twentieth century cases seemed to take that view, but contended that the Marshall and Taney Courts had dismissed appeals for want of jurisdiction when the state court had upheld federal rights. More recently, Professor Woolhandler has advanced "a middle ground between Amar's expansive view * * * and Meltzer's restrictive view," finding that the Court was more likely to accept the expansive view in cases involving the scope of federal statutes. She acknowledges that "no one seems to have thought review was available when [in 1911] the New York Court of Appeals struck down the state workers' compensation statute on federal constitutional grounds"—the decision that motivated Congress in 1914 to broaden the jurisdictional statute by eliminating the language that had made review depend on whether the state court had decided against the authority, title right, privilege, or immunity under federal law. Woolhandler, *Power, Rights, and Section 25*, 86 Notre Dame L.Rev.1241 (2011).

## Page 303.  Add a new Paragraph (4):

**(4) Jurisdiction Stripping, the Limits of Originalism, and Unconstitutional Motivation in Enacting Jurisdictional Legislation.** In a broad-ranging article, Professor Fallon contends that the interpretive approach of most analyses of jurisdiction-stripping has been excessively originalist. See Fallon, *Jurisdiction-Stripping Reconsidered,* 96 Va.L.Rev. 1043 (2010). He finds support for his rejection of originalism in the Supreme Court's 2008 decision in Boumediene v. Bush, Sixth Edition pp. 318, 1168, 1192. There, the Court, in ruling that Congress had violated the Suspension Clause of the Constitution when it sought to preclude both federal and state courts from exercising habeas corpus jurisdiction in specified cases, found the 18th century history indeterminate and proceeded to decide the case based on principles derived from recent decisions and functional considerations.

Putting aside any interpretive approach based on "exclusive originalism," Fallon contends that an unconstitutional purpose can render a jurisdiction stripping statute invalid, noting more broadly the prevalence of motive-based inquiries in constitutional adjudication. He suggests that a statute withdrawing from both the lower federal courts and the Supreme Court previously-conferred jurisdiction over a constitutional issue, based on Congress' anticipated disagreement with how federal courts would resolve that issue, would be unconstitutional because enacted "for the purpose of encouraging state courts to ignore, reject, or defy pertinent precedents." Fallon discounts the Court's declaration in Ex parte McCardle, Sixth Edition p. 286, that the Court may not inquire into Congress' motive. He finds McCardle distinguishable because another route to Supreme Court review remained and possibly because of the Court's decision in United States v. Klein, Sixth Edition p. 303, which he reads as approving inquiry into congressional motive.

Fallon does not argue, however, that a withdrawal of either the Supreme Court's appellate jurisdiction or the original jurisdiction of the lower federal courts over a particular constitutional issue would necessarily be unconstitutional. The former would not disturb lower federal courts, whose judges (unlike state court judges) enjoy tenure and salary protection, from enforcing the Constitution, while the latter would be consistent with "long-entrenched statutes and settled legal doctrines [that] tolerate the exclusion of cases presenting constitutional issues from the lower federal courts' jurisdiction.''

Fallon's argument calls attention to the far greater prominence of originalist arguments in debates about Article III than in debates about most other constitutional issues. Do you agree that a congressional decision, motivated by dislike of federal court constitutional decisions, to assign cases to state courts is necessarily an invitation to defy precedent, rather than an effort to seek decisions that the legislators think stand on a sounder constitutional footing? And if legislation precluding *all* federal court jurisdiction is constitutionally infirm because it is likely to rest on the unconstitutional purpose of encouraging courts to defy precedent, isn't legislation that strips lower federal courts alone of jurisdiction likely to rest on the same suspect motivation—especially given the infrequency of Supreme Court review of state court decisions?

**Page 305.   Add to the end of footnote 27:**

Some commentators contend that Klein stands for the principle that Congress may not deceive the electorate about the way in which legislation operates. They read the Klein opinion as holding that Congress had violated this principle by enacting evidentiary rules whose effect was to transform the meaning of the law that provided compensation to loyal owners of property. See Redish & Pudelski, *Legislative Deception, Separation of Powers, and the Democratic Process: Harnessing the Political Theory of United States v. Klein*, 100 Nw. U.L.Rev. 437 (2006); accord, Vladeck, *Why Klein (Still) Matters: Congressional Deception and the War on Terrorism*, 5 J.Nat'l Security L. & Pol'y 251 (2011).

Professor Young doubts that Klein's concern about separation of powers can plausibly be read as the source of a right not to be misled about the meaning of statutes, and he also questions the appropriateness of judicial evaluation of purported legislative deceptiveness. But in an article revisiting the Klein decision, Young now finds that Klein radiates more broadly than he had suggested in his 1995 article (cited in the Sixth Edition). See Young, *United States v. Klein, Then and Now*, 44 Loy.U.Chi.L.J. 265 (2012). On this broader reading, Congress may not regulate a federal court's deliberative processes in a variety of ways. Among the prohibited regulations would be some restrictions on fact-finding in constitutional cases (*e.g.*, conclusive presumptions or rebuttable presumptions that are probabalistically unreasonable) and some prescriptions of the interpretive methods to be followed when interpreting the Constitution and statutes.

**Page 314.   Add a new Paragraph (6a):**

**(6a) Preclusion of Review and Theories of Constitutional Remedies.**
For a careful analysis of congressional power to control jurisdiction, see Fallon, *Jurisdiction-Stripping Reconsidered,* 96 Va.L.Rev. 1043 (2010). After noting that Congress may be unable to point to a source of legislative authority to justify stripping all courts of jurisdiction, Fallon stresses that the scope of congressional power to preclude all jurisdiction is inextricably bound up with the scope of Congress' power to preclude the award of a particular remedy (or, in some cases, to preclude any and all remedies). He proceeds to analyze a broad set of situations, including the jurisdictional provision in Battaglia, limits on the writ of habeas corpus, limits on post-deprivation remedies, and limits on injunctive relief, in light of a theory of constitutionally-required remedies.

---

## SECTION 2.   CONGRESSIONAL AUTHORITY TO ALLOCATE JUDICIAL POWER TO NON-ARTICLE III FEDERAL TRIBUNALS

**Page 339.   Add a new footnote 11 at the end of Paragraph (7):**

**11.** As to these questions and, more generally, the material on administrative adjudication, see Merrill, *Article III, Agency Adjudication, and the Origins of the Appellate Review Model of Administrative Law*, 111 Colum.L.Rev.939 (2011). Professor Merrill provides a careful historical study of the origins of the appellate review model of agency adjudication, which he views as hardly inevitable. The nineteenth century, he suggests, featured a "bipolar", all-or-nothing model in which courts either reviewed administrative action under one of the prerogative writs (like mandamus or habeas corpus), on a record produced in court, or afforded no review at all. He locates the origins of the modern appellate review model in the Supreme Court's retreat from its aggressive, and politically controversial, review of decisions of the Interstate Commerce Commission in the 1890s and 1900s, and contends that the approach then spread to other areas. Merrill suggests that while today scholars worry about whether the appellate review model permits the dilution of judicial power, the earlier concern was that Article III courts would be contaminated by being drawn into matters of administration, a concern that the appellate review model largely eliminated. Moving to the present, he doubts that the current allocation of authority—in which judges decide legal issues, while deferring to agencies on factual matters—is optimal, given the close ties of law to policy and the greater expertise and accountability of agencies as policymakers. (The Chevron doctrine, Merrill suggests, is a partial but incomplete recognition of agency primacy in policymaking.) But he acknowledges that the appellate review model is so deeply entrenched as to make unlikely any significant departure from it.

**Page 349.   Add to Paragraph 8(e):**

Professor Fallon revisits appellate review theory in *Jurisdiction-Stripping Reconsidered*, 96 Va.L.Rev. 1043 (2010). While continuing to believe that the appellate review framework is correct, he acknowledges that its acceptance would call into question more adjudicative regimes (because of their lack of adequate appellate review) than he had initially anticipated.

**Page 363.   Add a new Paragraph (8):**

**(8) Stern v. Marshall.** In Stern v. Marshall, 131 S.Ct. 2594 (2011), its latest decision on non-Article III adjudication, the Supreme Court moved back toward the formal and categorical approach of Northern Pipeline and away from the more functional and pragmatic approach of Thomas and Schor.

**(a) The Facts.** The case was the latest chapter in a long dispute over the fortune of J. Howard Marshall II between his third wife, Vickie (formerly known as Anna Nicole Smith) and his son Pierce. Marshall died about a year after his marriage to Vickie, who was not included in his will. After Vickie filed for bankruptcy, Pierce filed a complaint in that bankruptcy proceeding, contending that Vickie had defamed him by inducing her lawyers to state that Pierce had defrauded her by inducing his father to sign a living trust that did not include Vickie. Pierce's complaint sought a determination that his defamation claim was not dischargeable in bankruptcy. (If the claim was dischargeable, a failure to file it in the bankruptcy court would result in its being foreclosed.). The bankruptcy trustee filed a counterclaim against Pierce, alleging that Pierce had wrongfully prevented J. Howard from taking the legal steps needed to carry out his asserted intention to provide Vickie with half of his property. Pierce later filed a proof of claim in the bankruptcy proceeding on his defamation claim.

The question before the Supreme Court was whether the bankruptcy court could constitutionally adjudicate the trustee's counterclaim against Pierce. In many respects the case resembled Northern Pipeline: a trustee was asserting a state common law claim against a private party. The key factual difference was that here, Pierce had filed a claim against the bankruptcy estate and was now being sued on a compulsory counterclaim rather than on a freestanding claim by the trustee.

**(b) The Majority Opinion.** In a 5–4 decision, the Court held that the bankruptcy court could not constitutionally adjudicate the counterclaim against Pierce. After stressing the importance of Article III's tenure and salary protection in preserving the separation of powers and thereby protecting individual liberty, Chief Justice Roberts' majority opinion stated that "in general, Congress may not 'withdraw from judicial cognizance any matter which, from its nature, is the subject of a suit at the common law, or in equity, or admiralty' " (quoting Murray's Lessee v. Hoboken Land & Improvement Co., Sixth Edition p. 332). With respect to the claim in question, the bankruptcy courts under the 1984 Act exercise the same powers that they possessed under the 1978 Act held unconstitutional in Northern Pipeline. Here, as in Northern Pipeline, the claim arose under state law; the bankruptcy court's jurisdiction was not limited by subject matter; the bankruptcy court issues enforceable judgments; and Article III review of those judgments occurs "under traditional appellate standards".

The Court proceeded to analyze the jurisdiction to adjudicate the counterclaim under two categories drawn from the Northern Pipeline plurality opinion—public rights cases and adjuncts—as well as to focus on the significance of the bankruptcy court's counterclaim jurisdiction.

**(i) The Public Rights Exception.** Acknowledging that the Court's discussion of the public rights exception "has not been entirely consistent, and the exception has been the subject of some debate," the majority found that the "case does not fall within any of the various formulations of the concept that appear in this Court's opinions." The Court's survey of precedents included the following observations:

• Decisions like Crowell v. Benson "contrasted cases within the reach of the public rights exception—those arising 'between the Government and persons subject to its authority in connection with the performance of the constitutional functions of the executive or legislative departments'—and those that were instead matters 'of private right, that is, of the liability of one individual to another' ".

• The decisions in Thomas and Schor "rejected the limitation of the public rights exception to actions involving the Government as a party. The Court has continued, however, to limit the exception to cases in which the claim at issue derives from a federal regulatory scheme, or in which resolution of the claim by an expert Government agency is deemed essential to a limited regulatory objective within the agency's authority. In other words, it is still the case that what makes a right 'public' rather than private is that the right is integrally related to particular Federal Government action."

• Thus, in Thomas the right to compensation was granted by a federal statute and did not depend on or replace a right to compensation under state law.

• The Court in Schor had stressed that "(1) the claim and the counterclaim concerned a 'single dispute'—the same account balance"; (2) the CFTC's jurisdiction was limited to " 'a narrow class of common law claims' in 'a particularized area of law' "; (3) that area " 'was governed by a specific and limited federal regulatory scheme' as to which the agency had 'obvious expertise' "; (4) the parties had freely elected to resolve their differences before the

CFTC; and (5) CFTC orders were " 'enforceable only by order of the district court' " (quoting Schor). "Most significantly, given that the customer's reparations claim before the agency and the broker's counterclaim were competing claims to the same amount, the Court repeatedly emphasized that it was 'necessary' to allow the agency to exercise jurisdiction over the broker's [counter]claim" (quoting Schor).

• In Granfinanciera, the Court had held that a fraudulent conveyance action filed on behalf of a bankruptcy estate against a noncreditor did not fall within in the public rights exception.

After that review of the precedents, the majority noted that the counterclaim in this case was between two private parties and was based on state common law. Unlike the claim in Thomas, it did not flow from a federal statutory scheme, nor was it " 'completely dependent upon' adjudication of a claim created by federal law, as in Schor" (quoting Schor). The Court further distinguished Schor on the ground that Pierce did not truly consent to bankruptcy court jurisdiction by filing a claim, as "[c]reditors who possess claims that do not satisfy the requirements for nondischargeability * * * have no choice but to file their claims in bankruptcy proceedings if they want to pursue the claims at all".

Acknowledging that the distinction between public and private rights may fail to provide guidance "as to whether, for example, a particular agency can adjudicate legal issues under a substantive regulatory scheme," the Court declared: "What is plain here is that this case involves the most prototypical exercise of judicial power: the entry of a final, binding judgment *by a court* with broad substantive jurisdiction, on a common law cause of action, when the action neither derives from nor depends upon any agency regulatory regime."

**(ii) The Significance of Pierce's Proof of Claim and Counterclaim Jurisdiction.** The Court then turned to the argument that Northern Pipeline and Granfinanciera were distinguishable because in this case Pierce, unlike the defendants in those cases, had filed a proof of claim in the bankruptcy proceedings. In Katchen v. Landy and Langenkamp v. Culp, Sixth Edition p. 360 n.2, after a creditor had filed a proof of claim against the bankrupt estate, the Supreme Court had upheld bankruptcy jurisdiction over a counterclaim asserting a voidable preference or a preferential transfer. (Such a counterclaim contends that the debtor had transferred assets to the creditor in anticipation of bankruptcy and that the creditor's claim should be disallowed as a result.) Chief Justice Roberts distinguished these cases "because it was not possible for the [bankruptcy court] to rule on the creditor's proof of claim without first resolving the voidable preference issue," and once that issue was resolved, nothing would remain for adjudication on the counterclaim. He also noted that in those cases, the counterclaim rested on *federal* bankruptcy law. By contrast, the counterclaim here rested on state law, and despite some factual overlap between Pierce's claim and the counterclaim, adjudicating the counterclaim required the bankruptcy court to make a number of factual and legal determinations not required to resolve Pierce's claim for defamation.

**(iii) Adjuncts.** Finally, the Court rejected the argument that bankruptcy courts under the 1984 Act are "adjuncts" of the district courts, essentially for the same reasons that the plurality in Northern Pipeline had rejected a similar argument: the bankruptcy courts have broad jurisdiction not limited by subject matter and can enter final judgments. Nor was it relevant that under the 1984 Act, bankruptcy judges are appointed by the Article III courts rather than by the President (as was true under the 1978 Act invalidated by Northern Pipeline); if the bankruptcy courts exercise the " 'essential attributes of judicial power' " (quoting Schor), it does not matter who appointed their judges.

**(iv) The Limits of Pragmatism**. In a concluding section of its opinion, the majority responded to the argument that restricting compulsory counterclaim jurisdiction will delay and impose additional costs on bankruptcy proceedings. The Court first stated that the efficiency or usefulness of a law, " 'standing alone, will not save it if it is contrary to the Constitution' " (quoting INS v. Chadha, 462 U.S. 919, 944 (1983)). In addition, the Chief Justice doubted that the practical consequences were so significant, given that under the 1984 Act, some specified state law claims are adjudicated in state courts rather than in the bankruptcy court, and that the bankruptcy court could still prepare proposed findings of fact and conclusions of law on counterclaims for review by the district court. He concluded by suggesting that even if the issue here is narrow and the counterclaim jurisdiction "may seem innocuous at first blush", there is a threat to the separation of powers from chipping away at the Judiciary's authority: " 'illegitimate and unconstitutional practices get their first footing * * * by silent approaches and slight deviations from legal modes of procedure' " (quoting Boyd v. United States, 116 U.S. 616, 635 (1886)).

**(d) Justice Scalia's Concurrence.** Although agreeing with the Court's interpretation of its precedents, Justice Scalia reiterated his view in Granfinanciera that a public rights case "must at a minimum arise between the government and others". He continued by stating that "[t]he sheer surfeit of factors that the Court was required to consider in this case should arouse the suspicion that something is seriously amiss with our jurisprudence in this area", listing seven different reasons the Court offered in determining that Article III adjudication was required. He then concluded: "Leaving aside certain adjudications by federal administrative agencies, which are governed (for better or worse) by our landmark decision in Crowell v. Benson, in my view an Article III judge is required in *all* federal adjudications, unless there is a firmly established historical practice to the contrary. For that reason—and not because of some intuitive balancing of benefits and harms—I agree that Article III judges are not required in the context of territorial courts, courts-martial, or true 'public rights' cases".

**(e) The Dissent**. Justice Breyer's dissent (joined by Justices Ginsburg, Sotomayor, and Kagan) objected to the majority's discussion of precedent and distanced the dissenters from a formal and categorical approach to the issue, favoring instead an approach stressing functional considerations.

Reviewing the precedents, he suggested that the Court's "watershed" opinion in Crowell did not hold narrowly, as the majority suggested, that an agency can make specialized, limited factual determinations in a particularized area of law as an adjunct of the district court. That narrow a view of Crowell needlessly cast doubt upon well established schemes in which federal agencies adjudicate disputes between private parties. (In this regard, the majority, after offering the narrow view of Crowell criticized by Justice Breyer, said that "Crowell may well have additional significance in the context of expert administrative agencies that oversee particular substantive federal regimes, but we have no occasion to and do not address those issues today.")

Justice Breyer also criticized the Court for relying so heavily on an approach supported only by a plurality in Northern Pipeline, rather than on the more pragmatic approach of the subsequent decision in Thomas and Schor, both of which commanded a majority. The question for him was whether "the challenged delegation of adjudicatory authority posed a genuine and serious threat that one branch of Government sought to aggrandize its own constitutionally delegated authority by encroaching upon a field of authority that the Constitution assigns exclusively to another branch." He stressed that Thomas and Schor rested their analysis on practical attention to substance and to a broad range of factors. "Insofar as the majority would apply more formal standards, it simply disregards recent, controlling precedent."

Justice Breyer then discussed the relevant factors under Thomas and Schor: First, while the nature of the counterclaim—which resembles a suit at common law—argues against the validity of non-Article III adjudication, this factor had less significance given that bankruptcy courts often decide claims that resemble common law claims. And though "the state-law question is embedded in a debtor's counterclaim, not a creditor's claim * * * the counterclaim is 'compulsory' " and thus its resolution will turn on facts related to the creditor's claim, which the bankruptcy court indisputably may resolve. Second, bankruptcy judges have considerable protection from improper political influence, as they are appointed by the Article III courts and are removable only by the judiciary and only for cause. Third, Article III judges supervise bankruptcy courts at least as much if not more than they supervised the agency in Crowell. Fourth, the parties consented—in Pierce's case, by voluntarily appearing in bankruptcy court to press a claim that he asserts is nondischargeable and hence that he could have pursued in another forum. Even as to private rights, non-Article III adjudication may be appropriate when both parties consent. And fifth, Justice Breyer stressed the importance of the legislative purpose served by counterclaim jurisdiction. A counterclaim may offset the creditor's claim or even augment the estate, and Congress had concluded that counterclaim jurisdiction is critical to efficient operation of the bankruptcy system.

In conclusion, Justice Breyer suggested that cases involving counterclaims against creditors arise with some frequency, and given the "staggering" volume of bankruptcy cases (1.6 million last year, compared to 280,000 civil and 78,000 criminal cases in the federal district courts), "a constitutionally required game of jurisdictional ping-pong between courts would lead to inefficiency, increased cost, delay, and needless suffering among those faced with bankruptcy."

**(f) The State of the Law after Stern v. Marshall.** Given all of the twists and turns since Northern Pipeline, and the close division in Stern v. Marshall, it seems clear that this area of the law remains unstable. On one view, the Court in Stern v. Marshall changed little: the precise issue was very close to that in Northern Pipeline, and the Court did not overturn any precedents. Moreover (as Justice Scalia complained), a number of features that seemed to be salient after Thomas and Schor figured in the Court's analysis, including whether the right is public or private, and more broadly the source of the right (state common law vs. federal statutory law); whether there is a federal regulatory program in the picture; whether the tribunal enters final judgments; the scope of Article III review; the substantive reach of the tribunal's adjudicatory authority; and whether the parties have consented to non-Article III adjudication.

On the other hand, whereas Thomas and Schor endorsed a broad, pragmatic, functional approach with considerable deference to congressional judgments about desirable institutional arrangements, the Court in Stern v. Marshall clearly rejects that understanding. Indeed, the Court's concluding warning about small incremental threats to the separation of powers echoes a similar warning by Justice Brennan in his dissent in Schor. The approach of the majority opinion is more formal and categorical than Thomas and Schor, and its tone is more skeptical of non-Article III adjudication.[8]

**(g) Additional Questions**. Consider, finally, these more particular questions about Stern v. Marshall:

(1) On the question of the voluntariness of consent, doesn't the majority have the better of the argument? Pierce's initial request for a declaration of non-dischargeability very likely stemmed from uncertainty on that score. If his choice was either to file in bankruptcy court or to accept a non-trivial risk of forfeiting his claim if it was later deemed to have been discharged, how "voluntary" was his constructive consent to counterclaim jurisdiction?

(2) Chief Justice Roberts emphasized that the non-Article III tribunal here was a court, not an agency. With respect to the concern about judicial independence, why should that fact alone matter? Indeed, aren't bankruptcy judges far freer from control by the political branches than adjudicators in administrative agencies, which are subject to congressional oversight and some measure of presidential influence and are typically led by political appointees?

(3) Suppose that bankruptcy judges begin preparing proposed findings of facts and conclusions of law for counterclaims, as suggested by the majority. Given the volume of cases noted by Justice Breyer, is it realistic to expect that district judges will truly engage in de novo decisionmaking?

**Page 370.  Add a new Subparagraph (3)(e):**

(e) Kontorovich, *The Constitutionality of International Courts*: *The Forgotten Precedent of Slave–Trade Tribunals*, 158 U.Pa.L.Rev. 39, 102, 104–05, 114 (2009), identifies two precedents bearing on the constitutionality of American participation in international courts (potentially including the International Criminal Court) that would have jurisdiction over U.S. nationals and U.S. territory. First, from the end of the War of 1812 through the 1840s, U.S. officials repeatedly rebuffed British entreaties to participate in a system of international courts to punish participation in the slave trade, with both administration officials and members of Congress citing objections founded on Article III and the Bill of Rights. Second, in 1862, the United States signed and the Senate swiftly ratified the Lyons–Seward Treaty, which authorized international courts including American judges to exercise a civil jurisdiction over vessels seized in the slave trade, but withheld criminal jurisdiction to try the crew. According to Professor Kontorovich, the central thread of consistency is that "[a]t all times there was consensus that [participation in international]

---

**8.** Indeed, it is possible that even reasonably well-established regimes could be open to question after Stern v. Marshall. The majority there, after noting the Court's statement in Granfinanciera that it did not mean to "suggest that the restructuring of debtor-creditor relations is in fact a public right", then said: "Because neither party asks us to reconsider the public rights framework for bankruptcy, we follow the same approach here."

If a party in a future case does ask for such reconsideration, what weight should the Court give to the tradition, which has deep roots in English and American practice, that bankruptcy adjudication extends to the administration of the estate and to the disposition of claims against it—but not to actions seeking to obtain property to be added to the estate? See Brubaker, *Article III's Bleak House (Part I): The Statutory Limits of Bankruptcy Judges' Core Jurisdiction*, 31 No.8 Bankr.L.Letter 1 (2011).

*criminal* tribunals would be unconstitutional", except possibly in cases involving universally cognizable offenses by service members; disagreement centered on "the acceptability of international courts to adjudicate cases that were less than criminal but more than pure 'public rights,' which all apparently agreed could be put before an international commission like the one created by the Jay Treaty."

However, Martinez, *International Courts and the U.S. Constitution: Reexamining the History*, 159 U.Pa.L.Rev. 1060 (2011), takes issue with Kontorovich's reading of the historical materials. In her view, the initial U.S. rejection of international slave-trade tribunals did not rest on objections to recognition of criminal jurisdiction over Americans—which, Martinez argues, those tribunals would not have been exercising. Rather, because through the 1840s, international law was not understood as banning the slave trade, the objection was to the tribunals' trying Americans for violations of *American* rather than of *international* law. By 1862, when the United States ratified the Lyons–Seward Treaty, the slave trade *was* understood to violate international law, alleviating the initial concern. As a result, Martinez argues, neither the initial U.S. resistance to nor its later acceptance of the slave-trade tribunals shows that participation in the International Criminal Court would be constitutionally suspect.

Whoever has the better of the historical argument, how much weight should nineteenth century extra-judicial constitutional analysis carry in current legal debates?

**Page 372.   Add a new footnote 2a at the end of Paragraph (4)(c):**

**2a.**   Paulsen, *The Constitutional Power to Interpret International Law*, 118 Yale L.J. 1762 (2009), draws on earlier work of other scholars and a detailed structural analysis of the Constitution to conclude that foreign and international tribunals cannot issue interpretations of international law (including treaties to which the United States is party) or judgments that bind American courts, and that the United States government cannot delegate that power to such tribunals.

**Page 382.   Add to Paragraph (3):**

Professor Seinfeld has recently elaborated upon Justice Jackson's argument. For discussion, see p. 89, *infra*.

---

## SECTION 3.   FEDERAL AUTHORITY AND STATE COURT JURISDICTION

———

**Page 404.   Add to footnote 5:**

In a subsequent article, Collins and Nash argue that the evidence from the Founding era—particularly the debate about the First Judiciary Act—is hard to square with state court authority to entertain federal criminal prosecutions. Collins & Nash, *Prosecuting Federal Crimes in State Courts*, 97 Va.L.Rev. 243 (2011). The authors contend that only one federal statute plainly authorized federal criminal prosecutions in state courts, and they note two state courts whose decisions suggested a lack of jurisdiction under it. They doubt that the non-discrimination principle associated with Testa v. Katt requires state courts, merely because they adjudicate state crimes, to also adjudicate federal crimes. And the authors highlight constitutional difficulties—primarily under the Take Care and Appointments Clauses—if federal crimes were prosecuted in state court by state prosecutors. If instead federal prosecutors brought cases in state court, a range of procedural problems (which they acknowledge may not be insurmountable) would arise, such as the application of double jeopardy principles, the location of the pardon power, and the applicability of federal constitutional provisions (such as the grand jury right and aspects of the petit jury right) that currently apply in federal but not state court prosecutions. They conclude that proposals to prosecute federal crimes in state courts are beset with constitutional and practical difficulties and should be rejected.

### Page 414.   Add a new Subparagraph (3)(c):

(c) In Haywood v. Drown, 556 U.S. 729 (2009), the Court rejected a state's claim that there was a "valid excuse" for its courts' refusal to entertain § 1983 claims against correction officials, even though the basis for the refusal did not discriminate against federal rights. At issue in the case was a New York statute that stripped the state's general trial courts of jurisdiction over prisoner suits seeking damages from state correction officials under either state or federal law. (The statute did not apply to suits for injunctive relief.) For damages actions against correction officials, the statute substituted an action directly against the state itself in the state's court of claims, but this alternative remedy was hedged with substantive and procedural limitations.

Although the state's jurisdiction-stripping statute was "neutral" in the sense that it treated claims founded on federal and on state law identically, the Court, in an opinion by Justice Stevens, held (5–4) that the state courts could not refuse to exercise jurisdiction over § 1983 damages claims against correction officers. "Ensuring equality of treatment" of state and federal causes of action is "the beginning, not the end, of the Supremacy Clause analysis," Justice Stevens wrote, and states may in no case withhold jurisdiction over federal claims based on substantive disagreement with federal law: "[H]aving made the decision to create courts of general jurisdiction that regularly sit to entertain analogous suits" against other state officials, New York "is not at liberty to shut the courthouse door to federal claims that it considers at odds with its local policy" of disfavoring prisoner litigation.

In a portion of his dissenting opinion that was joined by the Chief Justice and Justices Scalia and Alito, Justice Thomas maintained that the majority mistakenly pressed beyond the Court's precedents by invalidating a "neutral" statute that deprived state "courts of subject-matter jurisdiction over a particular class of claims on terms that treat federal and state actions equally." According to Justice Thomas, although the Court's precedents forbade the states to enforce substantive rules that discriminate against federal policy, a jurisdictional statute such as New York's is "incapable of undermining federal law" because it would merely require dismissal of the plaintiff's case without prejudice, leaving the plaintiff free to re-file in another forum (likely a federal court). He distinguished Howlett v. Rose, Sixth Edition p. 413, which barred a state court from recognizing a state law immunity defense in a § 1983 action against local officials, on the ground that Howlett involved a rule that was in effect substantive, not jurisdictional.

In a separate, lengthier part of his dissent in which he wrote only for himself, Justice Thomas argued that analysis should not begin with the Supremacy Clause, but instead with the question whether Article III requires state courts to entertain federal causes of action. Based largely on originalist grounds, he answered in the negative: "The Constitution's implicit preservation of state authority to entertain federal claims" under Article III, § 2 and the Madisonian Compromise "did not impose a duty on state courts to do so." In Justice Thomas' view, "the Supremacy Clause's exclusive function is to disable state laws that are substantively inconsistent with federal law—not to require state courts to hear federal claims over which the courts lack jurisdiction."

The New York statute that occasioned the dispute in Haywood did not cut off all state court jurisdiction over § 1983 actions against correction officials, who remained suable for declaratory and injunctive relief, but effectively immunized them from damages actions. It is not obvious whether the best label for such a rule is substantive, remedial, or jurisdictional, and the same could be said about the rule in Howlett v. Rose, which held that the label attached to the state law did not matter. Should the validity of a state's rule depend on the label chosen, especially when the choice of label will be anything but obvious?

Even assuming that the New York statute in Haywood should be deemed jurisdictional, consider whether Justice Thomas is persuasive that the central question in cases such as Haywood, Howlett, and Testa v. Katt, Sixth Edition p. 408, is whether Article III requires state courts to entertain federal causes of action, and that the sole function of the Supremacy Clause is to make the obligations established by other provisions of federal law paramount over contrary state law. Under his view, could a state refuse to confer on its courts jurisdiction over a federal cause of action merely because it *is* federal?[8] Could a state's courts refuse to entertain a plaintiff's claim that the Constitution guaranteed a right to judicial redress in the circumstances presented, even if Congress had not conferred federal court jurisdiction over the claim?

**8.** In Mims v. Arrow Financial Services, LLC, 132 S.Ct. 740 (2012), Congress, when prohibiting certain telemarketing practices, specified that a person "may, if otherwise permitted by the laws or rules of court of a State, bring in an appropriate court of that State" an action for damages and/or an injunction. The Supreme Court held that the recognition of state court jurisdiction did not bar the federal courts from exercising federal question jurisdiction. Explaining the significance of the statutory language authorizing state court suit, the Court said Congress "arguably gave States leeway they would otherwise lack" to decide whether to exercise jurisdiction over such actions. Should that language be read to authorize states to invoke any non-discriminatory basis for declining to hear such actions? To refuse to hear such actions even if their courts entertain analogous state law actions?

# CHAPTER V

# REVIEW OF STATE COURT DECISIONS BY THE SUPREME COURT

## SECTION 1.   THE ESTABLISHMENT OF THE JURISDICTION

**Page 432.   Add the following at the end of footnote 10:**

In an exhaustive analysis of Supreme Court practice dating to the early days of the Republic, Woolhandler, *Power, Rights, and Section 25*, 86 Notre Dame L.Rev. 1241 (2011), determines that even before the 1914 Act, the Supreme Court sometimes found a way to exercise jurisdiction in cases denying a federal claim of right. In particular, Professor Woolhandler notes that when the Court denies one party a federal right, one might characterize that action as giving the opposing party a federal immunity. For example, one might say that when a debtor successfully secured the discharge of a debt under federal bankruptcy law, the state court's ruling upheld a claim of federal right for purposes of Section 25. At the same time, the creditor who unsuccessfully resisted the debt's discharge under federal law might also seek review under Section 25 on the ground that he or she was denied a federal immunity against discharge in the circumstances of the case. Professor Woolhandler argues that the Court's attitude toward such characterizations varied in complex ways at different points in the Court's history. For further discussion of this question, see p. 41, *supra*.

**Page 444.   Add the following at the end of footnote 1:**

For an argument that the jurisdiction conferred upon the Supreme Court by Section 25 may be constitutionally required by the political compromise that made the Supremacy Clause, rather than a congressional veto, the mechanism for enforcing federal supremacy, see LaCroix, *On Being "Bound Thereby"*, 27 Const. Comm. 507 (2011). The author describes that position as a supra-textual structural understanding developed in common law fashion by "judges, politicians and the people." Is that reading a plausible implied limitation on Article III's Exceptions Clause? See Sixth Edition pp. 294–300.

**Page 445.   Add the following at the beginning of footnote 3:**

In particular, the Court established that, under Article III, the federal quality of the issues in the case, and not the relationship between the state courts and the Supreme Court, was determinative of the Court's jurisdiction. See LaCroix, *Federalists, Federalism, and Federal Jurisdiction*, 30 Law & Hist.Rev. 205, 237–40 (2012). What plausible interpretive methodology would make the initially secret drafting history of Article III determinative on this point? Compare Manning, *The Role of the Philadelphia Convention in Constitutional Adjudication*, 80 Geo.Wash.L.Rev. 1753 (2012).

**Page 445.   Add a new footnote 5a at the end of the first paragraph of Paragraph (5):**

**5a.**   In fact, some commentators believe that the Court's exercise of "vertical" authority to review state-court judgments helped it to establish and maintain "horizontal" authority to review the actions by the coordinate federal branches. For example, to the extent that national political leaders found it necessary to bolster the Court's final authority to enforce the supremacy of federal law against the states, those leaders often incidentally bolstered the Court's position as the final arbiter of legality more generally. In addition, particularly after the Court incorporated the Bill of Rights against the states, the exercise of federal judicial power to invalidate state statutes under provisions such as the First Amendment made it harder for Congress and the President to resist judicial enforcement of similar limitations against the federal government. See Friedman & Delaney, *Becoming Supreme: The Federal Foundation of Judicial Supremacy*, 111 Colum.L.Rev. 1137 (2011). Is this claim one of historical contingency, or is there a tight conceptual link between judicial review of state and federal action?

### Page 456.   Add the following at the end of footnote 1:

Section 25's proviso had restricted Supreme Court review to federal claims that appeared "on the face of the record." Professor Collins argues that the Reconstruction Congress repealed that proviso to remove this limitation on the reviewability of federal claims rather than to authorize review of state law. See Collins, *Reconstructing Murdock v. Memphis*, 98 Va.L.Rev. 1439 (2012).

### Page 456.   Add a new footnote 3a to the end of Paragraph (1):

**3a.**   Mitchell, *Reconsidering Murdock: State-Law Reversals as Constitutional Avoidance*, 77 U.Chi.L.Rev.1335 (2010), argues that nothing in the language of Article III or 28 U.S.C. § 1257(a) forecloses Supreme Court review of state law issues, and that the Court already reviews questions of state law in many contexts. Starting from those premises, Professor Mitchell argues that the Supreme Court should review state law rulings of state courts when necessary to avoid a "novel and contentious" federal constitutional question. Such an approach, he contends, would serve the interests of the avoidance doctrine and allow the Court to forestall error costs sometimes incurred in difficult constitutional cases. Can Professor Mitchell's reading of Article III be squared with the understanding of our federal system that underlies Erie R. Co. v. Tompkins, Sixth Edition p. 558? Even if his readings of Article III and § 1257 are correct, is it too late in the day to reconsider Murdock? If not, why does the Court have the discretion to pick and choose when to resolve state law issues in the way that he suggests? Compare Shapiro, *Jurisdiction and Discretion*, 60 N.Y.U. L. Rev. 543 (1985).

---

# SECTION 2.   THE RELATION BETWEEN STATE AND FEDERAL LAW

---

## SUBSECTION A: SUBSTANTIVE LAW

---

### Page 462.   Add a new footnote 1a to the end of Paragraph (1):

**1a.**   In Camreta v. Greene, 131 S.Ct. 2020 (2011), the Court adopted a position in some tension with the premise that the adequate-and-independent-state-ground doctrine has a constitutional underpinning. The suit brought in federal court under 42 U.S.C. § 1983 alleged that the defendants—a child protective services worker and a deputy sheriff—had violated the Fourth Amendment rights of a schoolchild by interviewing her without either a warrant or parental consent. The defendants defended on the merits and claimed that they were entitled to qualified immunity, in any case, because their conduct did not violate clearly established rights. See Sixth Edition pp. 1002–06. In cases including Pearson v. Callahan, Sixth Edition pp. 78, 1005–06, the Court had recognized that, in such cases, federal courts have discretion to reach the merits of a constitutional claim even when the presence of a meritorious qualified immunity defense makes it unnecessary to do so. The court of appeals in Camreta held that the defendants violated the Fourth Amendment but were entitled to qualified immunity. Although the defendant state officials prevailed below, they sought certiorari on the ground that they would have to conform their behavior to the lower court's Fourth Amendment ruling or risk liability in some future case. In an opinion for the Court, Justice Kagan upheld the Supreme Court's jurisdiction over the petition for certiorari and held that the state officers had standing. She reasoned that because the lower court's merits decision would constrain the state officers in the future conduct of their public duties, they had a constitutionally sufficient injury to sustain standing.

In dissent, Justice Kennedy argued that the Court's opinion contradicted the premises of the adequate-and-independent-state-ground doctrine. Relying on Herb v. Pitcairn, Sixth Edition pp. 461–62, he reasoned that if the Court's review could not alter the lower courts' judgment (the plaintiffs had not cross-petitioned on the issue of qualified immunity), then its decision of a question of law amounted to an advisory opinion.

Does Camreta suggest that it would be constitutionally permissible for the Court to exercise jurisdiction over state court cases that contain an adequate and independent ground but, like Camreta, impose federal constitutional constraints on state officials who prevailed below? Do federalism concerns distinguish the adequate-and-independent-state-ground doctrine from the Camreta doctrine? Should Camreta be understood as a context-specific response to the special challenges posed by qualified immunity cases?

**Page 472.   Insert the following at the end of Paragraph (1):**

For an extended defense of Justice Stevens' position, see Mazzone, *When the Supreme Court Is Not Supreme*, 104 Nw.U.L.Rev. 979 (2010).

**Page 476.   Add a new Paragraph (3)(d):**

(d) If the Court applied the opposite of the Long presumption—that ambiguity about the basis for a state court decision should preclude Supreme Court review—then "state courts could broadly evade accountability for their decisions. As Professors Vikram Amar and Alan Brownstein have written, if the Long presumption were reversed, state courts * * * might fuzz up their opinions to foreclose U.S. Supreme Court reversal of results they favor, but at the same time invoke enough federal law to suggest—even when such federal law isn't really constraining—federal responsibility for the outcome of controversial disputes." Amar & Brownstein, *When Avoiding Federal Questions Shouldn't Evade Federal Review*, 12 Green Bag 2d 381, 384 (2009). Because an ambiguous state court decision might rest on federal grounds, "attempts by state electorates to amend their constitutions or to impose electoral sanctions on state court judges could be discouraged by the not-unrealistic possibility that the state law options were constrained by federal requirements." How likely is such a result? Does it seem sufficient to sustain the Long presumption?

**Page 487.   Add at the end of Paragraph (1):**

A plurality of the Court recently reaffirmed Demorest's basic approach but for somewhat unusual reasons. In an opinion by Justice Scalia (joined by Chief Justice Roberts and Justices Thomas and Alito), a plurality in Stop the Beach Renourishment, Inc. v. Florida Department of Environmental Protection, 130 S.Ct. 2592 (2010), concluded that when any instrumentality of the state—including a state court—"declares that what was once an established right of private property no longer exists, it has taken that property" for purposes of the Takings Clause. The plurality also emphasized, however, that in determining whether such a taking has occurred, the Court should defer to the state court's understanding of state property law if the state court's decision has a "fair and substantial basis".

At issue was whether Florida's filling in of state-owned submerged lands to restore previous erosion deprived riparian property owners of their common law littoral right to any natural accretions that might have accrued to their property (under the doctrine of accretion) in the absence of the state-owned landfill. The Florida Supreme Court held that the statute that mandated the filling did not take the beach owners' property because a competing common law doctrine (the doctrine of avulsion) allowed the state to reclaim restored beach land on behalf of the public.

In reviewing the state court's decision, the plurality addressed the state's contention that the U.S. Supreme Court should not find a taking unless the state court decision lacked a "fair and substantial basis." Although noting that the "fair and substantial basis" test typically went to whether a state court decision supplied an adequate and independent state ground barring Supreme Court review (see Sixth Edition pp. 501–18), the plurality suggested that the substance of that test was implicit in its takings standard. The plurality noted that "we make our own determination, without deference to state judges, whether the challenged decision deprives the claimant of an established property right" and that this was part and parcel of the Court's more general obligation to determine "state-court compliance with *all* constitutional imperatives." Still, the plurality added, one could expect "a considerable degree of deference to state courts" in practice, under a test asking whether the state court decision resulted in the "deprivation of an *established* property right". As the plurality elaborated, no property right can be "established if there is doubt about its existence; and when there is doubt we do not make our own assessment but accept the determination of the state court."

Although Justice Kennedy (joined by Justice Sotomayor) and Justice Breyer (joined by Justice Ginsburg) wrote separately to state that it was unnecessary to determine whether a state court decision could itself unconstitutionally take property without just compensation, all eight Justices (Justice Stevens did not participate) joined the part of Justice Scalia's opinion holding that the Florida Supreme Court had not effected a taking of property because "[t]he Takings Clause only protects property rights as they are established under state law," and "[w]e cannot say that the Florida Supreme Court's decision eliminated a right of accretion established under Florida law."

Is the plurality correct to treat its deference to the state court's determination as a function of the need to find an "established" property interest? Does its approach to the Takings Clause offer a path to reconcile Brand and Demorest?

**Page 488.   Insert the following at the end of footnote 4:**

By the same token, because the procedures prescribed by state law do not define the scope of a liberty or property interest, a claimant cannot establish a due process violation merely by showing that the state has not complied with such procedures. In Swarthout v. Cooke, 131 S.Ct. 859 (2011) (per curiam), a prisoner filed a federal habeas petition alleging that the California state parole board had improperly denied his application for parole and that the state court had misapplied the state law standard of review requiring "some evidence" for the board's determinations. Treating the "some evidence" standard as a "component" of the state-created liberty interest in parole, the Ninth Circuit held that the state courts' failure to apply that standard denied the petitioner due process. The Supreme Court reversed, explaining that while the liberty interest at stake was the product of state law, the process due depended on federal constitutional rather than state-law criteria. To treat state procedure as a judicially enforceable component of the resultant liberty interest, the Court explained, "would subject to federal-court merits review the application of all state-prescribed procedures in cases involving liberty or property interests, including (of course) those in criminal prosecutions." This, the Court added, would contradict the settled principle that violations of state law do not necessarily violate the federal requirements of due process.

----

## SUBSECTION B: PROCEDURAL REQUIREMENTS

----

### Page 513.  Substitute the following for Paragraph (6)(d):

(d) Beard v. Kindler, 130 S.Ct. 612 (2009), clarified that a state procedural rule may supply the basis for an adequate and independent state ground even if the trial court has discretion to disregard the violation of the rule. Kindler had been convicted of murder in Pennsylvania state court in 1985. While his post-verdict motions were pending, he escaped to Canada, where he was captured, again escaped, and was recaptured. After fighting extradition for several years, Kindler was extradited to the United States in 1991. The Pennsylvania trial court had dismissed Kindler's original postverdict motions because of his escape. In 1991, the trial court rejected his motion to reinstate those earlier motions, reasoning that the original trial judge had not abused his discretion in dismissing them. The Pennsylvania Supreme Court affirmed, concluding that the trial court's dismissal of Kindler's postverdict motions constituted a "reasonable response" to his escape under Pennsylvania's fugitive forfeiture law. On state collateral review, the state courts again rejected Kindler's claims. Kindler then filed a petition for a writ of habeas corpus in federal court. The U.S. Court of Appeals for the Third Circuit held that because Pennsylvania's fugitive forfeiture law gave state courts "discretion" to hear an appeal by a fugitive who had been returned to custody, the fugitive forfeiture rule was not sufficiently "firmly established" to provide an adequate and independent state ground.

In reversing the court of appeals, Chief Justice Roberts, speaking for a unanimous Court, explained: "[A] discretionary state procedural rule can serve as an adequate ground to bar federal habeas review. Nothing inherent in such a rule renders it inadequate for purposes of the adequate state ground doctrine. To the contrary, a discretionary rule can be 'firmly established'—and 'regularly followed' even if the appropriate exercise of discretion may permit consideration of a federal claim in some cases but not others" (citing Meltzer, *State Court Forfeitures of Federal Rights*, 99 Harv.L.Rev. 1128, 1140 (1986)). The Court emphasized that a contrary principle would put states to a terrible choice. They "could preserve flexibility by granting courts discretion to excuse procedural errors, but only at the cost of undermining the finality of state court judgments." Alternatively, they could protect finality "by withholding such discretion, but only at the cost of precluding any flexibility in applying the rules." Noting that federal procedural norms frequently give the trial judge "broad discretion," the Court suggested that "the federalism and comity concerns that motivate the adequate state ground doctrine" would make it "particularly strange to disregard state procedural rules that are substantially similar to those to which we give full force in our own courts."

In Walker v. Martin, 131 S.Ct. 1120 (2011), the Court applied Kindler to California's rules governing state postconviction review. Instead of prescribing a set time for filing, the state rules direct prisoners to file habeas petitions "as promptly as the circumstances allow." In their filings, prisoners must state when they first learned of the claims asserted and why they did not seek postconviction relief sooner. A court may deny as untimely a petition deemed to be substantially delayed without justification. Alleging ineffective assistance of counsel, Martin filed for state postconviction relief nearly five years after his conviction became final, with no explanation for the delay. The California Supreme Court (in which he filed directly, as state law permits) denied the petition as untimely. On federal habeas review, the Ninth Circuit ruled that California's standard of "substantial delay" lacked the clarity and certainty necessary to constitute an adequate state ground. In a unanimous opinion by Justice Ginsburg, the Supreme Court reversed, ruling that California need not choose between imposing a specific deadline for petitions and preserving the flexibility of its practice " 'at the cost of undermining the finality of state court judgments' " (quoting Kindler). In holding that the lack of specificity in California's timeliness standards did not disqualify them from counting as "firmly established", the Court emphasized that time limits prescribed by its own opinions and by federal statutes (including the federal habeas statute) often relied on indeterminate language. In addition, the Court rejected the petitioner's contention that the state court rules were not "regularly followed" because the state supreme court's summary dismissals made it impossible to tell why the state court dismissed some delayed petitions as untimely and disposed of others on the merits. The Court made clear a state court may permissibly "opt to bypass the [timeliness] assessment and summarily dismiss a petition on the merits, if that is the easier path." Finally, the Court emphasized that "a showing of seeming inconsistencies" in application should not "automatically" negate the procedural bar. Noting that such "seeming inconsistencies" were often the price of applying a highly fact-dependent standard, the Court deemed it sufficient that the state court had not "exercised its discretion in a surprising or unfair manner."

Is there any reason to think that the Court's reasoning in Kindler and Walker should have less force in the context of applying the adequate-state-ground doctrine on direct review? If not, has the Court effectively rejected the majority's rationale in Sullivan v. Little Hunting Park, Inc., Sixth Edition p. 512? If Walker establishes that an adequate and independent state ground is no longer negated by the mere presence of state court discretion unless the state court has exercised that discretion in an "surprising or unfair manner", what must a petitioner do to make the requisite showing? If "seeming inconsistencies" in application do not alone suffice, does the petitioner have to show that the rules discriminate against federal rights? Might there be other grounds as well?[a]

**a.** Suppose, for example, that application of a state's plain error standard—under which a state court will sometimes reach an issue that was not properly raised—depends upon whether the issue is obviously meritorious or on whether any violation was prejudicial. Might not the Supreme Court be justified in reviewing and reversing on the federal issue, and then remanding to permit the state court to exercise its discretion in light of a correct understanding of federal law? *Cf.* Ake v. Oklahoma, 470 U.S. 68, 74–75 (1985)(state court ruling that defendant waived his federal constitutional claim by not repeating it in his motion for new trial was not an adequate and independent state ground because state waiver rule does not apply to federal constitutional error; hence, the state ground was not "independent" because it rests, implicitly or explicitly, on determination of the federal issue). For general discussion, see Hill, Sixth Edition p. 513 n. 1, at 985 n. 174; Sandalow, Sixth Edition p. 513 n. 1, at 225–26; Meltzer, Sixth Edition p. 513 n. 1, at 1139–42.

# CHAPTER VI

# THE LAW APPLIED IN CIVIL ACTIONS IN THE DISTRICT COURTS

## SECTION 1. PROCEDURE

**Page 537.  Add at the end of the first full paragraph:**

As indicated by the title of this Chapter, its focus is on the law applicable in *civil* cases in the federal district courts. But the limitations imposed on the Court as rulemaker by the Rules Enabling Act (see Sixth Edition pp. 539–43), and by related principles of the separation of powers between Congress and the judiciary, are also significant in the context of the criminal rules. For an important and innovative article exploring those limitations, both in general and in a number of specific instances involving the Federal Rules of Criminal Procedure, see Minzner, *The Criminal Rules Enabling Act*, 46 U. Richmond L.Rev. 1047 (2012).

**Page 541.  Add a new footnote 7a at the end of the first full paragraph:**

**7a.**  The Reporter for the Advisory Committee was Charles Clark, a leading member of the legal realist movement of the period. For a perceptive analysis of the role of rulemaking in realist jurisprudence (based in significant part on Clark's own writings) and a discussion of how Clark's jurisprudence helped shaped the Federal Rules, see David Marcus, *The Federal Rules of Civil Procedure and Legal Realism as a Jurisprudence of Law Reform*, 44 Ga.L.Rev. 433 (2010).

**Page 542.  Add a new footnote 9a at the end of the carry-over paragraph:**

**9a.**  In an order issued on April 28, 2010, approving certain proposed changes in the Rules of Criminal Procedure, the Court took the rare action of recommitting to the Advisory Committee for further consideration a proposed amendment to Rule 15 (dealing with depositions). 130 S.Ct. Ct.R.–179 (2010). There was no explanation.

**Page 542.  Add to footnote 13:**

The 70th anniversary of the Federal Rules, in 2008, was marked by a Symposium in 61 Okla.L.Rev. No. 2 (2008). Articles in this Symposium, which express starkly contrasting views, include: Bone, *Making Effective Rules: The Need for Procedure Theory*, *id.* at 319 (arguing that effective rulemaking requires the rulemakers themselves to develop a "coherent normative theory of civil adjudication," and giving as three examples the need for (1) more clearly articulating the "nature of the relationship between procedure and substantive law", (2) specifying "the precise role of settlement in any system of civil adjudication", and (3) "determining the proper way to value individual participation"); Richard Marcus, *Not Dead Yet*, *id.* at 299 (contending that, despite scholarly criticism, the rulemaking process is alive and well, that much of the criticism is directed to the retreat from the reforms of the 1970s, and that there is considerable evidence—including the recent reforms relating to electronic discovery—that the process continues to lead and to innovate); and Perschbacher & Bassett, *The Revolution of 1938 and Its Discontents, id.* at 275 (arguing that "the moment of the 1938 [Rules] is over" because the goal the rulemakers sought—to "assure more rapid advancement of law suits to the point of final decision on the merits"—has been gradually replaced by a desire to dispose of cases as expeditiously as possible, preferably by private resolution short of trial).

With respect to the notion that rules of civil procedure should apply across the range of substantive law, see David Marcus, *The Past, Present, and Future of Trans-substantivity in Federal Civil Procedure*, 59 DePaul L.Rev. 371 (2010). Marcus recognizes the decline of "trans-substantivity" in recent decades, especially in legislation merging substantive change with related and substance-specific procedural change. But, he argues, trans-substantivity can and should continue to operate "as an institutional restraint on *court-supervised* rulemakers" (emphasis added).

For an analysis of the rulemaking process based on a game-theoretic model, see Stancil, *Close Enough for Government Work: The Committee Rulemaking Game*, 96 Va.L. Rev. 69 (2010). Stancil concludes, and gives examples to support that conclusion, that the current committee-based system of rulemaking may lead Congress to accept rules that have substantive consequences "some distance away from its real preferences" in order "to avoid incurring the costs associated with informing itself and then acting." But, he adds, the present structure "may reduce certain other risks of strategic behavior, most notably interest-group hijacking of the rulemaking process." As a way of minimizing the costs while retaining the benefits, Stancil proposes revising the methods of selecting committee members in order to make them more "reflective of the bodies with constitutional responsibility for setting substantive policy."

### Page 542.    Add at the end of Paragraph (6):

Professor Paul Carrington, looking at the topic from a different perspective, is sharply critical of the Supreme Court for circumventing the rulemaking process. Carrington, *Politics and Civil Procedure Rulemaking: Reflections and Experience*, 60 Duke L.J. 597 (2010). Discussing a range of examples, including the Court's decision on the adequacy of the complaint in Ashcroft v. Iqbal, pp. 106–109, *infra*, he contends that "in recent decades, the Supreme Court has manifested dissatisfaction with its modest share of the power to make procedural law and has in its opinions proclaimed new rules having no basis in texts enacted through the established rulemaking process * * *." He concludes that the present rulemaking system is inadequate to remedy this trend, and proposes various ways in which Congress might address the problem.

### Page 549.    Add a new footnote 4a at the end of Paragraph (3):

**4a.**    In a valuable analysis of the Rules Enabling Act, the authors propose an interpretation that, they contend, best resolves the tensions and ambiguities in the Act and is most consistent with an objective determination of its purposes. Redish & Murashko, *The Rules Enabling Act and the Procedural–Substantive Tension: A Lesson in Statutory Interpretation*, 93 Minn.L.Rev. 26 (2008). Rejecting a "redundancy construction" under which the Act's prohibition on abridging, enlarging, or modifying any substantive right is merely repetitive of the authority to prescribe general rules of practice and procedure, as well as a "strict separation" approach, under which the prohibition constitutes a strict limitation on the authority granted, they advocate an interpretation that "permits rules to impact substantive rights if and only if they do so incidentally." As an example of a case effectively implementing their approach, the authors cite Burlington N.R.R. v. Woods, 480 U.S. 1 (1987), Sixth Edition p. 593 n.7 (holding that a federal appellate rule giving discretion to impose a penalty on a losing party preempts a state rule mandating such a penalty). Can this position be squared with the decision in 2010 in the Shady Grove case, *infra*?

With the approach of Redish & Murasko, compare Hendricks, *In Defense of the Substance–Procedure Dichotomy*, 89 Wash.U.L.Rev. 103 (2011) (acknowledging that it is "more accurate" to describe many legal rules as having both substantive and procedural aspects, but arguing that considerations of statutory interpretation [of the REA] and transparency require federal courts to classify each legal rule as either one or the other).

### Page 556.   Add to footnote 5:

Nelson, *A Critical Guide to Erie v. Tompkins*, 54 Wm. & Mary L.Rev. 921, 924–49 (2013) (containing an analysis of Swift similar to, and relying in part on, the work of Bridwell and Whitten).

---

## Section 2. The Powers of the Federal Courts in Defining Primary Legal Obligations That Fall Within the Legislative Competence of the States

---

### Page 564.   Add to footnote 3:

Aaron Nielson, *Erie as Nondelegation*, 72 Ohio St.L.J. 239 (2011), offers another constitutional basis for the Erie decision: that Congress cannot constitutionally authorize federal courts to formulate substantive law governing the Nation's commerce without providing an intelligible principle to limit the courts' exercise of that authority. See also Roosevelt, *Valid Rule Due Process Challenges: Bond v. United States and Erie's Constitutional Source*, 54 Wm. & Mary L.Rev. 987, 997–1000 (2013) (grounding Erie's constitutional source in the Due Process Clause, on the basis that the rule applied by the Second Circuit in the case was neither "federal" nor the law of any state, and thus "was law without a lawmaker, which is to say no law at all.")

In stark contrast to these justifications, Professor Sherry has attacked the Erie decision with a vehemence well-summarized in the title of an article appearing in a symposium on the Supreme Court's "Supreme Mistakes": *Wrong, Out of Step, and Pernicious: Erie as the Worst Decision of All Time*, 39 Pepp.L.Rev. 129 (2011). In a discussion reminiscent of that of Professor Crosskey (see Sixth Edition p. 555), though a good deal shorter, she contends that when Congress enacted the Rules of Decision Act, it "probably did not intend for federal courts sitting in diversity to apply *either* state statutory law or state common law, but rather to apply federal common law" (emphasis added). She goes on to contend that (1) Erie's rejection of Swift cannot be grounded in constitutional principles of federalism or separation of powers, and (2) Erie's pernicious effect is that by placing a "murky constitutional imprimatur" on judicial restraint it "threatens to deprive us of one of our oldest and most effective tools for avoiding majority tyranny."

For a more moderate, in-depth analysis and critique of Erie, see Nelson, *A Critical Guide to Erie v. Tompkins*, 54 Wm. & Mary L.Rev. 921 (2013) (concluding that the Rules of Decision Act did not require the federal courts to follow state courts' interpretation of unwritten (common) law and expressing skepticism about Justice Brandeis' constitutional arguments, but suggesting that the Erie doctrine may be appropriate as a matter of federal common law).

### Page 568.   Add a new footnote 3a at the end of the carry-over paragraph at the top of the page:

**3a.**  A thoughtful article by Professor Roosevelt, *Choice of Law in the Federal Courts: From Erie and Klaxon to CAFA and Shady Grove*, 106 N.W.U.L.Rev. 1 (2012), lends some support to the argument in text. He contends that Erie itself "is best understood as a choice-of-law case." Thus, in his view, an Erie problem should, like other choice-of-law problems, be subjected to a "two-step" analysis. First, the court should determine "which sovereigns might attach legal consequences to the events and which have in fact done so"—a question of the scope of the relevant sovereigns' laws. Second, if more than one sovereign has such an interest, the court "must decide which of the competing rights will get priority." Applying this analysis to Klaxon, Roosevelt argues that, as to step one, a federal court "must respect the [forum] state definition of rights and obligations, and choice-of-law rules about the scope of state law are part of that definition." As to step two, federal courts should "usually incorporate the rules of priority of the states in which they sit, but they reserve a 'federal veto'—the power to diverge from a state rule of priority that unreasonably disfavors foreign law."

**Page 569.   Add at the end of Paragraph (7):**

Still another area that may qualify for special consideration arises when the choice of law question is international in scope. For a thoughtful argument that (contrary to existing law declared in Day & Zimmermann, Inc. v. Challoner, 423 U.S. 3 (1975)), federal courts should develop "specialized federal common law in *international* conflict-of-laws cases", see Childress, *When Erie Goes International*, 105 Nw.L.Rev. 1531 (2011) (emphasis added).

**Page 569.   Add a new footnote 1 at the end of Paragraph (1):**

**1.** Another important question, explored in depth for the first time by Professor Abbe Gluck, is whether federal courts, in applying state statutory law, should follow the rules of statutory interpretation adopted by the courts of the relevant state. Gluck, *Intersystemic Statutory Interpretation: Methodology as "Law" and the Erie Doctrine*, 120 Yale L.J. 1898 (2011). Arguing that the ongoing debate over theories of interpretation has become an important part of our jurisprudence, Professor Gluck criticizes the failure of most federal courts to recognize that the interpretive rules adopted by a state (like those adopted by the federal courts in interpreting federal statutes or the Constitution) are integral to its substantive law. Such recognition, she contends, would have many benefits, including an enrichment of the debate itself. For her further exploration of the question of interpretive methodology—and the canons of interpretation in particular—as some kind of "law", see Gluck, *The Federal Common Law of Statutory Interpretation: Erie for the Age of Statutes*, 54 Wm. & Mary LRev. 753 (2013).

---

# Section 3.   Enforcing State-Created Obligations— Equitable Remedies and Procedure

---

**Page 576.   Add a new footnote a at the end of Paragraph (1)(b):**

**a.** For a thorough study of the development of federal equity prior to merger in 1938, see Collins, *"A Considerable Surgical Operation": Article III, Equity, and Judge–Made Law in the Federal Courts*, 60 Duke L.J. 249 (2010). This history, she states, shows that "federal courts [sitting in equity] applied a uniform body of judge-made equity principles with respect to procedure, remedial laws, and—in some instances—the primary rights of litigants." Thus, she concludes, Justice Frankfurter in his opinion in Guaranty, "[sought] to diminish federal equity's robust past" in order to further Erie's aim of allowing the states more leeway to pursue their (progressive) agendas.

**Page 578.   Add to footnote 2:**

Such use of state unconscionability doctrine suffered a severe setback in AT & T Mobility LLC v. Concepcion, 131 S.Ct. 1740 (2011). In a 5–4 decision, the Court held, in the context of a contracting party's effort to compel arbitration, that the FAA preempts a state's rule treating contractual class action waivers as unconscionable in certain consumer contracts of adhesion.

**Page 590. Add a new footnote a at the end of Part A:**

**a.** Of course, as indicated by the discussion at pp. 593–95 of the Sixth Edition, the line between matters covered by a Federal Rule of Civil Procedure and matters not covered can be a difficult one to draw. Thus, in an article advocating that in cases falling within the Erie doctrine, federal courts should follow state-law standards on summary judgment, class certification, and pleading, Adam Steinman argues, first, that these standards are not dictated by the Rules of Civil Procedure and, second, that if they were, the rules may to that extent run afoul of the Rules Enabling Act. See Steinman, *What Is the Erie Doctrine? (And What Does It Mean for the Contemporary Politics of Judicial Federalism?)*, 84 Notre Dame L.Rev. 245, 282–97 (2008). With the second of these arguments, compare Redish & Murashko, *supra*, the Court's decision in the Shady Grove case, *infra*, and Campos, *Erie as a Choice of Enforcement Defaults*, 64 Fla.L.Rev. 1573 (2012) (advocating, *inter alia*, a default rule favoring application of a Federal Rule of Civil Procedure in a difficult case as a method of forcing information from the state about the relationship of its rule to its substantive policies).

**Page 595. Add a new subparagraph (d) at the end of Paragraph (2):**

(d) In striking contrast to the Walker, Gasperini, and Semtek decisions, a fractured Supreme Court decided—in Shady Grove Orthopedic Associates, P.A. v. Allstate Ins. Co., 130 S.Ct. 1431 (2010)—that the provisions of Rule 23 (on class actions) conflicted with, and trumped, state law. The state law in question, N.Y. Civ. Prac. Law Ann. (CPLR) § 901(b), precludes the bringing of a class action to recover a "penalty", which—in the federal court's understanding of state law—includes statutory interest. Notwithstanding this prohibition, Shady Grove filed a diversity class action in a New York federal district court to recover certain statutory interest on behalf of itself and a similarly situated class. The trial court decided, and the court of appeals agreed, that whether or not the action met the criteria for class certification under Rule 23, it could not be maintained as a class action in view of the prohibition in New York law and, since Shady Grove's individual claim was for less than the jurisdictional amount, dismissed the case.[a] The Supreme Court reversed.

A majority of the Court, in an opinion by Justice Scalia (joined by Chief Justice Roberts and Justices Stevens, Thomas, and Sotomayor), held that there was a conflict between Federal Rule 23 and New York law. After stating that Rule 23—in providing that a class action "may be maintained" if certain conditions are met—confers "categorical permission" to maintain such an action, Justice Scalia rejected the argument that there was a distinction between the "eligibility" of a claim for class treatment and the "certifiability" of a class action with respect to that claim. Given the lack of such a distinction, the permission granted by Rule 23 could not be reconciled with the New York law that "prevents the class actions it covers from coming into existence at all." Reconciliation was not possible "because there is only one reasonable reading of Rule 23."

Justice Scalia, now speaking only for himself and three other Justices (Chief Justice Roberts and Justices Thomas and Sotomayor), went on to determine that because Rule 23 was a valid exercise of the authority granted by the Enabling Act, it trumped the conflicting state prohibition. Relying heavily on the holding of Sibbach v. Wilson, Sixth Edition p. 544, as well as its language (to the effect that the test of validity is whether the rule really regulates procedure—"the judicial process for enforcing rights and duties recognized by substantive law"), he concluded that "[a] class action * * *

**a.** Under the Class Action Fairness Act (CAFA), discussed at Sixth Edition pp. 1368–71, it might have been possible to meet the jurisdictional amount threshold by aggregating the damages of class members. But in an individual action, the general threshold in diversity actions provided by § 1332 could not be met.

merely enables a federal court to adjudicate claims of multiple parties at once, instead of in separate suits." Whether or not New York's prohibition of class actions in this context had a "substantive nature" or "substantive purpose", he insisted, *"makes no difference."* (Emphasis in original.) As long as the rule itself is procedural, it is "valid in all jurisdictions, regardless of its incidental effect upon state-created rights."

Justice Stevens, whose concurrence in part and concurrence in the judgment supplied the crucial fifth vote for the outcome, contended that in this case, Federal Rule 23 prevailed over New York law because that law "is a procedural rule that is not part of New York's substantive law." In contrast to the conclusion of Justice Scalia that in the event of conflict, the sole question was the validity of the federal rule as a rule of procedure, Justice Stevens emphasized that the rule had also to satisfy the limitation of subsection (b) of the Enabling Act, i.e., it could not "abridge, enlarge, or modify any substantive right."[b] Thus, a federal rule "cannot govern a particular case in which the rule would displace a state law that is procedural in the ordinary use of the term but is so intertwined with a state right or remedy that it functions to define the scope of the state-created right." Believing that the "bar for finding an Enabling Act problem is a high one", Justice Stevens then concluded that the bar had not been surmounted in this case. "The text of [New York's law] expressly and unambiguously applies not only to claims based on New York law but also to claims based on federal law or the law of any other State. * * * It is therefore hard to see how [the law] could be understood as a rule that, though procedural in form, serves the function of defining New York's rights or remedies." "In order to displace a federal rule, there must be more than just a possibility that a state rule is different than it appears."

Justice Ginsburg (joined by Justices Kennedy, Breyer, and Alito) dissented. The central theme of her dissent was that Federal Rule 23 need not, and should not, be read "to collide with New York's legitimate interest in keeping certain awards reasonably bounded." Citing and discussing at length a number of earlier decisions in which the Court had avoided such conflicts by interpreting the federal rules "with awareness of, and sensitivity to, important state regulatory policies", she went on to analyze the history and purpose of the New York limitation, and concluded that the state's decision "to block class-action proceedings for statutory damages [ ] makes scant sense, except as a means to a manifestly substantive end: Limiting a defendant's liability in a single lawsuit in order to prevent the exorbitant inflation of penalties". Implementation of the state's substantive purpose, she contended, was not in conflict with Rule 23 because that rule only "prescribes the considerations relevant to class certification and postcertification proceedings—but it does not command that a particular remedy be available when a party sues in a representative capacity."

Justice Ginsburg also rejected as not in any way dispositive the placement of the New York limitation in the state's Civil Practice Law—the same law in which the provision in the Gasperini case appeared. And as to the fact that the provision was not expressly limited to claims under New York law, she said that "the most likely explanation for the absence of limiting language [was that] New York legislators make law with New York plaintiffs and defendants

---

**b.**  In a portion of his opinion responding to Justice Stevens—a portion joined only by Chief Justice Roberts and Justice Thomas—Justice Scalia again relied heavily on the rationale of Sibbach, and conceded that "Sib-bach's exclusive focus on the challenged federal rule—driven by the very real fear that Federal Rules which vary from State to State would be chaos—is hard to square with § 2072(b)'s terms."

in mind". As in Gasperini, she said, the remedial provision could have been written, and should be understood, as a statutory cap.

Is there a rationale agreed on by a majority for the result reached in Shady Grove? How would you state it?[c]

Do you agree with Justice Scalia's premise that a class action is only a procedural device for aggregating individual claims? Compare Shapiro, *Class Actions: The Class as Party and Client*, 73 Notre Dame L.Rev. 913 (1998). If, as Shapiro contends, the availability of a class action has significant purposes and consequences that transcend the notion of joinder or aggregation, how does that affect the appropriate scope of Rule 23 under the Enabling Act?

Even if Justice Scalia's premise is accepted, do you agree with him that his reading of the rule is the only "reasonable" one? Is the dissent's reading of Rule 23 any more of a stretch than the Court's reading of Rule 42(b) in Semtek, or than its reading of other rules in the cases discussed in this Paragraph or earlier in this Chapter? Is it consistent with the Court's reading of the earlier version of Rule 23 in Cohen v. Beneficial Industrial Loan Corp., Sixth Edition p. 580 n.5?

If New York were to repeal CPLR § 901(b) and at the same time were to insert a provision in every law authorizing recovery of a statutory penalty that "the remedy herein provided may not be sought on behalf of a class but only on behalf of an individual plaintiff", would such a provision have to be honored in a federal diversity action brought to recover such a penalty?

Note the irony, emphasized by Justice Ginsburg, that the bringing of such a class action in a federal court was possible only because of the special provisions of CAFA, which, as she stated, was designed to result in "fewer—not more—class actions overall." Of course, as she also recognized, Congress itself can overrule the result in Shady Grove.

In any event, it remains true, over 70 years after the adoption of the Federal Rules of Civil Procedure, that no rule has been held invalid, on its face or as applied.

In the year since the Shady Grove decision, there has already been a good deal of scholarly comment. Because it is so far-ranging, and indicates disagreement among scholars on such basic questions as the meaning and scope of the Erie decision, the proper approach to questions arising under the Rules of

---

**c.** As a sign of the uncertain effect of the Shady Grove decision, several Justices disagreed on the appropriateness of the Court's subsequent per curiam decision granting certiorari, and summarily vacating and remanding for reconsideration in light of Shady Grove, the Second Circuit's refusal to permit a class action in another suit. See Holster v. Gatco, Inc., 130 S.Ct. 1575 (2010). (Justice Sotomayor did not participate.) In the view of Justice Ginsburg, whom Justice Breyer joined in dissent, the decision to vacate and remand was not warranted because the particular class action had been brought under a federal law (the Telephone Consumer Protection Act [TCPA]) that allowed a private action to be brought only if it was "otherwise permitted by the laws or rules of court of a State," and this language was relied on by the Second Circuit as a ground for rejecting a federal court class action that was "independent" of the Second Circuit's conclusion that the state's class action prohibition in CPLR § 901(b) was "substantive". But in the view of Justice Scalia, concurring in the per curiam, the remand was appropriate because the "independent ground" *may* have rested on an assumption (a) that Rule 23 did not "address whether class actions are available for specific claims" or (b) that the TCPA superseded Rule 23 because CPLR § 901(b) precludes an action under state law. In either event, he contended, the Shady Grove decision would affect the outcome in view of its holding that CPLR § 901(b) did not bar an *action* to recover a penalty but only the use of a procedural joinder device, and thus was trumped by Rule 23.

Decision and Rules Enabling Acts, and the question whether the validity of a Federal Rule of Civil Procedure should ever be considered on an "as applied" basis, much of that scholarship is cited and briefly summarized in the margin.[d]

---

# SECTION 4. THE EFFECT OF STATE LAW AND OF PRIVATE AGREEMENT ON THE EXERCISE OF FEDERAL JURISDICTION

**d.** Leading articles include Burbank & Wolff, *Redeeming the Missed Opportunities of Shady Grove*, 159 U.Pa.L.Rev.17 (2010) (arguing that Shady Grove was erroneous because Rule 23 is a *mechanism* for implementing aggregate liability policy, and not itself the source of that policy; in Shady Grove the source was the law of New York); and Tidmarsh, *Procedure, Substance, and Erie*, 64 Vand.L.Rev. 877 (2011) (defending the result in Shady Grove on the ground that the federal courts may properly apply their own rules (like Rule 23) to process a claim "as long as, in a world without transaction costs [including the costs of litigation], those rules do not affect the ex ante value of a claim") (In a federal diversity case arising in a state that did not allow attorney fee shifting, how would Tidmarsh regard a Federal Rule that a losing plaintiff in a common law tort case would be required to pay the winner's attorney's fees?)

In a Symposium in the Creighton Law Review, 44 Creighton L.Rev. 1–139 (2010), contributors were asked to rewrite one of the opinions in the case as they think it should have been written. The range of responses is striking: Bassettt, *Enabling the Federal Rules*, *id.* at 7 (concurring in the judgment on the ground that under the broad test of a Federal Rule's validity, which should be determined as of the time of its promulgation, Rule 23 is valid under the Enabling Act and thus trumps a conflicting state rule); Borchers, *The Real Risk of Forum Shopping: A Dissent from Shady Grove*, *id.* at 29 (dissenting on the ground that because of the substantial risk of vertical forum shopping created by the clash between Rule 23 and the substantive goal of New York law, application of Rule 23 in the particular context violates the Enabling Act); Cox, *Putting Hanna to Rest in Shady Grove*, *id.* at 43 (dissenting, on the ground that application of Rule 23, when a conflicting state provision is part of the state's substantive tort reform policy, would

violate Erie's constitutional mandate); Freer & Arthur, *The Irrepressible Influence of Byrd*, *id.* at 61 (arguing that the analysis in the Byrd decision, Sixth Edition p. 581, should be relevant to the resolution of problems arising under the Rules Enabling Act as well as in other contexts, and concluding that application of Byrd's analysis in Shady Grove itself supports the reasoning and conclusion of Justice Stevens' concurrence); Oakley, *Illuminating Shady Grove: A General Approach to Resolving Erie Problems*, *id.* at 79 (concurring on the ground that Rule 23 is a valid rule and expressly authorizes a class action in this case, and noting with approval the implicit rejection of the rationale of Gasperini, Sixth Edition p. 591); Rensberger, *Hanna's Unruly Family: An Opinion for * * * Shady Grove * * *, *id.* at 89 (dissenting on the ground that, while Rule 23 is valid rule, it is not applicable in this diversity case because it conflicts with a state rule that is intimately bound up with the state's substantive policy); Rowe, *Sonia, What's a Nice Person Like You Doing in Company Like That?*, *id.* at 107 (concurring in the judgment on the ground that Rule 23 is not invalid on its face *or* as applied, since the New York law that is in conflict with it does not create a substantive right that would be abridged, enlarged, or modified by allowing a federal class action); Whitten, *Shady Grove * * *: Justice Whitten Nagging in Part and Declaring a Pox on All Houses*, *id.* at 115 (dissenting on the alternative grounds that (a) Rule 23 does not allow a class action in a diversity case such as this, where state law would not permit use of that remedy, and (b) since the state rule is bound up with substantive rights, application of Rule 23 to allow a class action would violate the Enabling Act)

The outpouring of commentary on Shady Grove continued but slowed a bit after 2010 and early 2011. Two symposia of particular interest, both published in 2011, appear in 80 Notre Dame L.Rev. 939–1239 (2011), and in 44 Akron L.Rev. 897–1209 (2011).

**Page 600.   Add a new footnote 3a at the end of Paragraph (6)(b):**

**3a.**   Professor Heiser, in *The [2005] Hague Convention on Choice of Court Agreements: The Impact on Forum Non Conveniens, Transfer of Venue, Removal, and Recognition of Judgments in United States Courts*, 31 U.Pa.J. Int'l L. 1013 (2010), concludes, after a detailed analysis, that "in most cases [including those discussed in this Note], the Convention should have little impact on the enforcement of forum selection clauses [and the other topics covered in the title of the article]. However, in some areas, the Convention will require significant changes in domestic law."

**Page 602.   Add a new footnote 3 at the end of Paragraph (3)(c):**

**3.**   For a spirited defense of Justice Ginsburg's dissent in the Chicago v. ICS case (in which she argued that a federal district court lacked the authority under present law to engage in deferential closed-record review of a state agency proceeding), see Wolff, *Ruth Bader Ginsburg and Sensible Pragmatism in Federal Jurisdictional Policy*, 70 Ohio St.L.J. 839 (2010). In defending her dissent, Wolff advocates, in lieu of a strict textual approach to questions of federal court jurisdiction, a mode of interpretation grounded in an understanding of statutory purpose and a presumption in favor of preserving stable institutional arrangements—here, arrangements relating to judicial review of state administrative action.

# CHAPTER VII

# FEDERAL COMMON LAW

## SECTION 1. DEFINING PRIMARY OBLIGATIONS

## SUBSECTION B: CIVIL ACTIONS

**Page 619. Insert the following in place of the last paragraph in Paragraph (4)(b):**

How convincing is the federalism position and the related Supremacy Clause thesis? One line of criticism contests the textual basis for the Supremacy Clause thesis, arguing that it is unlikely that the term "Laws" in the previously quoted passage of the Supremacy Clause refers only to *enacted* federal law rather than federal common law. On that account, if "Laws" is given only the narrower reading, the clause may produce the anomalous result of preempting only state statute law, since it makes federal law supreme, "any Thing in the Constitution or *Laws* of any State to the Contrary notwithstanding." See, *e.g.*, Strauss, *The Perils of Theory*, 83 Notre Dame L.Rev. 1567, 1568–73 (2008). Another objection suggests that while Professor Clark's Supremacy Clause thesis has a textual basis, it cannot fully explain the history of the founding, or account for subsequent developments in, public law. See Monaghan, *Supremacy Clause Textualism*, 110 Colum.L.Rev. 731, 750–51 (2010). Monaghan acknowledges that the clause's reference to "Laws * * * *made* in pursuance of [this Constitution]" would have reached only statutes, since most lawyers at the time believed that the common law was found rather than made. Nevertheless, he claims that the history surrounding the clause's adoption belies any contention that it was framed to promote federalism. Its evident purpose, he adds, was to rectify weaknesses in the Articles of Confederation, and, during the ratifying debates, Anti-Federalists roundly criticized the clause's nationalizing tendency. More importantly, Monaghan argues that the Supremacy Clause thesis cannot account for the vast expanse of federal practice in the modern administrative state. For example, the Court has repeatedly approved congressional delegations of authority to administrative agencies to flesh out the details of broad—sometimes almost contentless—statutory standards. See, *e.g.*, American Power & Light Co. v. SEC, 329 U.S. 90, 104 (1946) ("fair and equitable"); NBC v. United States, 319 U.S. 190, 225–26 (1943) ("public interest, convenience, and necessity"). Such exercises of lawmaking authority do not comply with the procedural safeguards of federalism any more than does federal common lawmaking.

If Professor Monaghan is correct that the Supremacy Clause thesis cannot account for many settled features of the modern administrative state, does that conclusion further suggest that the thesis, even if supported by the constitutional text, should have *no* relevance in informing the Court's response to novel claims of federal lawmaking power? Conversely, if a given exercise of federal common lawmaking authority can be traced to a statutory or constitutional provision, does that resolve any federalism objection by ascribing the relevant authority to a legal source that was itself the product of the political safeguards of federalism?

### Page 620.   Insert a new footnote 7a at the end of Paragraph (5)(b):

**7a.** In a recent article, Professor Merrill further narrowed his view. He argues that several public law developments—including the Court's rejection of federal common law crimes, its recent trend away from recognizing new forms of federal common law, and its determination that the standard of judicial review of administrative action is a function of legislative intent—represent a cumulative judicial determination that Congress is the "exclusive repository" of the so-called "disposing power." See Merrill, *The Disposing Power of the Legislature*, 110 Colum.L.Rev. 452 (2010). Merrill defines the disposing power as being the power to decide "who has the authority to make law and under what circumstances." On his view, therefore, "neither the executive nor the judiciary has autonomous power to make law * * * unless delegated authority to do so by the legislature." Do Professor Merrill's examples convincingly rule out the possibility that some aspects of the constitutional structure may themselves implicitly authorize lawmaking of sorts by the executive or judiciary? Compare Sixth Edition pp. 653–85.

### Page 622.   Insert the following at the end of Paragraph (6):

Conversely, because "implied" delegation, by definition, supplies no intelligible principle to guide the judiciary's development of federal common law, might such a conception raise separation of powers concerns even under the Court's forgiving approach to the nondelegation doctrine? See Nielson, *Erie as Nondelegation*, 72 Ohio St.L.J. 239, 296301 (2011).

### Page 627.   Insert the following at the end of footnote 1:

See also General Dynamics Corp. v. United States, 131 S.Ct. 1900, 1906 (2011) (reaffirming the Court's "common-law authority to fashion contractual remedies in Government-contracting disputes").

### Page 646.   Add the following at the end of Paragraph (3)(b):

For the suggestion that the Court's standards for field preemption have become stricter in recent years, see Kurns v. Railroad Friction Products Corp., 132 S.Ct. 1261, 1270 (2012)(Kagan, J., concurring).

### Page 646.   Insert the following at the end of footnote 4:

In Arizona v. Inter–Tribal Council of Arizona, Inc., 133 S.Ct. 2247 (2013), the Court held that the presumption against preemption does not apply when Congress has regulated the manner of voting for federal office. In an opinion by Justice Scalia (joined by Chief Justice Roberts and Justices Ginsburg, Breyer, Sotomayor, and Kagan), the Court held that the National Voter Registration Act of 1993 (NVRA), 42 U.S.C. § 1973gg *et seq.*, which requires states to "accept and use" a uniform federal voter registration form, preempted a state law requirement that voters submit proof of citizenship with their registration. According to Justice Scalia, "*all* [congressional] action under the Elections Clause displaces some element of a pre-existing state regulatory regime, because the text of the Clause confers the power to do exactly (and only) that. By contrast, even laws enacted under the Commerce Clause * * * will not always implicate concurrent state power". In dissent, Justice Alito argued that the presumption against preemption applies "with full force" to election law, given the states' compelling interest in preserving the integrity of their elections. Do these sharply different readings of where to place a thumb on the scale raise questions about the utility of relying on clear statement rules to resolve preemption questions? Are such canons, like the presumption against preemption itself, a form of federal common law? See Gluck, *The Federal Common Law of Statutory Interpretation: Erie for the Age of Statutes*, 54 Wm. & Mary.L.Rev.753 (2013).

## Page 646.  Add a new footnote 6a at the end of the parenthetical in Paragraph (3)(c):

**6a.** In an opinion for the Court written by Justice Thomas and joined by Chief Justice Roberts and Justices Scalia, Kennedy, and Alito, the Court in PLIVA, Inc. v. Mensing, 131 S.Ct. 2567 (2011), held that, in the context of generic drugs, federal food and drug law preempted a state tort law action alleging that pharmaceutical companies had failed to warn consumers of potential side effects. The Court noted that federal law requires generic drugs to have "the same safety and efficacy labeling as their brand-name counterparts." Because it was therefore "impossible [for generics manufacturers] to simultaneously comply with both federal law and any state tort-law duty that required them to use a different label", the Court concluded that conflict preemption applied.

In a portion of Justice Thomas's opinion that Justice Kennedy declined to join, a plurality added that the presumption against preemption does not apply in conflict preemption cases based on impossibility. Relying on the historical analysis in Nelson, *Preemption*, 86 Va.L.Rev. 225 (2000), the plurality reasoned that the founders modeled the Supremacy Clause on *non obstante* clauses that eighteenth century legislatures had inserted into statutes to signal their intention to repeal earlier statutes on the same subject. In particular, the plurality emphasized, legislatures used *non obstante* clauses to signal the inapplicability of the traditional strong presumption against implied repeal—a presumption that required interpreters to strain to read potentially conflicting statutes as being in harmony. From that starting point, the plurality concluded that the *non obstante* language in the Supremacy Clause signaled that courts should not strain to find ways to avoid an evident conflict between state and federal law.

Does the plurality's approach pay too little heed to the federalism values that underlie the modern presumption against preemption? If the Supremacy Clause means what the plurality says it does, would it still be appropriate to enforce abstract federalism values through a clear statement rule? *Cf.* Manning, *Clear Statement Rules and the Constitution*, 110 Colum.L.Rev. 399, 432–34 (2010)(arguing that federalism-based clear statement rules raise certain legitimacy concerns).

## Page 648.  Add a new footnote 6b at the end of Paragraph (5):

**6b.** For a recent decision that broadly interpreted an awkwardly worded preemption clause without any mention of the presumption against preemption, see Bruesewitz v. Wyeth LLC, 131 S.Ct. 1068 (2011).

## Page 648.  Add to Paragraph (6):

In a concurring opinion, Justice Thomas announced that he would no longer subscribe to the Court's precedents that found preemption where a state law stood as an "obstacle" to achieving the "purposes and objectives" of a federal statute. Wyeth v. Levine, 129 S.Ct. 1187, 1204 (2009) (Thomas J., concurring in the judgment). Describing the Court's "entire body of 'purposes and objectives' pre-emption jurisprudence [as] inherently flawed", he argued that such cases "improperly rely on legislative history, broad atextual notions of congressional purpose, and even congressional inaction in order to pre-empt state law." To find preemption based on those indicia of unenacted statutory purpose, he reasoned, contradicts the safeguards of federalism found in the Supremacy Clause, U.S. Const. Art. VI, cl.2, which "gives 'supreme' status only to those [laws] that are 'made in Pursuance' of '[t]his Constitution.' " To respect that condition, he said, the Court may find preemption only when a state law conflicts with a statutory text (or a regulation authorized by such a text) that has cleared the hurdles of bicameralism and presentment set forth by

Article I, § 7. Finally, Justice Thomas stressed that the Court's finding preemption merely because a state law impedes a federal statutory purpose disregards the reality that the passage of federal statutes frequently requires compromise that may not pursue the legislative majority's goals " 'at all costs' " (quoting Geier v. American Honda Motor Co., 529 U.S. 861, 904 (2000) (Stevens, J., dissenting)); see also AT & T Mobility LLC v. Concepcion, 131 S.Ct. 1740, 1754 (2011) (Thomas, J., concurring) (renewing his objection to "purposes-and-objectives preemption"); Williamson v. Mazda Motor of America, Inc., 131 S.Ct. 1131, 1142–43 (2011) (Thomas, J., concurring in the judgment) (same).[a]

How convincing is Justice Thomas' reading of the Supremacy Clause? Compare Clark, *Separation of Powers as a Safeguard of Federalism*, 79 Tex. L.Rev. 1321 (2001) (arguing that the Supremacy Clause codifies the political safeguards of federalism), with Strauss, *The Separation of Powers as a Safeguard of Federalism*, 79 Tex.L.Rev. 1321 (2001) (replying that the text and history of the Clause cannot bear such a reading); see also Sixth Edition pp. 618–19. Apart from the Supremacy Clause, Justice Thomas' position seems to rest on views concerning legislative compromise and bicameralism that the Court has embraced in some of its recent opinions. See Sixth Edition pp. 623–24. Given that the other Justices who associate themselves in some degree with textualism (Justices Scalia and Kennedy) frequently emphasize those considerations in other contexts, why didn't they join Justice Thomas here? Compare Meltzer, *The Supreme Court's Judicial Passivity*, 2002 Sup.Ct.Rev. 343 (discussing the contradiction between textualism and implied preemption doctrine). Is it accurate to characterize Justice Thomas' opinion as suggesting that the presumption against preemption, at least as applied to "obstacle" preemption, might be rooted in separation-of-powers as well as federalism concerns? See, *e.g.*, Leske & Schweitzer, *Frustrated with Preemption: Why Courts Should Rarely Displace State Law Under the Doctrine of Frustration Preemption*, 65 N.Y.U.Ann.Surv.Am.L. 585 (2010); Sharkey, *Against Freewheeling, Extratextual Preemption: Is Justice Clarence Thomas the Lone Principled Federalist?*, 5 N.Y.U.J.L. & Liberty 63 (2010).

**a.** Williamson brought the legitimacy of obstacle preemption into particularly sharp focus. In that case, the Court held that a Department of Transportation regulation giving auto manufacturers the choice to install lap or shoulder belts in certain rear positions in a vehicle did not preempt a state tort action alleging that Mazda acted negligently by using a shoulder rather than a lap belt in such a position. By contrast, the Court in Geier v. American Honda Motor Co., *supra*, had previously held that, by giving manufacturers the choice between airbags or passive restraints, a prior version of the same regulation did preempt a state tort action alleging that an auto manufacturer had negligently failed to equip its vehicles with airbags. In Williamson, the majority distinguished Geier on the ground that both the drafting history and subsequent agency interpretations of the amended regulation revealed no agency intent to give manufacturers an affirmative choice between shoulder and lap belts. In his opinion concurring in the judgment in Williamson, Justice Thomas argued that the Court's reasoning, which he described as a free-ranging "psychoanalysis" of the agency's goals, confirmed that "[p]urposes-and-objectives pre-emption" necessarily "roams beyond statutory or regulatory text" and "is thus wholly illegitimate." If the constitutional structure does indeed establish a presumption against preemption, should the Court ever find preemption based on a conflict between state law and the implicit purposes and objectives of a regulation? Even if the Court does not insist that an organic act clearly provide for preemption, should it at least require the agency to provide some explicit statement of *its* intention to preempt?

**Page 648.  Add the following at the end of the second paragraph of Paragraph (6):**

Indeed, at least one scholar believes that the Court has shifted to a "centralization default"—a marked disposition toward finding preemption in cases of doubt. Sharpe, *Legislating Preemption*, 53 Wm. & Mary L.Rev. 163 (2011); see also Chemerinsky, *The Roberts Court at Age Three*, 54 Wayne L.Rev. 947, 968–72 (2008); Greve & Klick, *Preemption in the Rehnquist Court: A Preliminary Empirical Assessment*, 14 Sup.Ct.Econ.Rev. 43 (2006); Metzger, *Federalism and Federal Agency Reform*, 111 Colum.L.Rev. 1 (2011).

**Page 649.   Add a new footnote 7a at the end of Paragraph (7):**

**7a.**   Sharpe, *Toward (a) Faithful Agency in the Supreme Court's Preemption Jurisprudence*, 18 Geo. Mason L.Rev. 367 (2011), argues that various institutional limitations upon Congress, including the clash of interest groups and the limitations on legislative foresight, make it unlikely that Congress can address preemption questions in an adequately comprehensive manner. At the same time, Professor Sharpe argues that judges suffer from a legitimacy deficit when they try to develop federal common law criteria for determining when federal interests warrant preemption. Accordingly, he maintains that unless Congress has included a preemption clause in a statute, the Court should find preemption only when Congress has expressly delegated to an agency the power to preempt state law. In Sharpe's view, calibrating Congress's incentives in this way would produce greater flexibility than legislative preemption and greater legitimacy than a judge-centered federal common law approach. Under such a regime, would Chevron's applicability to agency preemption decisions be a foregone conclusion?

**Page 650.   Add the following in place of the last paragraph of Paragraph (8):**

The Court recently suggested that the trigger for preemption is lighter in the immigration context than in the usual case. In Arizona v. United States, 132 S.Ct. 2492 (2012), a divided Court held that federal immigration law occupies the field such that Arizona could not (a) make it a crime for an alien to fail to comply with federal registration requirements; (b) make it a crime for an unauthorized alien to work or apply for employment in the state; or (c) authorize state law enforcement to arrest a person on probable cause that he or she has committed an offense that makes that individual removable. At the outset of its analysis, the Court emphasized the federal government's "broad, undoubted power" over immigration and the potential foreign relations implications of the treatment of foreign nationals within U.S. borders. The Court also noted the pervasiveness of federal regulation of immigration. From that starting point, the Court found it relatively straightforward to conclude that the three provisions of state law mentioned above either entered a field that federal law had fully occupied or stood as an obstacle to the purposes of federal law. Citing Hines v. Davidovitz, Sixth Edition p. 650, the Court reasoned that Congress had "struck a careful balance" regarding the appropriate requirements for the registration of aliens and the sanctions for nonregistration, and that this "comprehensive" federal scheme precludes state regulation of the same field. Similarly, the Court found that because federal law imposed "comprehensive" sanctions on employers who hired unauthorized aliens—but deliberately omitted criminal sanctions on the employees themselves—states could not impose such sanctions on employees without interposing an obstacle to federal purposes. Finally, the Court found that the state's authorization to arrest persons based on probable cause of removability interfered with the purposes of federal law by intruding on the enforcement discretion of federal immigration officers. The Court upheld only one provision of the Arizona law, which provides that an officer who makes a lawful stop or arrest must take steps to ascertain immigration status if he or she has reasonable suspicion that the subject is an unauthorized alien.

Justices Scalia, Thomas, and Alito filed separate partial dissents. Justice Scalia argued that states have a traditional sovereign interest in the preservation of the integrity of their borders, and that courts should insist on a clear statement of legislative intent before reading a statute to abrogate that sovereign authority. Because none of the Arizona provisions squarely conflicts with federal law, Justice Scalia would have upheld them all. The fact that state laws strike a different balance from the federal laws on some issues, he argued, should not alone provide a ground for preemption. For example, he added, "[t]he sale of illegal drugs . . . violates state law as well as federal law, and no one thinks that the state penalties cannot exceed the federal." With respect to the employment provision in particular, Justice Scalia emphasized that Congress adopted an *express* preemption provision displacing "any state or local law imposing civil or criminal sanctions . . . upon those who employ, or recruit or refer for a fee for employment, unauthorized aliens." 8 U.S.C. 1324a(h)(2). For him, Congress's adoption of an express preemption provision precluded the Court's finding implied preemption of laws that did not fall within scope of the express provision.

Justice Alito agreed with the Court that under Hines v. Davidovitz, Arizona's registration provision was preempted. Relying on both the presumption against preemption and the limited scope of the express preemption provision cited above, he argued, however, that there was insufficient evidence that Congress wished to preempt the state's prescription of sanctions for unauthorized aliens seeking employment. Finally, he argued that the arrest authority conferred by the Arizona statute added little to state enforcement officers' background authority to arrest aliens for removable offenses, and that there is nothing in the state law that necessarily places its enforcement in conflict with the discretion of federal officials. Justice Thomas wrote a brief dissent reiterating his previously stated concerns about doctrines of implied preemption.

One interesting aspect of the case is that both the majority and Justice Scalia's dissent framed their respective analyses against the backdrop of broad structural presumptions—in the former case, a presumption of overriding federal interest and, in the latter, a presumption that a state possesses sovereign authority to exclude persons from its borders.[b] Where do these presumptions come from and how far do they go? Do they help or confuse judicial analysis? More generally, in other opinions, Justice Thomas has stated his reluctance to find implied preemption at all, reasoning that the analysis is too malleable and requires judges to delve into the unknowable realm of unstated congressional purpose. See pp. 73–74, *supra*. Does the complexity of the competing arguments in this case lend any support to this position? Or is it standard judicial practice to determine when Congress has struck an intricate

---

**b.** Abrams, *Plenary Power Preemption*, 99 Va.L.Rev. 601 (2013), describes the Court's approach as plenary power preemption—a phenomenon that "gives particular weight to federal interests where questions of national sovereignty are at stake." According to Professor Abrams, in areas of overriding national interest such as alienage, the Court has shown itself willing to find preemption even when conventional applications of conflict or obstacle preemption would not produce such a result.

federal balance that deliberately goes so far and no farther? Compare Buckman Co. v. Plaintiffs' Legal Comm., 531 U.S. 341, 347–348 (2001); Wisconsin Dept. of Industry, Labor & Human Relations v. Gould Inc., 475 U.S. 282, 288–289 (1986); Silkwood v. Kerr–McGee Corp., 464 U.S. 238, 249 (1984).

### Page 658.   Add a new footnote 10a to the last sentence of Paragraph (4):

**10a.**  In tension with its earlier position in Moragne, the Court in Atlantic Sounding Co. v. Townsend, 129 S.Ct. 2561 (2009), held that the common law of admiralty authorizes the recovery of punitive damages when a shipowner willfully denies a crew member maintenance and cure after an injury. See Sixth Edition p. 651 n.* (defining maintenance and cure). In so holding, the Court (5–4, per Justice Thomas) concluded that the traditional punitive damages remedy remained available despite the fact that such damages would *not* be recoverable in an action brought pursuant to the Jones Act, 46 U.S.C. § 30104, which removed a prior common law bar against negligence actions for certain maritime personal injuries. The Court noted that the Jones Act allows someone in the plaintiff's position to "elect" to bring a Jones Act claim and thus should not be read to preempt the plaintiff's existing maritime claim, especially given the Act's remedial purpose to expand maritime remedies.

In dissent, Justice Alito (joined by Chief Justice Roberts and Justices Scalia and Kennedy) argued that the plaintiff's common law claim—that the employer wrongfully withheld maintenance and cure—would be maintainable under the Jones Act, and that the Court should promote uniformity in maritime law by following the policies embedded in the Act as a matter of common law discretion. "[J]ust because the Jones Act was not meant to preclude general maritime claims or remedies," he wrote, "it does not follow that the Jones Act was meant to stop the development of a general maritime law by the courts." Noting that the Court looks to appropriate legislation for policy guidance in the admiralty context, the dissent would have followed the Jones Act's policy in determining the availability of punitive damages.

Does Atlantic Sounding signal further retrenchment from Moragne? Given the nature of legislative compromise, when, if ever, is it appropriate to borrow "policy" from enactments that Congress has not applied to the precise common law context before the Court? For an argument that courts possessing common law authority may properly use that power to broaden a statute's reach to new cases that text itself does not reach, see Pojanowski, *Statutes in Common Law Courts*, 91 Tex.L.Rev. 479 (2013).

### Page 661.   Add the following to the end of the footnote 16:

Sachs, *Constitutional Backdrops*, 80 Geo.Wash.L.Rev.1813 (2012), offers yet another take on the problem. Professor Sachs argues that a considerable body of common law predating the Constitution survived its adoption without having been formally incorporated into the document. He argues, for example, that no provision of the Constitution formally adopted the preexisting law of nations rules governing the resolution of inter-state boundary disputes. At the same time, nothing in the document displaced those rules. Accordingly, they survived the Constitution's adoption and became the relevant source of law for cases brought pursuant to the grant of jurisdiction for controversies between states. Professor Sachs adds, however, that even though the Constitution does not adopt the common law of interstate disputes, it gives those rules special status. In particular, because U.S. Const. Art. IV, § 3, preserves the territorial integrity of the states, except insofar as the legislatures of the affected states and Congress agree, Sachs argues that the Court may not retroactively alter the pre-existing common law rules for determining state boundaries without undermining territorial integrity.

### Page 661.   Add a new footnote 16a at the end of Paragraph (3):

**16a.**  In Montana v. Wyoming, 131 S.Ct. 1765 (2011), the Court used state law and general water law to decide a water rights question under an interstate compact guaranteeing such rights "in accordance with the laws governing the acquisition and use of water under the doctrine of appropriation". Emphasizing its obligation to construe a compact, much like any contract, in accordance with the parties' intent, the Court concluded that the relevant clause directed the parties to look "primarily to the doctrine of appropriation in Wyoming and Montana and to Western water law more generally". How could the Court draw that conclusion from general language referring to "the laws" governing the doctrine of appropriation? What should the Court have done if it had found that Montana and Wyoming had different water-law regimes?

**Page 662.   Insert a new heading for Paragraph (5):**

**(5) Interstate Pollution.**

**Page 663.   Insert a new Paragraph (5)(c):**

(c) In American Elec. Power Co. v. Connecticut, 131 S. Ct. 2527 (2011), the Court again addressed the criteria for statutory displacement of the federal common law of interstate pollution, this time in the context of air pollution. The plaintiffs—a number of states, the city of New York, and several private land trusts—filed public nuisance actions against several large power companies, alleging that the companies' carbon dioxide emissions contributed to global warming. The Second Circuit held that the plaintiffs had stated a claim under the federal common law of nuisance and that the Clean Air Act did not displace that federal common law right of action.

In an opinion by Justice Ginsburg, joined in full by Chief Justice Roberts and Justices Scalia, Kennedy, Breyer, and Kagan, the Court reversed. Given its previous holding in Massachusetts v. EPA, Sixth Edition pp. 144–46, that the Clean Air Act authorized the EPA to regulate greenhouse gases, the Court concluded that the Act displaced any federal common law right of action that the plaintiffs might otherwise have had.[c] Emphasizing that the standard for such displacement was lower than the standard for preemption of state law, the Court stated that "[t]he test for whether congressional legislation excludes the declaration of federal common law is simply whether the statute 'speak[s] directly to [the] question at issue'" (quoting Mobil Oil Corp. v. Higginbotham, 436 U.S. 618, 625 (1978)). Since Massachusetts v. EPA "made plain that emissions of carbon dioxide qualify as air pollution subject to regulation under the [Clean Air] Act," the Court held that the Act "speaks directly" to the claims brought by the plaintiffs. It made no difference that the EPA had not yet fully implemented its previously recognized regulatory authority. If the EPA declined to set emissions standards for a particular pollutant or pollution source, the remedy would lie in the judicial review prescribed by the Act itself. The important point, for the Court, was that Congress entrusted the "complex balancing" of environmental, energy, and economic considerations, in the first instance, to an expert agency. For that reason, the Court found it inappropriate to attribute parallel authority to inexpert, unelected federal judges.[d]

Does American Elec. Power apply as stringent a test for displacement of federal common law as did Milwaukee v. Illinois, Sixth Edition p. 662? In Milwaukee, the Court emphasized that the Clean Water Act "occupied the field through the establishment of a comprehensive regulatory program supervised by an expert administrate agency." In contrast, the American Elec. Power Court found displacement simply because the Clean Air Act authorized the EPA to address the subject matter of the lawsuit. Does this apparent relaxation

**c.** The Court declined to reach the question of whether the plaintiffs would have had a federal common law right of action if the Clean Air Act did not address the question at issue.

**d.** Justices Thomas and Alito wrote separately to express their continuing dis-

agreement with the Court's decision in Massachusetts v. EPA, but stated that the Court's judgment in American Elec. Power followed if Massachusetts v. EPA was good law. Justice Sotomayor did not participate.

of the displacement standard signal a broader reticence on the part of the Court about the federal common law of interstate pollution?

**Page 663.  Add a new footnote 17a at the end of Paragraph (5)(b):**

**17a.**  The BP Deepwater Horizon oil spill raises interesting questions about the contemporary significance of judge-made admiralty law. See, *e.g.*, *Symposium: Big Oil, Big Consequences, and the Big Unknown: Exploring the Legal, Regulatory, and Environmental Impact of the Gulf Oil Spill*, 74 Alb.L.Rev. 475 (2011); *Symposium: Deep Trouble: Legal Ramifications of the Deepwater Horizon Oil Spill*, 65 Tul.L.Rev. 889 (2011).

**Page 674.  Add a new Paragraph 2(f):**

In Samantar v. Yousuf, 130 S.Ct. 2278 (2010), the Court held that the immunity conferred upon "a foreign state" by the Foreign Sovereign Immunities Act of 1976 (FSIA), 28 U.S.C. § 1604, did not extend to foreign *officials* when sued in their personal capacities for alleged wrongs committed while in office. As the Court explained, the doctrine of foreign sovereign immunity had originally developed "as a matter of common law", rooted in the notion that " 'the United States had impliedly waived jurisdiction over certain activities of foreign sovereigns' " (quoting Verlinden B.V. v. Central Bank of Nigeria, 461 U.S. 480, 486 (1983)). Traditionally, if the State Department granted a "suggestion of immunity" requested by a foreign sovereign, district courts would dismiss for lack of jurisdiction. If the State Department did not recognize immunity, the district court was free to decide the question itself under the common law. Although rare, cases involving suits against foreign *officials* were handled according to the same procedure.

In 1952, the State Department announced the adoption of a "restrictive" view of foreign sovereign immunity, declaring that it would grant such immunity only with respect to a foreign sovereign's "public acts", and not with respect to commercial activities. This approach was thought to be consistent with then-prevailing norms of international law. Because of perceived inconsistencies in the State Department's application of this new policy, however, Congress enacted the FSIA in order to codify the restrictive view of the doctrine and to shift responsibility for its implementation primarily to the district courts.

Finding that the FSIA's definition of "foreign state" evokes "a body politic that governs a particular territory", Justice Stevens' opinion for the Court in Samantar concluded that the FSIA did not extend to suits against foreign officials and, correlatively, that it did not displace whatever common law immunity such officials enjoyed prior to the FSIA's enactment. Because the scope and application of sovereign immunity and official immunity were not fully coextensive, the Court found no reason to infer that the codification of the former body of common law implicitly also codified the latter. Indeed, because questions about official immunity prior to the FSIA were "few and far between," the Court concluded that such immunity "simply was not the particular problem to which Congress was responding". The Court indicated that the district court would have to determine, on remand, whether petitioner was entitled to raise common law immunity.

The Court did not specify the nature of the common law of official immunity left intact by the FSIA. Would such immunity properly be characterized as federal common law? Might it instead be understood as an inference from the constitutional structure about how best to allocate diplomatic authority between the political branches and the courts? See Paragraph (4)(c), *infra*.

Even if the FSIA did not directly apply to official immunity, should the approach take by the FSIA to foreign sovereign immunity inform—or even dictate—the approach federal courts should take in crafting the common law of official immunity? *Cf.* Moragne v. States Marine Lines, Sixth Edition pp. 657–58.

### Page 679.  Add a new footnote 13a at the end of the penultimate paragraph of Paragraph (4)(c):

**13a.**  Bellia & Clark, *The Law of Nations as Constitutional Law*, 98 Va.L.Rev. 729 (2012), goes one step farther and argues that courts cannot understand certain constitutional powers assigned to the political branches except by reference to the state-state relations branch of the law of nations. These powers include Congress' powers to declare "war," grant "letters of marque and reprisal," and make rules governing "captures." They also include presidential powers to receive "ambassadors" and (with the requisite Senate approval) to make "treaties." These Article I and Article II powers, the authors argue, all are terms of art whose meaning the founders drew from the law of nations. Bellia and Clark contend that this understanding helps explain why the Supreme Court has treated the law of state-state relations as part of U.S. law throughout American history, up to and including Sabbatino. Compare Vázquez, *Customary International Law as U.S. Law: A Critique of the Intermediate Positions and a Defense of the Modern Position*, 86 Notre Dame L.Rev.1495 (2011) (arguing that Bellia and Clark's structural argument is "thoroughly convincing" but that it "actually provides substantial support for most of the modern position").

### Page 679.   Add a new footnote 13b at the end of Paragraph (4)(c):

**13b.**  Professor Bederman has suggested yet another alternative to the modern and revisionist positions. See Bederman, *Law of the Land, Law of the Sea: The Lost Link Between Customary International Law and the General Maritime Law*, 51 Va.J.Int'l L. 299 (2011). Emphasizing the common origins of CIL and general maritime law in the law of nations and the similar treatment that the Court gave to both forms of law during much of our history, he suggests that the Court use the post-Southern Pac. Co. v. Jensen, Sixth Edition p. 655–56, admiralty framework to determine the status and effect of CIL. On that account, Bederman argues, CIL would be "supreme, impliedly preemptive of state law, and permissive of direct Supreme Court review of state court decisions as to its content, but [would] not constitute a federal question for the purposes of that head of jurisdiction." See Sixth Edition, pp. 837–39 (noting that judge-made admiralty law does not give rise to federal question jurisdiction). According to Bederman, this approach strikes the appropriate balance between federalism and promoting the needed uniformity in CIL.

Even if CIL and general maritime law share common origins, should the problems of judicial administrability associated with the post-Jensen approach to admiralty law give the Court pause before extending that approach to CIL? Compare Sixth Edition pp. 656–57. Does the existence of an explicit Admiralty Clause in Article III make it more legitimate for the Court to develop a federal common law of admiralty than to do the same for CIL?

### Page 681.  Add a new footnote 5a at the end of the first sentence in the penultimate paragraph in Paragraph (4):

**5a.**  Kontorovich, *Discretion, Delegation, and Defining the Constitution's Law of Nations Clause*, 106 Nw.U.L.Rev. 1675 (2012), argues that limiting offenses cognizable under the ATS to clearly established international norms saves the ATS from effecting an impermissible delegation to the federal courts of Congress's power to "define and punish * * * offenses against the Law of Nations". U.S. Const. Art. I, § 8, cl. 10. In the absence of such a standard, Professor Kontorovich argues, the ATS would lack the intelligible principle required for its validity. Is the grant of common lawmaking authority supplied by the ATS any vaguer than the one at issue in Textile Workers Union v. Lincoln Mills, Sixth Edition p. 663? Does the foreign relations context give the Court greater reason for caution in approving delegations to federal courts?

**Page 684.  Add the following at the end of Paragraph (4):**

(4) Do these anomalies cast doubt on whether the Court in Sosa has advanced a convincing account of the congressional design underlying the ATS? Is there an intelligible way to understand the ATS without assuming that Congress meant to authorize the federal courts to develop a specialized federal common law of international torts?[e]

**Page 685.  Add a new Paragraph (6):**

**(6) The Extraterritorial Application of the ATS:** In Kiobel v. Royal Dutch Petroleum Co., 133 S.Ct. 1659 (2012), the Supreme Court unanimously affirmed the dismissal of an Alien Tort Statute (ATS) suit by a foreign national against foreign corporations for conduct that occurred in a foreign country. Although the Court granted certiorari to resolve a conflict in authority on the availability of corporate liability under the ATS, after briefing and argument, it set the case for reargument and ordered the parties to brief the following question: "Whether and under what circumstances the [ATS] allows courts to recognize a cause of action for violations of the law of nations occurring within the territory of a sovereign other than the United States?"

In an opinion by Chief Justice Roberts (joined by Justices Scalia, Kennedy, Thomas, and Alito), the Court held that a familiar canon of construction—the presumption against extraterritorial application of U.S. law—governs claims brought pursuant to the ATS. The Court acknowledged that the presumption, which serves to prevent the U.S. from becoming embroiled in international disputes that might arise from conflicts between U.S. and foreign law, ordinarily reaches only the extraterritorial application of statutes that "regulat[e]

**e.** Professors Bellia and Clark argue that the original meaning of the ATS did not authorize the development of a CIL of torts; rather, in their view, the First Congress understood the statute to permit an alien to sue a U.S. citizen for any intentional tort to person or personal property because *any such tort* would have violated the law of nations in 1789. See Bellia and Clark, *The Alien Tort Statute and the Law of Nations*, 78 U.Chi. L.Rev. 445 (2011). Under law of nations principles, a nation became responsible for its citizens' intentional torts against an alien unless it extradited the offender, imposed criminal punishment, or gave the alien a civil remedy. Failure to take one of these steps gave the victim's nation just cause to retaliate against the tortfeasor's nation. Bellia and Clark maintain that by granting federal courts jurisdiction to hear alien tort claims against U.S. citizens, the First Congress sought to establish a self-executing means of satisfying the United States' obligations under the law of nations. They agree with the Court's conclusion that the ATS was merely a "grant of jurisdiction" that did not confer "power to mold substantive law". But they contend that, rather than authorizing common lawmaking authority under the ATS,

Congress would have expected the right of action to come instead from power conferred by Section 14 of the Judiciary Act of 1789 and the Process Acts of 1789 and 1792, which authorized federal courts to employ common law writs (including trespass on the case) in the exercise of their jurisdiction. If correct, this approach would be broader than Sosa's by extending to all intentional torts, but narrower by reaching only tort actions by aliens against citizens of the United States.

Would such an approach supply a plausible framework for understanding the ATS without creating the anomalies implicit in Sosa's reading of the statute? If CIL no longer requires a sovereign to provide civil relief for all intentional torts committed by a citizen against an alien, would that make the ATS obsolete? Compare Wuerth, *The Alien Tort Statute and Federal Common Law: A New Approach*, 85 Notre Dame L.Rev.1931, 1934 (2010)(arguing that the Court should not derive rules of decision in ATS cases from CIL norms alone but should develop "judge-made, post-Erie federal common law" that filters CIL "through the particular history and origins of the ATS itself, along with other factors unique to the United States").

conduct". The ATS, in contrast, is strictly jurisdictional and thus "does not directly regulate conduct or afford relief." Still, the Court found that "the principles underlying the canon of interpretation similarly constrain courts considering causes of action that may be brought under the ATS." In particular, because Sosa v. Alvarez–Machain, Sixth Edition p. 680, concluded that the ATS authorizes federal courts "to recognize certain causes of action based on * * * international law," the Court in Kiobel asserted that the risk of "unwarranted judicial interference" in U.S. foreign policy is, if anything, "magnified". Nor, said the Court, was there sufficient evidence of congressional intent to rebut the presumption against extraterritoriality. Noting that Sosa had held that the ATS was designed to address three main offenses against the law of nations—violation of safe conducts, wrongs against ambassadors, and piracy— the Court reasoned that the first two of those offenses "have no necessary extraterritorial applications" and that the third "typically occurs on the high seas," which do not lie within another sovereign's jurisdiction. The Court also found it implausible to think that Congress intended to make "their fledgling Republic" the guardian of international morals. Indeed, rather than serving the ATS's apparent purpose of "avoiding diplomatic strife," applying it extraterritorially "could have generated it." Because all relevant conduct in Kiobel occurred outside the United States, the Court held that the ATS supplied no jurisdiction over the case.[f]

Justice Breyer, joined by Justices Ginsburg, Sotomayor, and Kagan, concurred only in the judgment and disputed the majority's reliance on the presumption against extraterritoriality. Justice Breyer emphasized that the presumption was inapt as applied to a statute that "was enacted with 'foreign matters' in mind." Indeed, noting that Congress passed the ATS "to permit recovery of damages from pirates and others who violated basic international law norms as understood in 1789," Justice Breyer emphasized that piracy was extraterritorial and often required the application of U.S. law to ships that flew the flag of foreign nations and thus lay within their jurisdiction. Accordingly, Justice Breyer explained that he would read the ATS in light of its evident purpose "of compensating those who have suffered harms at the hands of, *e.g.,* torturers or other modern pirates." Invoking the jurisdictional principles of foreign relations law, Justice Breyer concluded that jurisdiction should lie under the ATS "where (1) the alleged tort occurs on American soil, (2) the defendant is an American national, or (3) the defendant's conduct substantially and adversely affects an important American national interest, and that includes a distinct interest in preventing the United States from becoming a safe harbor (free of civil as well as criminal liability) for a torturer or other common enemy of mankind." He added that he would rely on doctrines such as exhaustion, comity, and *forum non conveniens* to ensure the workability of the invocation of any such jurisdiction relating to events occurring abroad. Because

**f.** In a brief concurring opinion, Justice Kennedy noted that the Court left open a number of questions regarding the reach and interpretation of the ATS, and that the proper implementation of the presumption against extraterritorial application may require some further elaboration and explanation. Justice Alito, joined by Justice Thomas, also joined the Court's opinion but wrote separately to emphasize that he reads Morrison v. National Australia Bank Ltd., 130 S.Ct. 2869 (2010), and Sosa broadly to bar ATS claims like the one before the Court unless such claims include domestic conduct sufficient to violate an international law norm that satisfies Sosa's requirements of definiteness and acceptance among civilized nations.

the facts of Kiobel did not satisfy any of the criteria for jurisdiction, he would have dismissed the case.

Two centuries after the fact, it is obviously difficult to reconstruct the purposes of a statute with very little legislative history, especially when one can find but few interpretations of the statute before modern times. Does that underlying indeterminacy elevate the importance of tie-breaking rules of thumb such the presumption against extraterritorial application? Does the Court convincingly explain why it makes sense to apply that presumption to a statute enacted, in part, to deal with piracy? For symposia discussing Kiobel, see *Agora: Kiobel*, 106 Am.J.Intl L. 509 (2012); Symposium, *Corporate Responsibility and the Alien Tort Statute*, 43 Geo.J. Int'l L. 1089 (2012).

# SECTION 2.   ENFORCING PRIMARY OBLIGATIONS

## SUBSECTION A:  CIVIL ACTIONS

**Page 712.   Add a new footnote 10a at the end of last sentence of Paragraph (5):**

**10a.**   In Douglas v. Independent Living Center of Southern California, 132 S.Ct. 1204 (2012), the Court was presented with—but found it unnecessary to resolve—the question whether the Supremacy Clause provides litigants with an implied right of action to enforce federal preemption of state law under a federal statute that contains no express right of action. In a dissenting opinion joined by Justices Scalia, Thomas, and Alito, Chief Justice Roberts reached the question left open by the Court, concluding that the Supremacy Clause creates no right of action, but merely makes supreme any right of action created by statute. To conclude otherwise, Chief Justice Roberts argued, "would effect a complete end-run around this Court's implied right of action and 42 U.S.C. 1983 jurisprudence."

**Page 713.   Insert the following in place of the second paragraph in footnote 11:**

Ernest Young argues that Medellín adopts the correct approach even if one assumes, as Professor Vázquez does, that the Court should approach treaties the same way as statutes and constitutional provisions, given their like placement in the Supremacy Clause. See Young, *Treaties as "Part of Our Law"*, 88 Tex.L.Rev. 91 (2009). Young emphasizes that not all statutes are themselves "self-executing": some provide no private right of action; others contain some purely aspirational provisions; still others lack any binding legal effect absent administrative implementation. The form and extent of a statute's binding legal effect thus depends upon congressional intent. Since "[d]omestic law approaches these statutory questions through a variety of local doctrines", Young argues that "a blanket presumption of self-execution for treaties * * * would create an exceptional rule quite different from the regime governing statutes." On that view, Medellín tends "to 'normalize' the treatment of treaties" with that of domestic law.

The question of self-execution has produced a broad-ranging and sharply divergent set of views concerning historical understandings of treaties' domestic force. See, *e.g.*, Flaherty, *History Right?: Historical Scholarship, Original Understanding, and Treaties as "Supreme Law of the Land,"* 99 Colum.L.Rev. 2095 (1999); Parry, *Congress, the Supremacy Clause, and the Implementation of Treaties*, 32 Fordham Int'l L.J. 1209 (2009); Sloss, *Non-Self-Executing*

*Treaties: Exposing a Constitutional Fallacy*, 36 U.C. Davis L.Rev. 1 (2002); Vázquez, *Treaty-Based Rights and Remedies of Individuals*, 92 Colum.L.Rev. 1082 (1992); Yoo, *Globalism and the Constitution: Treaties, Non-Self-Execution, and the Original Understanding*, 99 Colum.L.Rev. 1955 (1999). For example, Professor Yoo argues that the Federalists gained crucial support for ratification through assurances that treaties would not have domestic legal effect without implementing legislation. See Yoo, *supra*. Professor Flaherty, in contrast, contends that the majority view at the time of the ratification was that treaties were judicially enforceable. See Flaherty, *supra*. Others assert that the founders expressed a broad range of (sometimes ambiguous) views on the subject. See, *e.g.*, Parry, *supra*. If history cannot decisively identify the proper framework for determining a treaty's self-executing status, does it make sense, as Professor Young suggests, for the Court to handle the question of treaty self-execution in light of the same separation-of-powers assumptions that guide its treatment of analogous subjects, such as the implication of private rights of action under statutes?

---

## SUBSECTION B: REMEDIES FOR CONSTITUTIONAL VIOLATIONS

---

**Page 734. Add a new footnote 2a at the end of the first, carryover sentence:**

    **2a.** Khan, *The Path of the Constitution: The Original System of Remedies, How It Changed, and How the Court Responded*, 87 N.Y.U.L.Rev. 132 (2012), argues that the common law remedies available to vindicate constitutional rights at the beginning of the Republic either withered or became inadequate to vindicate new forms of constitutional rights, thereby provoking the Court to derive implied federal remedies for constitutional violations.

**Page 736. Insert the following in place of the last paragraph in Paragraph 5(a):**

    In Hui v. Castaneda, 130 S.Ct. 1845 (2010), the Court rejected a Bivens claim alleging that Public Health Service (PHS) officials had shown "deliberate indifference" to Casteneda's "serious medical needs," in violation of the Fifth, Eighth, and Fourteenth Amendments, while he was in the custody of U.S. Immigration and Customs Enforcement (ICE). In a unanimous opinion for the Court, Justice Sotomayor held that the Bivens action was precluded by 42 U.S.C. § 233(a), which provides: "The [FTCA] remedy against the United States provided by [28 U.S.C. §§ 1346(b) and 2672] for damage for personal injury, including death, resulting from the performance of medical * * * or related functions * * * by any [PHS] commissioned officer or employee * * * while acting within the scope of his office or employment, shall be exclusive of any other civil action or proceeding by reason of the same subject-matter against the officer or employee." Applying Carlson v. Green, Sixth Edition p. 735, the lower courts had held that a Bivens action is foreclosed only if Congress has expressly declared an alternative remedy to be a substitute for a Bivens action *and* if the alternative is equally effective, or if special factors militate against finding an implied right of action. Carlson had held that an FTCA remedy was not equally effective because (a) the relief did not run against the individuals; (b) punitive damages are not available under the FTCA; (c) a Bivens plaintiff is entitled to a jury trial; and (d) Bivens actions are determined by federal law, not state law as under the FTCA.

    Noting, however, that Carlson had also stated that "Congress follows the practice of explicitly stating when it means to make FTCA an exclusive remedy," the Court in Castaneda reasoned that § 233(a) "grants absolute immunity to PHS officers and employees for actions arising out of the performance of medical or related functions within the scope of their employment by barring all actions against them for such conduct." The Court emphasized that even if a Bivens action would ordinarily be available for the "particular constitutional violation," that issue was distinct from the question of whether Congress has given the particular defendants absolute immunity from suit. Because none of the officials in Carlson had invoked immunity, the only question before the Court was whether a constitutional claim was cognizable under Bivens.

Does Castaneda eliminate Carlson's requirement of an "equally effective" alternative remedy where Congress has *expressly* made the alternative remedy exclusive? If so, what does that reveal about the extent of Congress's authority to control constitutional remedies under Bivens? Notice that when the respondents argued that denying a Bivens claim would be contrary to the public interest and would undermine the development of an adequate standard of care in PHS cases, the Court replied that "the confines of [the] judicial role" did not permit it to take into account such considerations because the text of § 233(a) "plainly precludes a Bivens action" in this case.

**Page 738.   Add at the end of footnote 5:**

For a contrasting view of the efficacy of Bivens actions, see Reinert, *Measuring the Success of Bivens Litigation and its Consequences for the Individual Liability Model*, 62 Stan.L.Rev. 809 (2010)(arguing, based on data collected from five district courts over three years, that "Bivens cases are much more successful than has been assumed" and that "[d]epending on the procedural posture, presence of counsel, and type of case, success rates for Bivens suits range from 16% to more than 40%").

**Page 738.   Add a new footnote 5a at the end of the penultimate paragraph in Paragraph (8)(a):**

**5a.**   In an intriguing article, Pfander and Baltmanis argue that whatever the legitimacy of Bivens as an original matter, Congress effectively "ratified" the doctrine. See Pfander & Baltmanis, *Rethinking Bivens: Legitimacy and Constitutional Adjudication*, 98 Geo.L.J. 117 (2009). First, in amending the FTCA in 1974, Congress rejected legislation proposed by the Justice Department that would have substituted the government for individual defendants on constitutional tort claims. Second, in 1988, the Westfall Act, Pub. L. No. 100–694, 102 Stat. 4563 (1988), made the FTCA the exclusive remedy for certain nonconstitutional torts by federal officials and expressly assumed the continuing existence of Bivens actions for constitutional torts. See also Vázquez & Vladeck, *State Law, the Westfall Act, and the Nature of the Bivens Question*, 161 U.Pa.L.Rev. 509 (2013)(drawing similar inferences from the Westfall Act). Accordingly, on the theory that these measures gave a congressional imprimatur to the Bivens action, Pfander and Baltmanis argue that the Court should not hesitate to apply Bivens to factual contexts other than those recognized in Bivens, Davis, and Carlson.

How convincing are these claims of ratification? With respect to Congress' rejection of the Justice Department's proposal in 1974, the authors' contention runs up against the Court's general view that failed legislation may tell us little because "[a] bill can be proposed for any number of reasons, and it can be rejected for just as many others." Solid Waste Agency of Northern Cook County v. U.S. Army Corps of Engineers, 531 U.S. 159, 170 (2001). If Pfander and Baltmanis are on stronger ground in suggesting that the Westfall Act affirmatively "ratified" the Bivens framework, should the Court assume that the Act ratified the framework as of 1971, when Bivens was decided, or as of 1988, when the Court had already begun its retrenchment in cases such as Bush v. Lucas, Sixth Edition p. 736; Chappell v. Wallace, Sixth Edition p. 737; and United States v. Stanley, Sixth Edition p. 737? Did the existence of those decisions in 1988 suggest at the very least that the Bivens doctrine, like any common law doctrine, is a dynamic one?

**Page 740. Substitute the following for Paragraph (8)(c) and add new Paragraphs (8)(d) & (e):**

(c) In an opinion that ostensibly dealt with the standards of pleading in Bivens actions, the Court in Ashcroft v. Iqbal, 556 U.S. 662 (2009) (also discussed in Chapter IX, *infra*), further signaled its apparent intention to limit Bivens strictly to the domain already recognized by previous opinions of the Court. In the course of a massive federal law enforcement effort following the September 11, 2001, terrorist attacks, FBI and Immigration and Naturalization Service agents arrested Iqbal, a Pakistani national, on charges that he had engaged in fraud in relation to his identification documents. Iqbal's lawsuit alleged that because of his race, national origin, and Muslim faith, various federal officers—including then-Attorney General Ashcroft and FBI Director Mueller—designated him as a person of "high interest", which resulted in his placement in highly restrictive conditions of confinement. Iqbal alleged that the defendants' actions violated his rights under the Free Exercise Clause of the First Amendment and the equal protection component of the Due Process Clause of the Fifth Amendment.

Justice Kennedy's opinion for a divided (5–4) Court held that Iqbal's allegations concerning Ashcroft's and Mueller's involvement were too general and conclusory to satisfy Federal Rule of Civil Procedure 8(a)(2)'s requirement of a "short and plain statement of the claim showing that the pleader is entitled to relief." In two respects, however, the Court used the occasion to signal a further intention to pare back relief under Bivens.

First, the Court noted that "[b]ecause implied causes of action are [now] disfavored," it has been reluctant to recognize new Bivens claims. Thus, even though the parties had not challenged Bivens' applicability to free exercise claims, the Court went out of its way to note that it had never before recognized "an implied damages remedy under the Free Exercise Clause" and that it was merely assuming but not deciding that such a claim was available.

Second, citing a long line of cases involving the liability of public officers in related areas, the Court concluded that a Bivens action against officials such as Ashcroft and Mueller could not be sustained under a theory of "supervisory liability". Accordingly, it held that to state a claim that they had violated clearly established constitutional rights (and thus to overcome qualified immunity, see Sixth Edition pp. 1102–04), Iqbal's complaint needed to allege that Ashcroft and Mueller had *themselves* acted with a discriminatory purpose, in violation of the First and Fifth Amendment guarantees at issue. Mere knowledge that their subordinates had acted with such a purpose would not suffice.

In dissent, Justice Souter argued that the majority's rejection of all "supervisory liability" claims rested on a misreading of precedents that had merely rejected a superior officer's liability based on a theory of *respondeat superior*, which broadly holds an employer liable for the actions of an employee acting within the scope of employment. Identifying a "spectrum" of available standards of supervisory liability lying between *respondeat superior* and the majority's outright rejection of any supervisory liability, the dissent complained that the question of supervisory liability had not been briefed or argued and that its resolution was unnecessary to the decision, given the majority's conclusion that "all of the allegations in the complaint that Ashcroft and Mueller authorized, condoned, or even were aware of their subordinates' discriminatory conduct are [too] 'conclusory'" to survive a motion to dismiss.

What should guide the Court in the exercise of its authority to decide questions such as the appropriate standard of supervisory liability, if any? To the extent that Bivens constitutes an implied right of action devised by the Court, should the Court have substantial latitude in shaping the resultant right of action to effectuate the goals of compensation and deterrence without unduly chilling the performance of public functions?[g]

(d) Although Carlson v. Green, Sixth Edition p. 735, held that a plaintiff may bring a Bivens action to vindicate an Eighth Amendment claim that federal prison officials showed deliberate indifference to his medical needs, the Court in Minneci v. Pollard, 132 S. Ct. 617 (2012), concluded that a prisoner at a federal prison *operated by a private company* could not bring such a claim against company employees. In an opinion by Justice Breyer, the Court reasoned that the plaintiff's Eighth Amendment claim alleged conduct "that typically falls within the scope of traditional state tort law" and that, in the case of a private prison, state tort law was "capable of protecting the constitutional interests at stake." While the plaintiff argued that state tort remedies might be less generous than those available under Bivens, the Court emphasized that the two sets of remedies need not be congruent as long as "state tort law remedies provide roughly similar incentives for potential defendants to comply with the Eighth Amendment while also providing roughly similar compensation to victims of violations."

Justice Scalia, joined by Justice Thomas, wrote a concurring opinion reaffirming his view that Bivens is out of step with the Court's approach to implied rights of action more generally and should not be extended beyond its facts.

Justice Ginsburg dissented, reasoning that the distinction between Pollard's case and Carlson was too thin to justify denying Pollard a federal remedy. She argued, moreover, that this case was distinguishable from the suit against the private prison contractor in Correctional Services Corp. v. Malesko, Sixth Edition p. 738, because Pollard brought his action against the individual employees rather than against the corporation. Accordingly, she believed that Pollard's action would have the deterrent effect contemplated by Bivens.

(e) Given that the Court has consistently refused to recognize a Bivens remedy since its 1980 decision in Carlson v. Green, is it fair to conclude that the Court's decisions have now begun to cut into Bivens' core? See Tribe, *Death by a Thousand Cuts: Constitutional Wrongs Without Remedies After Wilkie v. Robbins*, 2007 Cato Sup.Ct.Rev. 23, 70. So long as Bivens is not squarely overruled, is it sufficiently alive that it is capable of reinvigoration? See

---

**g.** Although the Court did not frame Iqbal as a national security case, might national security considerations have informed the Court's hesitation to recognize a new Bivens claim? See, *e.g.*, Huq, *Against National Security Exceptionalism*, 2009 Sup.Ct.Rev. 225, 248 (arguing that despite its national security setting, Iqbal did not materially alter the procedural hurdles that Bivens plaintiffs already faced); Vladeck, *National Security and Bivens After Iqbal*, 14 Lewis & Clark L.Rev. 255 (2010) (arguing that courts should be more willing to recognize Bivens actions in the national security context, given the pressures on government officials to act aggressively and given the availability of the state secrets privilege, qualified immunity, and governmental indemnification as defenses to such actions). What bearing, if any, do military cases such as Chapell v. Wallace, Sixth Edition p. 737, and United States v. Stanley, Sixth Edition p. 737, have on whether the Court should treat national security considerations as "special factors" counseling hesitation in recognizing new Bivens actions?

Shapiro, *The Role of Precedent in Constitutional Adjudication: An Introspection*, 86 Tex.L.Rev. 929, 940 n.41 (2008).

**Page 742.  Add at the end of the penultimate paragraph in Paragraph (11):**

Given that Carlson v. Green, Sixth Edition p. 735, held that an action under the FTCA is not an equally effective alternative to a Bivens remedy, does Hui v. Castaneda, pp. 84–85, *supra*—which held that Congress made the FTCA the exclusive remedy in certain types of actions—make plain that Congress has the authority to prescribe an exclusive substitute remedy even if that remedy is *not* equally effective? Given that the FTCA provided some form of remedy, does Hui leave open the possibility that some minimum remedy must be available for constitutional torts?[8]

---

**8.**  Preis, *Constitutional Enforcement by Proxy*, 95 Va.L.Rev. 1663, 1669 (2009), suggests that the Court's increased willingness to treat statutory or administrative remedies as adequate proxies for constitutional enforcement through Bivens actions "allows the judiciary to retain its power to check abuses by non-Article III actors and, at the same time, allows these same entities a role in particularizing the norms of acceptable government behavior."

# CHAPTER VIII

# THE FEDERAL QUESTION JURISDICTION OF THE DISTRICT COURTS

## SECTION 1. INTRODUCTION

**Page 744. Add at the end of footnote 6:**

For a rich discussion of the Judiciary Act of 1801, see LaCroix, *Federalists, Federalism, and Federal Jurisdiction*, 30 Law & Hist.Rev. 205 (2012).

**Page 748. Add at the end of the first full paragraph:**

The "forthcoming" article by Professor Seinfeld summarized in the Sixth Edition has been published. See Seinfeld, *The Federal Courts as a Franchise: Rethinking the Justifications for Federal Question Jurisdiction*, 97 Calif.L.Rev. 95 (2009).

## SECTION 2. THE SCOPE OF THE CONSTITUTIONAL GRANT OF FEDERAL QUESTION JURISDICTION

**Page 771. Add a new Paragraph (8a):**

**(8a) A Broader Model of Congressional Power to Extend Jurisdiction.** In *Article I, Article III, and the Limits of Enumeration*, 108 Mich.L.Rev. 1389 (2010), Professor Seinfeld considers the relationship between the limited enumerated powers in Article I and the enumerated heads of jurisdiction in Article III, and argues that Congress has very broad power to assign cases to the federal courts, notwithstanding the enumeration of limited categories of subject matter jurisdiction in Article III, Section 2.

Seinfeld presents what he describes as two conventional stories. The first is that the enumeration of legislative power in Article I has failed; decisions recognizing unenumerated power over immigration and foreign affairs, and the nearly unlimited scope of the commerce and (conditional) spending powers, have given Congress almost plenary authority to legislate. The second story is that the enumeration of limited categories of federal judicial power in Article III has succeeded. Seinfeld views the second story as false. Surveying the decisions, he doubts that they significantly restrict congressional power to assign cases to the federal courts. He notes that the Supreme Court has not found any statute to fall outside the scope of the nine heads of jurisdiction, while numerous decisions have had to stretch conceptions of "arising under" in order to uphold statutory grants of jurisdiction.

Seinfeld then sketches what he calls the congressional power model of jurisdiction, which posits that Congress may vest jurisdiction in the federal courts whenever the jurisdictional legislation can be viewed as within the scope of an enumerated power in Article I and the Necessary and Proper Clause. His approach, he suggests, is a "cousin" of theories of protective jurisdiction; what distinguishes it is his acknowledgment that the enumerated categories in Article III don't matter; by contrast, theories of protective jurisdiction contend that the cases fall within the arising under jurisdiction. Viewing that contention as unpersuasive, he prefers to acknowledge the scope of congressional power without resorting to what he deems to be labored constructions of Article III.[a]

Seinfeld discussed two cases in which the Court adopted narrowing constructions to avoid constitutional problems under Article III: Mesa v. California, Sixth Edition p. 771, and Hodgson v. Bowerbank, Sixth Edition p. 1363 (a diversity case construing the First Judiciary Act as not authorizing jurisdiction based solely on the alienage of one of the parties). Both decisions, he suggests, are consistent with his model, because in both it is arguable that there was no legislative power because no legitimate federal interest would be served by the exercise of federal jurisdiction. (But isn't it equally arguable that there was such an interest in each case and hence that the cases do not fit comfortably within his model?)

As to federal question cases, Seinfeld's approach is quite similar to Professor Wechsler's theory of protective jurisdiction. Are there differences between the two approaches other than the fact that Wechsler contends that cases falling within his theory do arise under federal law, while Seinfeld suggests that Congress' power is not limited by Article III's enumeration of heads of subject matter jurisdiction? How significant is that difference?

# SECTION 3.   THE SCOPE OF THE STATUTORY GRANT OF FEDERAL QUESTION JURISDICTION

---

**a.** Seinfeld's theory is very similar to that of Justice Jackson in his plurality opinion in National Mut. Ins. Co. of Dist. of Colum. v. Tidewater Transfer Co, 337 U.S. 582 (1949). Tidewater upheld a statute granting jurisdiction over a state law claim brought by a citizen of the District of Columbia against a citizen of Virginia. Viewing the plaintiff as not being a citizen of a "State" within the meaning of Article III's diversity clause, Justice Jackson, joined by Justices Black and Burton, nonetheless voted to uphold the statute, on the theory that Congress, acting under Article I, may assign to the federal courts cases or controversies that fall outside the nine heads of subject matter jurisdiction enumerated in Article III. Six of the nine Justices rejected Justice Jackson's view (although two of the six voted to uphold the statutory grant on the distinct ground, rejected by Justice Jackson, that a citizen of D.C. was a citizen of a "State" within the meaning of Article III's Diversity Clause). For fuller discussion, see the Sixth Edition pp. 381–83.

SUBSECTION A:   THE STRUCTURE OF "ARISING
UNDER" JURISDICTION UNDER THE
FEDERAL QUESTION STATUTE

———

**Page 779.  Add to Paragraph (2):**

Professor Field proposes expanding removal jurisdiction so that, subject to some possible exceptions, it would embrace cases in which the defendant's answer, or possibly further pleadings, "reveal that the case is likely to turn upon federal law." Field, *Removal Reform: A Solution for Federal Question Jurisdiction, Forum Shopping, and Duplicative State Litigation*, 88 Ind.L.J. 611, 642 (2013). As her title suggests, one advantage that she claims for that approach is that it would reduce the number of cases in which pending suits in federal and state court overlap, for under her scheme the party that prefers federal court would likely be able to remove an overlapping state court action.

**Page 780.  Add to Paragraph (4):**

Two post-Holmes Group developments, one decisional, one statutory, are worth noting:

(a) In Vaden v. Discover Bank, 556 U.S. 49 (2009), the Court divided 5–4 on a difficult issue involving the implications of the Holmes Group decision in a federal court action seeking to compel arbitration. This litigation began when Discover Bank (through a servicing affiliate) filed a state court action against Vaden to recover past-due charges on a credit card. Vaden counterclaimed that the charges and fees in question violated state law, though both parties later agreed, and the Supreme Court assumed, that the counterclaims were entirely based on federal law, because a provision of the Federal Deposit Insurance Act (FDIA) "completely preempted" any applicable state law. (See Sixth Edition p. 813.)

At this point in the litigation, Discover filed a federal court action against Vaden seeking to compel arbitration of the counterclaims under § 4 of the Federal Arbitration Act (FAA), a statute discussed at Sixth Edition pp. 577–78. (The credit-card agreement called for arbitration of any claim or dispute arising out of the account.) Section 4 authorizes a party to seek federal district court enforcement of an agreement to arbitrate if "save for such agreement, [the district court] would have jurisdiction * * * of the subject matter of a suit arising out of the controversy between the parties".

The Supreme Court held that the federal district court lacked jurisdiction over Discover's petition to compel arbitration. Resolving a circuit conflict, the Court unanimously agreed that the quoted language in § 4 did not refer to a "controversy" over the existence, applicability, or enforceability of an arbitration agreement but rather directed the federal court to "look through" the dispute over arbitrability to see whether the court would have had subject matter jurisdiction over the underlying substantive controversy between the parties. The majority, per Justice Ginsburg, went on to hold that the "whole" controversy between the parties was one arising under state law (based as it was on Discover's claim for unpaid charges and fees), and that under the well-pleaded complaint rule as interpreted in Holmes Group, federal question jurisdiction could not rest on a counterclaim.

In dissent, Chief Justice Roberts (joined by Justices Stevens, Breyer, and Alito) contended that federal question jurisdiction did exist because the "controversy" referred to in § 4 was the controversy allegedly subject to arbitration, in this instance Vaden's federal law counterclaim. He noted that Discover was not seeking arbitration of its state law claim against Vaden, and argued that since federal question jurisdiction would clearly have existed had the only litigation been an original action by Vaden for violation of the FDIA (or, perhaps, by Discover for a declaratory judgment that the FDIA had not been violated), the sequence of the actual litigation in the case should not control. That Discover could also have sought arbitration of the counterclaim in state court (a point made by the majority) should not, the Chief Justice argued, deprive it of access to a federal forum.

In her counterclaims, Vaden sought to represent a class of Discover credit card holders, and her desire to avoid arbitration was described by the majority as "unsurprising" because the arbitration clause "framed by Discover" prohibited presentation of any claims on behalf of a class. Do you think Vaden's preference for litigating her counterclaim as a class action in state court affected the result in this case? If so, should it have?

The "look through" approach required by the FAA resembles the approach developed by the Supreme Court in the context of declaratory judgment actions (see Sixth Edition pp. 800–06). Does the result reached by the majority in Vaden indicate the need for corrective legislation, at least as to federal question jurisdiction over compulsory counterclaims filed in state court actions? The Vaden majority noted that to date Congress has not responded to numerous suggestions that it revise the law to allow "responsive pleadings that may be dispositive" to "count in determining whether a case 'arises under' federal law."

(b) Although Congress has not taken action to deal with the issue in Vaden or broadly to address the reach of federal question jurisdiction over counterclaims based on federal law, the Leahy–Smith America Invents Act, 125 Stat. 284 (2011), a major patent reform measure, includes a set of jurisdictional provisions that partially overturn the Holmes Group decision. As amended by that Act, 28 U.S.C. § 1338, the statute that grants the federal courts exclusive jurisdiction over patent, plant variety protection, and copyright cases, reads as follows:

"(a) The district courts shall have original jurisdiction of any civil action arising under any Act of Congress relating to patents, plant variety protection, copyrights and trademarks. No State court shall have jurisdiction over any claim for relief arising under any Act of Congress relating to patents, plant variety protection, or copyrights. For purposes of this subsection, the term 'State' " includes any State of the United States, the District of Columbia, the Commonwealth of Puerto Rico, the United States Virgin Islands, American Samoa, Guam, and the Northern Mariana Islands."

The first sentence is unchanged; the second and third sentences substitute for the second sentence of the previous provision.[b]

Note that while the first sentence of section § 1338(a), like § 1331 and many other jurisdictional grants in Title 28, speaks of federal court jurisdiction

---

**b.** Before 2011, the second sentence read: "Such jurisdiction shall be exclusive of the courts of the states in patent, plant variety protection and copyright cases."

over *a civil action*, the second sentence of § 1338(a) excludes state court jurisdiction over *a claim for relief*. Fed. R. Civ. Proc. 8(a) makes clear that a claim for relief includes counterclaims, not merely a claim in the plaintiff's complaint. If § 1338(a)'s reference to a claim for relief should be understood the same way, § 1338(a) appears to preclude a state court from hearing a patent, plant variety, or copyright counterclaim.

The Leahy–Smith America Invents Act also contains a new provision, codified as 28 U.S.C. § 1454, that authorizes *any party* to remove a civil action in state court in which any party asserts a claim for relief under the patent, plant variety, or copyright laws. By comparison, the general removal statute, 28 U.S.C. § 1441, which previously governed removal of civil actions filed under § 1338(a), authorizes only the defendant to remove. New § 1454 also specifies that removal is not precluded because the state court lacked jurisdiction over the claim.

Thus, the jurisdictional provisions of the Act appear to contemplate that a state court defendant may file a patent, plant variety, or copyright counterclaim in state court (and perhaps must if the counterclaim is compulsory under state law)—even though under § 1338(a) the state courts lacks jurisdiction to decide that counterclaim—and then the defendant or the plaintiff may, under § 1454, remove the action to federal court.[c]

The limited reach of these provisions no doubt arises from their inclusion in an act dealing with patent reform. Is there any reason of policy why the jurisdictional rules for claims for relief arising under the patent, plant variety, and copyright laws should differ from those governing claims for relief arising under other schemes where federal jurisdiction is exclusive (for example, the antitrust laws, or ERISA)? Indeed, should Congress more broadly permit removal on the basis of any compulsory counterclaim that itself arises under federal law, without regard to its relationship to schemes of exclusive federal jurisdiction? On the basis of any counterclaim that arises under federal law?

**c.**   The 2011 Act also changes the jurisdiction of the Court of Appeals for the Federal Circuit. Under 28 U.S.C. § 1295(a)(1), that court was initially given exclusive appellate jurisdiction over patent and plant variety cases arising under § 1338, in order to centralize appellate resolution of such matters in a specialized court. The Holmes Group case, see Sixth Edition p. 780 n.1, held that a civil action in which a defendant asserted a patent counterclaim did not arise under the patent laws within the meaning of § 1338, and hence appellate jurisdiction lay in the regional court of appeals, not in the Court of Appeals for the Federal Circuit. As amended in 2011, 28 U.S.C. § 1295(a)(1) now gives the Federal Circuit exclusive jurisdiction "in any civil action arising under, *or any civil action in which a party has asserted a compulsory counterclaim arising under*," any Act of Congress relating to patents or plant variety protection. For reasons noted in the Sixth Edition, the grant of appellate jurisdiction to the Federal Circuit to review patent and plant

variety claims was too narrow to ensure centralized appellate review of patent cases, and the grant in 2011 of appellate jurisdiction over counterclaims makes enormous sense. (Indeed, what is the reason, under current law, to exclude from the Federal Circuit's appellate jurisdiction review of patent counterclaims that are not *compulsory*?).

But the jurisdiction that remains after the 2011 Act is also too broad. Imagine a case in which a plaintiff files a patent infringement action in federal court, the defendant counterclaims for a state law business tort, and the only issue raised on appeal concerns the trial court's decision of the business tort counterclaim. Under § 1295(a)(1), both before and after 2011, the Federal Circuit would have exclusive jurisdiction over the appeal, because the civil action arose under the patent laws. But does it make sense to direct that appeal, which includes no patent law issue, to the Federal Circuit rather than to the regional court of appeals?

**Page 785.  Add a new Paragraph (5), just before the "Introductory Note on Jurisdiction under § 1331 Based on the Presence of a Federal Element":**

**(5) The Standard for Congressional Divestment of § 1331 Jurisdiction.** In Mims v. Arrow Financial Services, LLC, 132 S.Ct. 740 (2012), the Court held that an explicit grant of state court jurisdiction over a federal cause of action did not oust federal court jurisdiction under § 1331. The Telephone Consumer Protection Act of 1991 (TCPA) prohibits some telemarketing practices that generate unwanted nuisance calls. The TCPA authorizes States to bring civil actions on behalf of their citizens when there is a pattern or practice of violation; the federal courts have exclusive jurisdiction over such actions. The TPCA also authorizes private parties to seek judicial redress "if otherwise permitted by the laws or rules of court of a State, ... in an appropriate court of that State"; private plaintiffs may recover the greater of actual damages or $500 per violation.

In Mims, the lower courts held that Congress had vested jurisdiction over actions by private parties exclusively in the state courts and hence dismissed the plaintiffs' federal court lawsuit. The Supreme Court unanimously reversed. Justice Ginsburg's opinion noted the deeply rooted presumption that an explicit grant of federal court jurisdiction does not oust concurrent state court jurisdiction—a presumption that can be overcome only " 'by an explicit statutory directive, by unmistakable implication from legislative history, or by a clear incompatibility between state-court jurisdiction and federal interests' " (quoting Gulf Offshore Co. v. Mobil Oil Corp., 453 U.S. 473, 478 (1981), Sixth Edition pp. 385, 394). " '[D]ivestment of district court jurisdiction,' " she stated, "should be found no more readily than 'divestmen[t] of state court jurisdiction,' given 'the longstanding and explicit grant of federal question jurisdiction in 28 U.S.C. § 1331' " (quoting ErieNet, Inc. v. Velocity Net, Inc., 156 F.3d 513, 523 (3d Cir.1998) (Alito, J., dissenting).

The defendant argued that in view of the presumption of concurrent state court jurisdiction, the Act's specific acknowledgment of state court jurisdiction would be superfluous if it merely gave state courts a non-exclusive jurisdiction. Justice Ginsburg responded that given the exclusive federal jurisdiction provided by the Act in suits by States, "Congress may simply have wanted to avoid any argument that" federal court jurisdiction over private actions is also exclusive. As for concern about flooding the federal courts with small cases seeking $500 in damages, or about defendants removing cases filed in state small claims court in order to subject plaintiffs to a more expensive federal forum, Justice Ginsburg doubted that a party would file a $500 case in, or remove it to, federal court when the filing fee is $350. She added that of the 91 TCPA cases located in Lexis or Westlaw that had been filed in or removed to federal court, 89 were class actions.

**Page 785.  Add a new footnote a at the end of Paragraph (1):**

a.  Professors Woolhandler & Collins, in *Federal Question Jurisdiction and Justice Holmes*, 84 Notre Dame L.Rev. 2151 (2009), contend, on the basis of extensive research, that cases in which federal law was a substantial ingredient but not the source of the cause of action may well have constituted the "paradigm" of "arising under" cases both before and after passage of the 1875 general federal question jurisdiction statute. They conclude, however, that allowing all such cases to fall within federal question jurisdiction today might prove unworkable, and suggest that "federal ingredient" cases might appropriately be limited to those in which the ingredient was a constitutional (and not merely a statutory) one.

**Page 799.   Add a new Paragraph (2)(e):**

(e) In Gunn v. Minton, 133 S.Ct. 1059 (2013), the Supreme Court considered a case that was similar in most respects to Merrell Dow—a state law tort action in which the determination of the defendant's negligence turned on an issue of federal law. However, the incorporated issue was one of patent law, and under 28 U.S.C. § 1338(a), federal courts have exclusive jurisdiction over cases arising under the patent laws. Indeed, in 2011, Congress departed from the well-pleaded complaint rule in patent litigation, providing that federal jurisdiction (and federal exclusivity) extends even to patent claims (such as a counterclaim) not asserted in the plaintiff's complaint. See pp. 92–93, *supra*. The Gunn case thus presented the question of how to apply Grable's framework to a case involving such exclusivity.

The story began when, in Minton's action for patent infringement, the federal district court found Minton's patent invalid, on the basis that the invention had been on sale more than a year prior to the patent application. In a motion for reconsideration, Gunn, the lawyer for Minton, raised for the first time an argument that the prior uses of the invention were "experimental" and thus, under the patent laws, did not render the patent invalid. The district court denied the motion, and the Court of Appeals for the Federal Circuit affirmed, ruling that the district court had properly found Minton's experimental-use argument to have been waived by its belated assertion.

Minton then sued Gunn for malpractice in Texas state court, complaining of Gunn's tardiness in raising the experimental-use argument. After losing in the trial court on the merits, Minton argued on appeal that the state courts lacked subject matter jurisdiction. He contended that his malpractice claim, because it was founded on a question of patent law, arose under federal patent law and hence was within the exclusive jurisdiction of the federal courts. On review, the Supreme Court unanimously held that the case did not arise under federal law and that the state courts had therefore properly entertained the malpractice case. (In so holding, the Court reaffirmed that the standard for arising under jurisdiction is the same under § 1331 and § 1338(a).)

Chief Justice Roberts' opinion observed that the Court has identified a "slim category" in which claims originating under state law nonetheless arise under federal law. The boundaries of that category, he said, were ill-defined prior to the Grable decision, which sought "to bring some order to this unruly doctrine" by providing that federal jurisdiction lies over a state claim "if a federal issue is: (1) necessarily raised, (2) actually disputed, (3) substantial, and (4) capable of resolution in federal court without disrupting the federal-state balance approved by Congress." Applying those four requirements, the Court acknowledged that the federal patent issue was necessarily raised and actually disputed, but it concluded that the last two requirements were not satisfied. As to substantiality, the Court held that it did not suffice that the issue was important to the plaintiff's case; rather, the relevant question was "the importance of the issue to the federal system as a whole." In both Grable and Smith v. Kansas City Title & Trust, the issue of federal law embedded in the state law claim for relief was of general importance to the federal government. Here, the federal question—whether, if Minton's counsel had raised a timely experimental-use argument, the patent infringement lawsuit would have yielded a different outcome—would not change the prior patent litigation, nor would it threaten the uniformity of federal law. The Chief Justice also noted that a state court determination of the patent issue would not bind the federal courts and that state courts addressing patent issues could be expected to "hew closely to the pertinent federal precedents." Even novel questions of patent law arising for the first time in state court will likely be raised at some point in federal court, with review in the Federal Circuit. And the Chief Justice expressed some doubt that a possibly erroneous state court decision would have preclusive effect; at most, he said, it could bind the parties with regard to the patents at issue. Finally, as to Grable's fourth requirement, the Court noted that it was the states' responsibility to maintain standards of practice for members of their bars. Thus, the Court determined broadly that "state legal malpractice claims based on underlying patent matters will rarely, if ever, arise under federal patent law for purposes of § 1338(a)."

Consider the fourth requirement, concerning the federal-state balance. As a result of the Court's decision, the standards of practice before a federal administrative agency (the Patent and Trademark Office) and the federal courts, for lawyers whose practice may be almost exclusively before those bodies, will be regulated by state law, and enforced by state courts that generally lack jurisdiction to consider issues of patent law—issues sufficiently distinctive that Congress saw fit to centralize federal appellate review in the Court of Appeals for the Federal Circuit. Is that a cause for concern?

Note that unlike in Grable, no Justice in Gunn v. Minton advocated return to Justice Holmes' "cause of action" test as the exclusive measure of arising under jurisdiction.

**Page 800.  Add to footnote 7:**

For a thorough analysis of the Court's decisions from Smith v. Kansas City Title & Trust through Empire Healthcase, see Field, p. 91, *supra*.

---

# SECTION 4.  FEDERAL QUESTION REMOVAL

———

**Pages 817–18.  Add to footnote 7:**

In Watson v. Philip Morris Companies, Inc., 551 U.S. 142 (2007), a state court action alleging false advertising by the defendant tobacco company in violation of state law, the Court unanimously rejected the defendant's effort to remove the case under § 1442(a)(1) on the ground that the plaintiffs were attacking a testing process that was mandated and supervised by the Federal Trade Commission. After discussing the history and purpose of the statute, the Court concluded that a private person's acting under a federal officer or agency, within the meaning of § 1442(a)(1), requires more than compliance with federal regulations; rather, the private person seeking to remove must have been engaged in "an effort to *assist*, or to help *carry out*, the duties or tasks of the federal superior."

---

# SECTION 5.  SUPPLEMENTAL (PENDENT) JURISDICTION

———

**Page 833.   Add to Paragraph (6)(c):**

The Federal Courts Jurisdiction and Venue Clarification Act of 2011, Pub.L. 112–63, 125 Stat. 758, has clarified the operation of § 1441(c) and resolved longstanding constitutional uncertainties. The amended provision authorizes removal of a state court action that contains both a removable claim falling within the district court's original federal question jurisdiction (within the meaning of § 1331) and a claim *not* within the federal court's original or supplemental jurisdiction. But once the entire state court action has been removed, § 1441(c) now requires the severance and remand to the state court of any claim in the latter category. The general rule requiring that all parties agree to removal is modified; only those parties to the removable claim(s) are required to agree to removal.

# CHAPTER IX

# SUITS CHALLENGING OFFICIAL ACTION

## SECTION 1.   SUITS CHALLENGING FEDERAL OFFICIAL ACTION

**Page 843.   Add to footnote 6:**

Figley & Tidmarsh, *The Appropriations Power and Sovereign Immunity*, 107 Mich.L.Rev. 1207, 1267 (2009), seek to revise understandings of sovereign immunity on both sides of the Atlantic. The authors maintain that by the early eighteenth century, settlement of claims against the crown for money had emerged as a parliamentary prerogative, no longer subject to common law forms of action, in accord with newly won parliamentary powers over finance. On this side of the Atlantic, the authors depict the Appropriations Clause as embodying an understanding that "Congress—rather than the President, the judiciary, * * * or even the people—is the organ that must give consent" to suits against the United States. From the premise that the Appropriations Clause would preclude the payment of money judgments against the United States in the absence of congressional appropriations, does it follow that the United States is immune from suit in the absence of congressional authorization? *Cf.* Glidden Co. v. Zdanok, Sixth Edition p. 91.

**Page 844.   Add to Paragraph (3):**

Pfander & Hunt, *Public Wrongs and Private Bills: Indemnification and Government Accountability in the Early Republic,* 85 N.Y.U.L.Rev 1862 (2010), maintain that the seeming harshness of officer liability in tort actions was ameliorated in practice by congressional enactment of private bills indemnifying officials—such as Captain Little in Little v. Barreme, Sixth Edition p. 843— who were held liable for good faith efforts to discharge their official duties. According to the authors, Congress relied on a special House Committee on Claims to determine entitlements to indemnification, and the Committee developed criteria for decision that it applied with remarkable consistency. Those criteria generally followed common law agency rules, under which principals were liable for the actions of agents acting within the scope of their instructions and in good faith. The petition-and-indemnification practice became so well known, Pfander and Hunt report, that courts during the antebellum years routinely decided tort actions against federal officials on the assumption that the government, not the nominal defendant, would pay adverse judgments. On this account, sovereign immunity was little more than a formalism, except in cases in which common law agency rules would have adjudged any principal not responsible for the misconduct of an agent. Although Pfander & Hunt do not precisely date the demise of what they refer to as the antebellum system, they characterize modern doctrines under which government officers frequently possess "official immunity" from suit—which are discussed in Chap. IX, Sec. 3

**99**

of the Sixth Edition—as reflecting "a remarkable feat of judicial creativity" by the twentieth-century Supreme Court. According to the authors, "[o]ne can fairly ask whether victims of positive government wrongdoing would fare better in 1810 or 2010."

**Page 859.   Add a footnote 2a at the end of the paragraph immediately preceding Paragraph (B)(1):**

**2a.**   In addressing a question about the scope (rather than the existence) of a waiver of sovereign immunity, Federal Aviation Administration v. Cooper, 132 S.Ct. 1441 (2012), held, by 5–3, that an authorization of suits for "actual damages" under the Federal Privacy Act did not waive immunity from suits to recover for mental and emotional distress. Writing for the Court, Justice Alito concluded that "[a]mbiguity exists", and thus precludes the conclusion that Congress has waived immunity under the rule requiring that waivers must be unequivocally expressed, "if there is a plausible interpretation of the statute that would not authorize money damages against the Government." Justice Sotomayor, joined by Justices Ginsburg and Breyer, dissenting, argued that "both as a term of art and in its plain meaning, 'actual damages' connotes compensation for proven injuries or losses" regardless of whether they are "pecuniary in nature." Should Congress be presumed not to have waived sovereign immunity when ordinary indicia of statutory meaning would indicate that it had done so, but there is a merely "plausible" argument to the contrary?

**Page 864.   Add to footnote 14:**

Although the FTCA does not bar Bivens claims altogether, the lower courts have held consistently that the judgment in an FTCA action will preclude any subsequent Bivens claim based on the same underlying facts. For an argument that this result overreaches Congress' assumptions and purposes in enacting the FTCA, see Pfander & Aggarwal, *Bivens, the Judgment Bar, and the Perils of Dynamic Textualism*, 8 U.St. Thomas L.J. 417 (2011).

**Page 866.   Add a new footnote 15a at the end of Paragraph (3):**

**15a.**   According to Sisk, *The Jurisdiction of the Court of Federal Claims and Forum Shopping in Money Claims Against the Federal Government*, 88 Ind.L.J. 83 (2013), more recent decisions by both the Supreme Court and the Court of Appeals for the Federal Circuit resolve uncertainties created by Bowen v. Massachusetts and establish that when a plaintiff ultimately wants monetary relief, and the Court of Federal Claims can provide an adequate remedy, suit must be brought in that court.

**Page 866.   Add to footnote 17:**

See also United States v. Tohono O'Odham Nation, 131 S.Ct. 1723 (2011) (holding that a statute bars Court of Federal Claims jurisdiction whenever a suit in another court is based on substantially the same operative facts, even if neither court alone could provide the plaintiff with complete relief).

---

# SECTION 2.   SUITS CHALLENGING STATE OFFICIAL ACTION

———

## SUBSECTION A: THE ELEVENTH AMENDMENT AND STATE SOVEREIGN IMMUNITY

———

**Page 871. Add to footnote 3:**

See also Clark, *The Eleventh Amendment and the Nature of the Union*, 123 Harv.L.Rev. 1817 (2010), discussed below; Lash, *Leaving The Chisholm Trail: The Eleventh Amendment and the Background Principle of Strict Construction*, 50 Wm. & Mary L.Rev. 1577 (2009) (arguing that public debate about state sovereign immunity was underway well prior to Chisholm and that the Eleventh Amendment should be read as exemplifying the principle—which is also embodied in the Ninth and Tenth Amendments—that federal powers, including the judicial power under Article III, should be construed narrowly).

**Page 872. Add to Paragraph (4)(b):**

According to Pfander & Hunt, *Public Wrongs and Private Bills: Indemnification and Government Accountability in the Early Republic*, 85 N.Y.U.L.Rev 1862 (2010), also discussed p. 99, *supra*, the "party of record" rule followed naturally from the assumption, which prevailed in antebellum suits for damages against federal officials, that sovereign immunity was "a matter of mere form" and that the government would indemnify its officers against liability incurred in the discharge of official responsibility. Even if Pfander & Hunt are correct about the prevalence of indemnification in suits for damages against federal officers, is it plausible to think that the Eleventh Amendment could always be evaded by the expedient of pleading an action as one against a state officer, rather than the state itself?

**Page 879. Add to Paragraph (2):**

Clark, *The Eleventh Amendment and the Nature of the Union*, 123 Harv. L.Rev. 1817 (2010), argues that, contrary to the Supreme Court's assumption in Hans, the narrow language of the Eleventh Amendment made perfect sense in the historical context in which it was written. According to Professor Clark, the founding generation understood it as implicit in the nature of the union created by the Constitution—which, unlike the Articles of Confederation, authorized the federal government to issue commands directly to individuals—that Congress could not impose statutory duties on the sovereign states and that states could not be sued for constitutional violations. With the possibility of suits against the states based on federal law being ruled out by a widely shared original understanding, Professor Clark argues, the Eleventh Amendment had the clear, limited purpose of correcting Chisholm's mistaken (and anomalous) conclusion that Article III permitted out-of-state citizens to sue states in federal court based on diversity of citizenship. In other words, by barring federal suits against the states by out-of-state citizens, the Eleventh Amendment closed the only possible loophole that might have permitted any kind of suit against unconsenting states. In Clark's view, most of the modern doctrine of state sovereign immunity, beginning with Hans, cannot be predicated directly on the Eleventh Amendment. But he acknowledges the force of stare decisis and the possibility of "dynamic" constitutional interpretation and says little about how, if at all, current doctrine ought to be revised in light of his historical conclusions.

Vazquez, *The Unsettled Nature of the Union,*123 Harv.L.Rev. Forum 79 (2011), maintains that most of the evidence that Professor Clark cites to support his claim that the federal government lacked the power to regulate the states unequivocally supports only the narrower conclusion that Congress could not subject the states (rather than their officers) to coercive suits.

**Page 884.    Add a new footnote 15a at the end of Paragraph (7)(b):**

**15a.**  In Alabama v. North Carolina, 130 560 U.S. 330 (2010), a case within the Supreme Court's original jurisdiction, the majority, in an opinion by Justice Scalia, held that the Eleventh Amendment and principles of state sovereign immunity did not bar an interstate commission's suit against a state insofar as the commission "makes the same claims and seeks the same relief" as co-plaintiff states whose actions were concededly not barred. Chief Justice Roberts, joined by Justice Thomas, dissented. Although acknowledging that Arizona v. California, 460 U.S. 605 (1983), supported the Court's decision, the Chief Justice argued that subsequent cases, including Federal Maritime Commission v. South Carolina Ports Authority, Sixth Edition p. 938, showed the error of the earlier ruling: "Our Constitution does not countenance such 'no harm, no foul' jurisdiction."

**Page 891.    Add at the beginning of footnote 5:**

So understood, the Young cause of action depends on the premise that a state official has violated or will imminently violate the Constitution. As brought out in the discussions on pages 712 and 806–08 of the Sixth Edition, complex issues can arise in the application of this premise to cases in which plaintiffs allege that state officials' failure to comply with federal *statutory* law violates the Supremacy Clause. For example, in Douglas v. Independent Living Center of Southern California, 132 S.Ct. 1204 (2012), the plaintiffs sought to enjoin California state officials from restricting Medicaid payments, allegedly in violation of applicable federal statutes. The Court, in an opinion by Justice Breyer, avoided the question whether the Supremacy Clause gave the plaintiffs a cause of action by holding that administrative action by the federal Department of Health and Human Services had changed the posture of the case and thus called for a remand to the court of appeals. In a dissenting opinion joined by three other Justices, Chief Justice Roberts maintained that no cause of action would lie under the Supremacy Clause. To hold otherwise, he argued, "would effect a complete end-run around this Court's implied right of action" jurisprudence, which "would serve no purpose if a plaintiff could overcome the absence of a statutory right of action by invoking a right of action under the Supremacy Clause to exactly the same effect." The Chief Justice distinguished Ex parte Young and similar subsequent cases on the ground that they "present[ed] quite different questions involving 'the preemptive assertion in equity of a defense that would otherwise have been available in the State's enforcement proceedings at law.' " In doing so, the Chief Justice appeared to accept, although without citation, the thesis of Harrison, *Ex Parte Young,* 60 Stan.L.Rev. 989 (2008), discussed in the Sixth Edition, p. 891 n.5.

Vladeck, *Douglas and the Fate of Ex Parte Young*, 122 Yale L.J. Online 13 (2012), rejects the Chief Justice's (and Professor Harrison's) analysis: "[I]f the Supremacy Clause divests state officers of the power to act in violation of *any* federal law (as Ex parte Young holds), then a plaintiff who seeks injunctive relief in a case like Douglas is seeking as much to enforce the Constitution against the state officer as he or she is seeking to enforce the relevant federal statute. An inability to bring such a suit would leave plaintiffs without a remedy for an ongoing constitutional violation." Is it analytically helpful to characterize suits to enjoin Fourteenth Amendment violations (such as that in Young) as enforcing the Supremacy Clause (rather than, more simply, as enforcing the Fourteenth Amendment)? If reference to the Supremacy Clause were analytically superfluous, then a case such as Douglas would indeed be distinguishable from Young (in which the Court made no direct reference to the Supremacy Clause). But further complicating the analysis are cases that recognize the existence of a cause of action directly under the Supremacy Clause to enjoin the coercive enforcement of a state statute that is allegedly preempted by federal statutory law. For further discussion of the perplexities of determining when federal causes of action arise under the Supremacy Clause, see Sixth Edition pp. 712, 806–08.

**Page 891.    Add to Paragraph (2):**

Shapiro, *Ex parte Young and the Uses of History*, 67 N.Y.U.Ann.Surv.Am.L. 69 (2011), hypothesizes that scholars who have characterized Young as either dramatically pathbreaking or as marking no extension of traditional federal equitable practice have done so as a result of reading this now iconic precedent in light of ideologically charged preferences and expectations. Relying heavily on the work of Professor Woolhandler that is cited on p. 891 of the Sixth Edition, as well as on case law and treatises available at the time of the Young decision, Shapiro depicts Young as being situated in but not the culmination of "two gradual transitions: (1) from the granting of relief against wrongs to tangible property to the granting of relief against the constitutional wrong of enforcing an invalid law, and (2) from the development of remedies without concern over the source of law to the federalization, and even constitutionalization, of those same forms of relief." He concludes: "[A]rguments about the case have become a proxy for a more important debate: To what extent, if any, should federal law (especially the Constitution) be available for use not only as a shield against state action but as a sword, and to what extent should litigants be able to unsheathe that sword in a suit against a state or local government, or its officers, in federal court? Young is certainly not irrelevant to that debate, but its significance should not be exaggerated."

**Page 892. Add to footnote 5:**

Note, *Pleading Sovereign Immunity: The Doctrinal Underpinnings of Hans v. Louisiana and Ex Parte Young*, 61 Stan.L.Rev. 1233 (2009), echoes Professor Harrison's assertion that Ex parte Young reflected a standard application of nineteenth century pleading conventions but offers a different account of those conventions. The Note also argues more broadly that pleading conventions—rather than concerns about state treasuries or a tort/contract distinction—were the "mainspring" that drove sovereign immunity doctrine up to and including Hans v. Louisiana and Ex parte Young.

For a variety of perspectives on Young and its significance, see *Ex parte Young Symposium: A Centennial Recognition*, 40 U. Toledo L.Rev. 819 (2009) (including articles by Professors Bobroff, Copeland, Leonard, McCormick, Purcell, Sloss, and Solimine).

**Page 895. Add a new Paragraph (5)(c):**

(c) In Virginia Office for Protection and Advocacy v. Stewart, 131 S.Ct. 1632 (2011), the Court relied on Ex parte Young to hold, by 6–2,[a] that sovereign immunity did not bar a suit for prospective relief brought against a state official by an agency of the same state. Although acknowledging that "the relative novelty" of the lawsuit "does give us pause", Justice Scalia's opinion for the Court concluded that "there is no warrant in our cases for making the validity of an Ex parte Young action turn on the identity of the plaintiff." Justice Kennedy, joined by Justice Thomas, concurred in the Court's opinion but also wrote separately to reiterate his view that correct application of Ex parte Young required a balancing test sensitive to "the need to preserve 'the dignity and respect afforded a State, which [sovereign] immunity is designed to protect' " (quoting Idaho v. Coeur d'Alene Tribe, Sixth Edition p. 894, at 268). Among pertinent considerations, Justice Kennedy emphasized that "state law must authorize an agency or official to sue another arm of the State" in order for a state agency to sue a state official.

Chief Justice Roberts, joined by Justice Alito, dissented. In his view, the "fiction" of Ex parte Young constituted " 'a narrow exception' to a State's sovereign immunity", the extension of which was unjustified. In Alden v. Maine, Sixth Edition p. 928, the Court had held that Congress could not force an unconsenting state to defend itself in a suit in its own courts: "Here extending Young" subjected the state to the greater indignity of being required "to defend itself *against* itself in federal court." Chief Justice Roberts did not question, however, that a state court would need to entertain a suit by a state

**a.** Justice Kagan did not participate.

agency against a state official seeking prospective relief under federal law. Is the Chief Justice's concession of that point consistent with his reliance on Alden to oppose the "extension" of Ex parte Young?

### Page 923.   Add at the end of Paragraph (4)(e):

Deep divisions about the scope of Congress' Section 5 power were again on display in Coleman v. Court of Appeals of Maryland, 132 S.Ct. 1327 (2012), in which the Court, without a majority opinion, held that Congress had no authority under the Fourteenth Amendment to abrogate the states' immunity from suit under a provision of the Family and Medical Leave Act (FMLA) that requires employers to provide up to twelve weeks of unpaid leave per year for an employee's own health issues. Writing for a four-Justice plurality, Justice Kennedy found that Congress had not adequately linked the provision to a pattern of constitutional violations and, in particular, had not shown it to be a response to sex discrimination in sick leave policies. Justice Thomas joined the plurality opinion but wrote separately to state his view that Nevada Dep't of Human Resources v. Hibbs, Sixth Edition p. 921, which upheld other provisions of the FMLA and which the plurality distinguished, was wrongly decided. Justice Scalia concurred in the judgment only: "[O]utside of the context of racial discrimination (which is different for *stare decisis* reasons)," he "would limit Congress's § 5 power to the regulation of conduct that *itself* violates the Fourteenth Amendment." In a dissenting opinion that she summarized from the bench, Justice Ginsburg, joined in full by Justice Breyer and in pertinent parts by Justices Sotomayor and Kagan, relied heavily on the legislative history in arguing that the FMLA provision involved in the case was directed at the exclusion of women from the workplace based on pregnancy-related health issues, even though it was deliberately framed in gender-neutral terms (in response to the concerns of "equal-treatment feminists" who objected to legislation subjecting men and women to formally different legal treatment). In light of the record before Congress, Justice Ginsburg concluded that the statute was congruent and proportional to an identified pattern of sex discrimination. (She also argued at length that the Court should revisit and overrule the holding of Geduldig v. Aiello, 417 U.S. 484 (1974), that discrimination on the basis of pregnancy does not constitute discrimination on the basis of sex. But she maintained that the Court erred in its § 5 analysis "even if Aiello"—which the plurality did not discuss—"senselessly holds sway".)

### Page 938.   Add at the end of Paragraph (7)(b):

Sossamon v. Texas, 131 S.Ct. 1651 (2011), affirmed that Congress can condition grants of federal funds on state waivers of sovereign immunity, but held that statutory language authorizing suits for "appropriate relief against a government" that accepts federal money did not constitute a waiver of immunity from suits for money damages. Writing for the majority, Justice Thomas echoed prior admonitions that "[a] State's consent to suit must be 'unequivocally expressed'" and that the scope of any waiver "'will be strictly construed * * * in favor of the sovereign.'" The term "appropriate relief", he then concluded, was too "open-ended and ambiguous" to elicit a waiver of immunity from damages actions.

Justice Sotomayor dissented in an opinion joined by Justice Breyer. According to her, it was "self-evident" that "money damages are 'appropriate relief'". Even the majority, she noted, "appears to accept" that by taking federal funds Texas had waived its immunity from suits for equitable relief. She continued: "But sovereign immunity is not simply a defense against certain classes of remedies—it is a defense against being sued at all. As a result, there is no inherent reason why the phrase 'appropriate relief' would provide adequate notice as to equitable remedies but not as to monetary ones. In fact, * * * in light of general remedies principles the presumption arguably should be the reverse."

For critical commentary on the relatively recently minted rule that a general waiver of sovereign immunity will not encompass suits for money relief absent clear authorization of that remedy, see Tang, *Double Immunity*, 65 Stan.L.Rev. 279 (2013).

———

## Subsection C: Federal Statutory Protection Against State Official Action: Herein of 42 U.S.C. § 1983

———

**Page 958.  Add at the end of Paragraph (2):**

The Court held that there can be no "supervisory liability" in Bivens and § 1983 actions, and that "each Government official, his or her title notwithstanding, is only liable for his or her own misconduct" in Ashcroft v. Iqbal, 556 U.S. 662 (2009), also discussed at p. 86, *supra*, and p. 106, *infra*. In an opinion by Justice Kennedy, the Court, by a 5–4 vote, ordered the dismissal of claims against a former Attorney General and FBI Director predicated, *inter alia*, on their " 'knowledge and acquiescence in' " lower officials' alleged violations of the rights of a Pakistani Muslim arrested and detained in the aftermath of 9/11. "[M]ere knowledge" is not enough to establish a constitutional violation, Justice Kennedy wrote: "In a § 1983 suit or a Bivens action * * * the term 'supervisory liability' is a misnomer."

Dissenting, Justice Souter, joined by Justices Stevens, Ginsburg, and Breyer, protested that the majority had ruled ill-advisedly on a question that the petitioner defendants had not presented: "[T]hey conceded * * * that they would be liable if they had 'actual knowledge' of [unconstitutional] discrimination by their subordinates and exhibited 'deliberate indifference' to that discrimination." The Court, Justice Souter continued, "is not narrowing the scope of supervisory liability; it is eliminating * * * supervisory liability entirely" based on a false assumption that the only two possible standards are respondeat superior liability and "no supervisory liability at all. * * * In fact, there is quite a spectrum of possible tests for supervisory liability: it could be imposed where a supervisor has actual knowledge of a subordinate's constitutional violation and acquiesces; or where supervisors 'know about the conduct and facilitate it, approve it, condone it, or turn a blind eye for fear of what they might see'; or where the supervisor has no actual knowledge of the violation but was reckless in his supervision of the subordinate; or where the supervisor was grossly negligent. I am unsure what the general test for supervisory liability should be, and in the absence of briefing and argument I am in no position to choose or devise one." (Citations and some internal quotations omitted.)

Justice Souter is correct, isn't he, that "supervisory liability" is not necessarily an all-or-nothing proposition? Consider also whether the Court should have distinguished between the questions (1) when, if ever, supervisors violate the Constitution by failing to exercise adequate control over their subordinates and (2) when, if ever, state officials should be deemed to have "cause[d]" a constitutional violation within the meaning of § 1983. Was the Court justified in deciding the second question in the context of a Bivens action? See Levinson, *Who Will Supervise the Supervisors? Establishing Liability for Failure to Train, Supervise, or Discipline Subordinates in a Post–Iqbal/Connick World,* 47 Harv.C.R.-C.L. L. Rev. 273 (2012) (answering in the negative and arguing that "supervisory liability should follow the same interpretation of causality and culpability that the Supreme Court acknowledged in § 1983 government liability cases, although recognizing and incorporating the immunity defense for individuals").

### Page 960.  Add a new footnote 11a at the end of the first paragraph in Paragraph (5).

**11a.**  Based on research in the Justices' papers, Achtenberg, *Frankfurter's Champion: Justice Powell, Monell, and the Meaning of "Color of Law",* 80 Fordham L.Rev. 681 (2011), speculates that Justice Powell, whose vote was necessary for Justice Brennan to write for a majority in Monell, likely agreed with Justice Frankfurter about the meaning of "under color of law". According to Achtenburg, Powell, more than any other Justice, successfully pushed Justice Brennan to make municipal liability hinge on the same distinction that Justice Frankfurter thought should govern officer liability under § 1983.

### Page 962.  Add at the beginning of footnote 14:

The Court, by 5–4, once again rejected a claim of local governmental liability predicated on a failure-to-train theory in Connick v. Thompson, 131 S.Ct. 1350 (2011). The petitioner Orleans Parish District Attorney's Office, for which Connick was at relevant times the sole policymaker, conceded that assistant district attorneys had failed to disclose potentially exculpatory physical evidence (a blood sample) to the plaintiff, who spent 18 years in prison on robbery and murder convictions (14 of them on death row), before both convictions were vacated. In his § 1983 action, Thompson alleged that the failure of District Attorney Connick to train his subordinates regarding their obligations to disclose exculpatory evidence under Brady v. Maryland, 373 U.S. 83 (1963), manifested "deliberate indifference" to plainly foreseeable constitutional violations and was causally responsible for his wrongful convictions. In an opinion by Justice Thomas, the Court emphasized that Thompson "did not contend that he proved a pattern of * * * Brady violations" that were "similar" to the one that occurred in his case. Although Louisiana courts had overturned four convictions obtained by the Orleans Parish District Attorney's Office in the 10 years preceding Thompson's prosecution, the previous incidents had not involved failures to disclose physical evidence, and thus "could not have put Connick on notice that the office's Brady training was inadequate with respect to the sort of Brady violation at issue here." Nor should Connick have anticipated that in the absence of training prosecutors would commit Brady violations of the kind at issue. Although other officials might require constitutional training, attorneys not only have legal educations, but also possess the tools to perform legal research when uncertain of their obligations.

In a dissent joined by Justices Breyer, Sotomayor, and Kagan, Justice Ginsburg argued that "the evidence demonstrated that misperception and disregard of Brady's disclosure requirements were pervasive in Orleans Parish" and that, under the circumstances, failure to provide training reflected actionable "deliberate indifference" to the kind of wrong that Thompson suffered.

### Page 965.  Add to Paragraph (4):

The Court found the plaintiffs' pleadings inadequate to survive a motion to dismiss in Ashcroft v. Iqbal, 556 U.S. 662 (2009), also discussed at pp. 86, 105, *supra*, which involved claims against former Attorney General John Ashcroft and FBI Director Robert Mueller based on alleged unconstitutional acts in the period following September 11, 2001. Iqbal, a Pakistani Muslim who was arrested for and pleaded guilty to fraud and subsequently was removed to Pakistan, alleged that Ashcroft and Mueller adopted a policy of discriminatorily designating Arab Muslims as persons of "high interest" to the 9/11 investigation and of detaining them in a maximum security facility—in which detainees were kept in lockdown for 23 hours a day and spent the sole hour outside their cells in handcuffs and leg irons—on account of their race, religion, or national origin. The complaint further averred that Ashcroft and Mueller knew of and condoned Iqbal's subjection to the policy. In finding Iqbal's complaint insufficient to survive a motion to dismiss, the Court (5–4), in an opinion by Justice Kennedy, did not purport to lay down a special pleading rule for § 1983 and Bivens actions, but instead to apply Rule 8 of the Federal Rules of Civil Procedure, which says that a pleading must contain a "short and plain statement of the claim showing that the pleader is entitled to relief," as interpreted in Bell Atlantic Corp. v. Twombly, 550 U.S. 544 (2007), a case that had ordered dismissal of an antitrust complaint.

Twombly, Justice Kennedy wrote, had established two pertinent principles. First, "the tenet that a court must accept as true all of the allegations contained in a complaint is inapplicable to legal conclusions. Threadbare recitals of the elements of a cause of action, supported by mere conclusory statements, do not suffice." Applying this principle, the Court rejected as inadequate Iqbal's averments that the petitioners knew of and condoned his alleged mistreatment; that the mistreatment reflected a policy of discrimination based on race, religion, or national origin; "that Ashcroft was the 'principal architect' of this invidious policy"; and that "Mueller was 'instrumental' in adopting and executing it." Justice Kennedy explained that "we do not reject these bald allegations on the ground that they are unrealistic or nonsensical. * * * It is the conclusory nature of respondent's allegations, rather than their extravagantly fanciful nature, that disentitles them to the presumption of truth."

The second principle that the Court extracted from Twombly was that "only a complaint that states a plausible claim to relief survives a motion to dismiss. Determining whether a complaint states a plausible claim for relief will * * * be a context-specific task that requires the reviewing court to draw on its judicial experience and common sense." Applying this principle both to Iqbal's conclusory averments and to more specific assertions intended to support them, Justice Kennedy found Iqbal's claim that the defendants had "adopted a policy of classifying post-September–11 detainees as 'of high interest' because of their race, religion, or national origin" not to be sufficiently plausible to survive a motion to dismiss "given more likely explanations" for the defendants' alleged conduct: "The September 11 attacks were perpetrated by 19 Arab Muslim hijackers * * *. * * * It should come as no surprise that a legitimate policy directing law enforcement to arrest and detain individuals because of their suspected link to the attacks would produce a disparate, incidental impact on Arab Muslims, even though the purpose of the policy was to target neither Arabs nor Muslims." Even on the assumption that the defendants had adopted a policy of subjecting some terrorist suspects to the rigors of maximum security facilities, "the complaint does not show, or even intimate," that they did so for invidiously discriminatory reasons. The more plausible inference was that "the Nation's top law enforcement officers, in the aftermath of a devastating terrorist attack, sought to keep suspected terrorists in the most secure conditions available until the suspects could be cleared of terrorist activity. * * * [Iqbal] would need to allege more by way of factual content to 'nudg[e]' his claim of purposeful discrimination 'across the line from conceivable to plausible.' Twombly, 550 U.S., at 570."

Justice Souter, joined by Justices Stevens, Ginsburg, and Breyer, dissented. Twombly, he said, made clear that "a court must take the allegations [in a complaint] as true, no matter how skeptical the court may be", subject to a "sole exception" for "allegations that are sufficiently fantastic to defy reality as we know it: claims about little green men, or the plaintiff's recent trip to Pluto, or experiences in time travel. That is not what we have here." Nor was this a case, like Twombly, in which the plaintiff's factual allegations, although " 'consistent with' " alleged illegality, were " 'just as much in line with' " a lawful course of conduct (quoting Twombly). "[T]he allegations in the complaint are neither confined to naked legal conclusions nor consistent with legal conduct. The complaint alleges that FBI officials discriminated against Iqbal solely on account of his race, religion, and national origin, and it alleges * * * knowledge and deliberate indifference [by the defendants.] * * * Iqbal's complaint therefore contains 'enough facts to state a claim to relief that is plausible on its face' " (quoting Twombly).

In a separate dissenting opinion, Justice Breyer wrote that he, "like the Court, believe[d] it important to prevent unwarranted litigation from interfering with" government operations, but that he could not "find in that need adequate justification for the Court's interpretation" of the pleading requirements of the Federal Rules of Civil Procedure. According to Justice Breyer, trial judges already have other mechanisms for preventing unwarranted discovery: "A district court, for example, can begin discovery with lower level government defendants before determining whether a case can be made to allow discovery related to higher level government officials."

However wise or unwise as a matter of policy, can the Court's ruling be justified as an interpretation of Rule 8 of the Federal Rules of Civil Procedure?[a] What exactly does it mean to say that a court assessing whether the allegations of a complaint are sufficiently "plausible" to survive a motion to dismiss must make judgments "that draw on its judicial experience and common sense"?

Fitzpatrick, *Twombly and Iqbal Reconsidered*, 87 Notre Dame L.Rev. 1621 (2012), characterizes Iqbal (and the prior decision in Twombly) as sensibly aimed "to recalibrate plaintiffs' discovery rights in light of the exponential increases in discovery costs that have developed in the years since the Federal Rules of Civil Procedure were first promulgated in 1938". Among the purposes of the qualified immunity doctrine of Harlow v. Fitzgerald, Sixth Edition p. 986, is to facilitate the dismissal of insubstantial suits against governmental officials prior to discovery. If the Court believes that discovery costs have gotten

---

**a.** Consider the pertinence of Form 11, which is attached to the Rules and which, under Rule 84, "suffice[s] under these rules". It is a "Complaint for Negligence", which, on the question of liability, states simply "On *date* and *place*, the defendant negligently drove a motor vehicle against the plaintiff."

Iqbal has been widely criticized. See, e.g., Meier, *Why Twombly Is Good Law (But Poor-*

*ly Drafted) and Iqbal Will Be Overturned*, 87 Ind.L.J. 709 (2012); Miller, *From Conley to Twombly to Iqbal: A Double Play on the Federal Rules of Civil Procedure*, 60 Duke L.J. 1 (2010); Steinman, *The Pleading Problem*, 62 Stan.L.Rev. 1293 (2010). For a rare defense, see Moline, *Nineteenth–Century–Principles for Twenty–First Century–Pleading*, 60 Emory L.J. 159 (2010).

out of hand, is the "recalibrat[ion]" of pleading standards an appropriate response?

**Page 965.   Add a new footnote 19a at the end of the first paragraph of Paragraph (5):**

    **19a.**   Fox v. Vice, 131 S.Ct. 2205 (2011), held unanimously that when a plaintiff asserts both frivolous and non-frivolous claims in a § 1983 action, a court may award the defendant only such attorney's fees as would not have been incurred anyway in defending against the non-frivolous claims.

**Page 967.   Add a new Paragraph (3):**

**(3) Prisoner Litigation and Structural Injunctions.** In Brown v. Plata, 131 S.Ct. 1910 (2011), a sharply divided Supreme Court, by 5–4, upheld a three-judge district court's mandate that California reduce its prison population or otherwise alleviate prison overcrowding in order to remedy ongoing Eighth Amendment violations. The case involved two consolidated class actions alleging that inadequacies in care given to inmates with mental and serious medical conditions violated the Eighth Amendment. District courts found constitutional violations in both cases and entered remedial orders, but when those orders proved ineffective over 12 years in one case and five years in the other, both district courts granted motions for the convening of three-judge district courts, which are the only courts empowered under the Prison Litigation Reform Act to enter orders with the effect of reducing or limiting prison populations. 18 U.S.C. § 3626(a)(3). A three-judge court heard the consolidated cases, found prison overcrowding to be the root cause of the ongoing constitutional violations to which the plaintiffs were subjected, and ordered the defendants to reduce California prison populations to 137.5% of prisons' design capacities (from current levels of nearly 200%) within two years.

    In an opinion by Justice Kennedy, the Supreme Court affirmed. The majority began with an overview of the conditions underlying the lawsuit: "California's prisons are designed to house a population just under 80,000, but at the time of the three-judge court's decision the population was almost double that. * * * Prisoners are crammed into spaces neither designed nor intended to house inmates. As many as 200 prisoners may live in a gymnasium, monitored by as few as two or three correctional officers. As many as 54 prisoners may share a single toilet. * * *

    "Prisoners in California with serious mental illness do not receive minimal, adequate care. Because of a shortage of treatment beds, suicidal inmates may be held for prolonged periods in telephone-booth sized cages without toilets. * * * Other inmates awaiting care may be held for months in administrative segregation, where they endure harsh and isolated conditions and receive only limited mental health services. Wait times for mental health care range as high as 12 months. In 2006, the suicide rate in California's prisons was nearly 80% higher than the national average for prison populations * * *. * * *

    "Prisoners suffering from physical illness also receive severely deficient care. California's prisons * * * have only half the clinical space needed to treat the current population. A correctional officer testified that, in one prison, up to 50 sick inmates may be held together in a 12–by 20–foot cage for up to five hours awaiting treatment. The number of staff is inadequate, and prisoners face significant delays in access to care. A prisoner with severe abdominal pain died after a 5–week delay in referral to a specialist; a prisoner with 'constant and extreme' chest pain died after an 8–hour delay in evaluation by a doctor; and a prisoner died of testicular cancer after a 'failure of MDs to work up for cancer in a young man with 17 months of testicular pain.' * * * Many more prisoners, suffering from severe but not life-threatening conditions, experience prolonged illness and unnecessary pain.''

After having laid out the plaintiffs' grievances, Justice Kennedy stated the test that the three-judge court had needed to apply in order to grant injunctive relief that potentially included a mandated reduction in prisoners to reduce overcrowding: It must "find by clear and convincing evidence that 'crowding is the primary cause of the violation of a Federal right' and that 'no other relief will remedy the violation of the Federal right.' 18 U.S.C. § 3626(a)(3)(E). * * *. The three-judge court must [also] find that the relief is 'narrowly drawn, extends no further than necessary * * *, and is the least intrusive means necessary to correct the violation of the Federal right.' [18 U.S.C. § 3626(a)(1)(A).] In making this determination, the three-judge court must give 'substantial weight to any adverse impact on public safety or the operation of a criminal justice system caused by the relief.' Ibid.

"Applying these standards, the three-judge court found a population limit appropriate, necessary, and authorized in this case", and the majority agreed. "[C]rowding [was] the primary cause of the violation of a Federal right" because excess populations created unsanitary living conditions, led to increased violence, and overtaxed health care facilities and providers. Clear and convincing evidence established that "no other relief will remedy the violation" of the right at issue because, although the building of new facilities would suffice in theory, "the three-judge court found no realistic possibility that California would be able to build itself out of this crisis." In addition, the remedy was narrowly drawn: An otherwise proper remedy did not become impermissible merely because it would have "positive effects beyond the plaintiff class." Moreover, the three-judge court had given " 'substantial weight' to any potential adverse impact on public safety from its order". Justice Kennedy explained: "Expert witnesses produced statistical evidence that prison populations had been lowered without adversely affecting public safety in a number of jurisdictions." The state could make expanded use of good-time credits to the prisoners least likely to re-offend and could rely more on devices such as electronic monitoring of parolees.

In a concluding section, Justice Kennedy noted that the three-judge court retained authority and responsibility to amend its order as events warranted and appeared to endorse one modification in particular: "The State may wish to move for modification * * * to extend the deadline for the required reduction to five years * * *. The three-judge court may grant such a request provided that the State * * * ensure[s] that measures are taken to implement the plan without undue delay.''

Justice Scalia, joined by Justice Thomas, filed a sharp dissent in which he accused the majority of affirming "perhaps the most radical injunction issued by a court in our Nation's history: an order requiring California to release the staggering number of 46,000 convicted criminals." In his view, no class action should ever have been certified: No two plaintiffs had suffered the same injury, unless on the untenable theory that it was cruel and unusual punishment merely to be incarcerated in a prison with inadequate medical facilities, regardless of whether an inmate actually needed medical treatment.

Justice Scalia continued: "Even if I accepted the implausible premise that the plaintiffs have established a systemwide violation of the Eighth Amendment, I would dissent from the Court's endorsement of a decrowding order. That order is an example of what has become known as a 'structural injunction.' As I have previously explained, structural injunctions are radically different from the injunctions traditionally issued by courts of equity", which "usually required 'a single simple act.' H. McClintock, Principles of Equity § 15, pp. 32–33 (2d ed. 1948). * * * The court did not engage in any ongoing supervision of the litigant's conduct, nor did its order continue to regulate its behavior. International Union, UMW v. Bagwell, 512 U.S. 821, 841–842 (1994) (Scalia, J., concurring).

"Structural injunctions depart from that historical practice, turning judges into long-term administrators of complex social institutions such as schools, prisons, and police departments. Indeed, they require judges to play a role essentially indistinguishable from the role ordinarily played by executive officials. * * * The drawbacks of structural injunctions have been described at great length elsewhere. See, *e.g.,* Missouri v. Jenkins, 515 U.S. 70, 124–133 (1995) (Thomas, J., concurring); Horowitz, Decreeing Organizational Change: Judicial Supervision of Public Institutions, 1983 Duke L.J. 1265. This case illustrates one of their most pernicious aspects: that they force judges to engage in a form of factfinding-as-policymaking that is outside the traditional judicial role. * * *

"This feature of structural injunctions is superbly illustrated by the District Court's proceeding concerning the decrowding order's effect on public safety." Although acknowledging that the judges heard witnesses, Justice Scalia insisted that "they were relying largely on their own beliefs about penology and recidivism. And *of course* different district judges, of different policy views, would have 'found' that rehabilitation would not work and that releasing prisoners would increase the crime rate. * * *

"But structural injunctions do not simply invite judges to indulge policy preferences. They invite judges to indulge *incompetent* policy preferences. Three years of law school and familiarity with pertinent Supreme Court precedents give no insight whatsoever into the management of social institutions. * * *

"In my view, a court may not order a prisoner's release unless it determines that the prisoner is suffering from a violation of his constitutional rights, and that his release, and no other relief, will remedy that violation. Thus, if the court determines that a particular prisoner is being denied constitutionally required medical treatment, and the release of that prisoner (and no other remedy) would enable him to obtain medical treatment, then the court can order his release; but a court may not order the release of prisoners who have suffered no violations of their constitutional rights, merely to make it less likely that that will happen to them in the future.

"This view follows from the PLRA's text * * *. '[N]arrowly drawn' means that the relief applies only to the 'particular [prisoner] or [prisoners]' whose constitutional rights are violated; 'extends no further than necessary' means that prisoners whose rights are not violated will not obtain relief; and 'least intrusive means necessary to correct the violation of the Federal right' means that no other relief is available. * * * The District Court's order that California release 46,000 prisoners extends 'further than necessary to correct the violation of the Federal right of a particular plaintiff or plaintiffs' who have been denied needed medical care. 18 U.S.C § 3626(a)(1)(A). It is accordingly forbidden by the PLRA—besides defying all sound conception of the proper role of judges."

Justice Alito, joined by Chief Justice Roberts, also dissented: "The decree in this case is a perfect example of what the Prison Litigation Reform Act * * * was enacted to prevent." According to Justice Alito, "the three-judge court improperly refused to consider evidence concerning present conditions in the California prison system." He also thought that the majority misapplied the statutory criteria that it purported to find satisfied. In his view, "the [three-judge] court erred in holding that no remedy short of a massive prisoner release can bring the California system into compliance with the Eighth Amendment". In addition, "the court gave inadequate weight to the impact of its decree on public safety": "The three-judge court would have us believe that the early release of 46,000 inmates will not imperil * * * public safety. Common sense and experience counsel greater caution."

For further discussion of structural reform litigation and related issues, including bibliographical citations, see Sixth Edition pp. 73–75, 219–22.

**Page 969.   Add to footnote 3:**

On the question whether § 1983 creates a cause of action for violations of treaty rights, see Parry, *A Primer on Treaties and § 1983 After Medellin v. Texas*, 13 Lewis & Clark L.Rev. 35 (2009) (arguing that it does).

---

# SECTION 3.   OFFICIAL IMMUNITY

**Page 996.   Add at the end of Paragraph (2)(a):**

Fallon, *Asking the Right Questions About Officer Immunity*, 80 Fordham L.Rev. 479 (2011), takes issue with the claim of both Harlow and Gregoire v. Biddle that immunity necessarily involves a "balance between * * * evils": "[O]fficial immunity is not a variable among constants but * * * one potential variable among others. * * * In the absence of official immunity, even some currently well-established constitutional rights and authorizations to sue to enforce them would likely *shrink*, and sometimes appropriately so." (For example, if there were no official immunity, the Court might hold that searches are not unreasonable under the Fourth Amendment unless no reasonable official could have thought them unreasonable, or that no cause of action runs against judges whose only constitutional violation is to rule erroneously on constitutional claims.) Nevertheless, Professor Fallon is equivocal about existing immunity doctrine. Viewing immunity as "a potential mechanism for achieving the best overall bundle of rights and correspondingly calibrated remedies," he maintains that "there has been too little thinking about" alternatives to official immunity (such as non-retroactivity doctrines applicable to path-breaking rulings recognizing new rights or straitened pleading requirements as a way of weeding out frivolous suits) and the distinctive features of immunity, if any, that might make it—"in comparison with other potentially adjustable variables"—the best "tool for defining or redefining packages of rights and enforcement mechanisms that confer meaningful guarantees but are not intolerably [socially] costly".

**Page 997.   Add to Paragraph (2)(b):**

Consider the potential relevance of the historical argument of Pfander & Hunt, *Public Wrongs and Private Bills: Indemnification and Government Accountability in the Early Republic,* 85 N.Y.U.L.Rev 1862 (2010), that federal officials generally enjoyed no immunity from suit during the antebellum era and that Congress routinely provided indemnification for official action taken in good faith discharge of official duties. Although the authors assert that "[n]o one would argue for a return to the world of the early republic and * * * an indemnity practice managed through petitions to Congress", they see considerable virtues in a regime in which "[c]ourts evaluated legality" and Congress took responsibility for "adjust[ing] official incentives".

**Page 999.   Add to footnote 2:**

Rehberg v. Paulk, 132 S.Ct. 1497 (2012), held unanimously that a witness in a grand jury proceeding enjoys the same absolute immunity from suit as a witness at trial.

**Page 1000.   Add to footnote 3:**

For further attacks on absolute prosecutorial immunity, largely predicated on the claim that current law includes too few deterrents to prosecutorial misconduct, see Johns, *Unsupportable and Unjustified: A Critique of Absolute Prosecutorial Immunity,* 80 Fordham L.Rev. 509 (2011); Rudin, *The Supreme Court Assumes Errant Prosecutors Will Be Disciplined by Their Offices or the Bar: Three Case Studies that Prove that Assumption Wrong,* 80 Fordham L.Rev. 537 (2011).

**Page 1002.   Add a new footnote 7a at the end of the first paragraph of Paragraph (7):**

**7a.** For a discussion of lower courts' difficulties in applying the "clearly established" standard and some "modest" suggestions for doctrinal clarification, see Jeffries, *What's Wrong With Qualified Immunity?,* 62 Fla.L.Rev. 851 (2010).

**Page 1002.   Add to Paragraph (7)(a):**

In Camreta v. Greene, 131 S.Ct. 2020 (2011), which is further discussed at pp. 13 and 27, *supra,* and p. 115, *infra,* the Supreme Court posited that a Ninth Circuit ruling that a defendant had violated a constitutional right would not be "mere dictum" in subsequent cases within the circuit, even if the court ordered the suit dismissed on qualified immunity grounds. The Court also asserted that "district court decisions—unlike those from the courts of appeals—do not necessarily settle constitutional standards or prevent repeated claims of qualified immunity." In conjunction, do these assertions imply that a squarely on-point court of appeals decision suffices to "clearly establish" the law within the circuit in which it was issued? Would it matter if other circuits or state supreme courts had decided the same question differently?

The Court also addressed the significance of district court rulings in Ashcroft v. al-Kidd, 131 S.Ct. 2074 (2011), which is further discussed at p. 117, *infra,* holding that dictum in a single district court decision could not "clearly establish" that a course of action by the Attorney General violates the Constitution: "[A] district judge's * * * holding is not 'controlling authority' in any jurisdiction, much less in the entire United States; and his *ipse dixit* of a footnoted dictum falls far short of what is necessary absent controlling authority: a robust 'consensus of cases of persuasive authority.' Wilson v. Layne, 526 U.S. 603, 617 (1999)."

In a concurring opinion in al-Kidd, Justice Kennedy argued that the criteria for identifying clearly established law might vary with the office that an official holds: "In contrast [with officials operating within a single jurisdiction,] the Attorney General occupies a national office and so sets policies implemented in many jurisdictions throughout the country. * * * A national officer intent on retaining qualified immunity need not abide by the most stringent standard adopted anywhere in the United States." Imagine that the Attorney General and a county sheriff are both sued in the Ninth Circuit for ordering seizures that would be unreasonable under Ninth Circuit precedent. Is it possible that the latter has violated clearly established law but the former has not?

### Page 1003.  Add to footnote 8:

In Reichle v. Howards, 132 S.Ct. 2088 (2012), the Court upheld a claim of qualified immunity by Secret Service agents who were alleged to have violated the First Amendment by arresting a suspect, admittedly with probable cause (for making a materially false statement to a federal official), but purportedly in retaliation for speech uttered in an encounter with Vice President Cheney. In an opinion joined by five other Justices, Justice Thomas held (in line with earlier cases) that the question was not whether there is a "general right to be free from retaliation for one's speech", but whether there was a clearly established "right to be free from a retaliatory arrest that is otherwise supported by probable cause." After concluding that Supreme Court cases had not established such a right, he overturned the Tenth Circuit's holding that one of its cases had done so. An intervening Supreme Court decision had created reasonable uncertainty about the Tenth Circuit precedent's continuing validity, he ruled. Justices Ginsburg and Breyer concurred in the judgment only. Justice Kagan did not participate.

Brown, *The Fall and Rise of Qualified Immunity: from Hope to Harris*, 9 Nev.L.J. 185 (2008), reports, on the basis of an empirical study of qualified immunity cases in the Sixth and Eleventh Circuits, that the defense's success rate is lowest with respect to claims of race-and gender-based discrimination, followed by Eighth Amendment "deliberate indifference" claims, and highest with respect to substantive due process.

### Page 1004.  Add at the beginning of footnote 9:

Jeffries, *The Liability Rule for Constitutional Torts*, 99 Va.L.Rev. 207 (2012), argues for shifting the immunity inquiry "from whether the defendant violated a 'clearly established' right to whether the defendant's actions were 'clearly unconstitutional.'" According to Professor Jeffries, the latter standard would "signal a less technical requirement, less tied to specific precedent, and more accommodating of notice through 'common social duty'" in cases involving egregious official misconduct but no closely on-point judicial precedents clearly establishing constitutional rights.

### Page 1004.  Add at the end of Paragraph (7)(c):

The Court cited uncertainty among lower court judges as its principal ground for upholding a qualified immunity defense in Safford Unified School Dist. #1 v. Redding, 557 U.S. 364 (2009). In an opinion by Justice Souter, the Court first held that the defendant school officials had violated the Fourth Amendment when they strip-searched a thirteen-year-old middle school student without adequate reason to suspect her of hiding dangerous contraband in her underwear. But the defendants possessed qualified immunity, the Court said, largely because lower courts had "reached divergent conclusions regarding how" the controlling precedent allowing school searches under a reasonableness standard, New Jersey v. T.L.O., 469 U.S. 325 (1985), applied to strip searches: "We would not suggest that entitlement to qualified immunity is the guaranteed product of disuniform views of the law in the other federal, or state, courts, and the fact that a single judge, or even a group of judges, disagrees about the contours of a right does not automatically render the law unclear.

That said, however, the cases viewing strip searches differently from the way we see them are numerous enough, with well-reasoned majority and dissenting opinions, to counsel doubt that we were sufficiently clear in the prior statement of the law." Justice Stevens, joined by Justice Ginsburg, dissented, asserting that "the clarity of a well-established right should not depend on whether jurists have misread our precedents."

When, if ever, would "disuniform views" among lower courts fail to demonstrate that the law was not "clearly established"? In thinking about this question, note that in Groh v. Ramirez, 540 U.S. 551 (2004), a five-Justice majority held that the defendant had violated clearly established rights, even though Justices Scalia and Thomas concluded that the defendants had not violated the Constitution at all.

In Anderson v. Creighton, 483 U.S. 635, 640 (1987), the Court said that for qualified immunity to be defeated, "[t]he contours of the right must be sufficiently clear that a reasonable official would understand that what he is doing violates that right." In Ashcroft v. al-Kidd, 131 S.Ct. 2074, 2083 (2011), Justice Scalia's Court opinion quoted that language but interrupted the quotation to replace "a reasonable official" with "every 'reasonable official.'" See also Reichle v. Howards, 132 S.Ct. 2088, 2093 (2012) (quoting the al-Kidd formulation). How large a change in the law, if any, does that substitution make?

**Page 1004.   Add at the end of the second paragraph of Paragraph (7)(d):**

The Court appeared to attach greater significance to a magistrate's issuance of a search warrant in Messerschmidt v. Millender, 132 S.Ct. 1235 (2012), in which it characterized "the fact that a neutral magistrate has issued a warrant" as a legally relevant indicator that "the officers acted in an objectively reasonable manner". Chief Justice Roberts' majority opinion described Malley v. Briggs, Sixth Edition p. 1004, as establishing an "exception" to the principle that a magistrate's decision to issue a warrant normally establishes the objective legal reasonableness of its execution, an exception that applies only when "the magistrate so obviously erred that any reasonable officer would have recognized the error." Justice Sotomayor, in a dissenting opinion joined by Justice Ginsburg, and Justice Kagan, in an opinion concurring in part and dissenting in part, protested that the majority misread Malley. According to the dissenting Justices, an officer's unreasonable decision to seek an overbroad warrant could not be rendered objectively reasonable by a magistrate's issuance of such a warrant.

**Page 1004.   Add to footnote 10:**

In Filarsky v. Delia, 132 S.Ct. 1657 (2012), a unanimous Court distinguished Wyatt v. Cole and Richardson v. McKnight, Sixth Edition p. 1004, and held that a person hired directly by the government to work on its behalf need not be a permanent or full-time employee in order to claim official immunity.

**Page 1006.   Add a new Paragraph (8)(c):**

(c) The Court's struggle with issues involving the proper order of decision in qualified immunity cases took a series of further, tortuous turns in Camreta v. Greene, 131 S.Ct. 2020 (2011), with Justice Kagan's Court opinion pronouncing at one point that "[i]n general, courts should think hard, and then think hard again, before turning small cases into large ones" by ruling on the merits when a case could be easily dismissed on qualified immunity grounds. In early

2003, Camreta, a child services worker, and a deputy sheriff interviewed the respondent Greene's then 9–year-old daughter, S.G., at her Oregon elementary school about allegations that her father had sexually abused her. In a § 1983 action brought on her daughter's behalf, Greene alleged that the interview, conducted in the absence of parental consent, judicial authorization, or exigent circumstances, constituted an unreasonable seizure forbidden by the Fourth Amendment. The District Court granted summary judgment for the defendants. In its view, the "seizure" of S.G. was objectively reasonable, and the defendants were in any case entitled to qualified immunity because the right that the defendants were alleged to have violated was not clearly established. In affirming, the Ninth Circuit held for the defendants on the ground of qualified immunity, but also determined that "government officials investigating allegations of child abuse" should not assume "that a 'special need' automatically justifies dispensing with traditional Fourth Amendment protections in this context." It said that it had decided the merits before reaching the qualified immunity issue in order to "provide guidance to those charged with the difficult task of protecting child welfare within the confines of the Fourth Amendment". Although the plaintiff Greene did not seek review in the Supreme Court, Camreta, the prevailing defendant, did, alleging that the court of appeals' ruling on the merits of the Fourth Amendment issue interfered with his capacity as a child services worker to protect his clients against abuse.

Writing for the majority, Justice Kagan ultimately dismissed the case as moot. Because S.G. was nearly 18, was about to graduate from high school, and had moved out of state, she faced no realistic prospect of ever again being subjected to interrogation as a suspected victim of child abuse within the Ninth Circuit. The proper disposition, the Court held, was to vacate the part of the judgment holding that the defendants' conduct violated the Constitution (even though the part of the judgment involving qualified immunity should remain intact), in order to prevent Camreta from being bound by a lower court decision of which he had no opportunity to seek review.

On its way to that determination, the Court pronounced on a number of issues of potential relevance to future qualified immunity cases presenting order-of-decision issues:

(1) The language of 28 U.S.C. § 1254(1), authorizing a petition for certiorari by "any party", permitted Camreta and a co-defendant to seek Supreme Court review even though they were prevailing parties in the Ninth Circuit.

(2) Camreta retained a continuing "personal stake" sufficient to satisfy the Article III case-or-controversy requirement: Because he "regularly engages" in conduct that the court of appeals found to be illegal, "he suffers injury caused by the adverse constitutional ruling."

(3) The policy of judicial avoidance of constitutional issues did not bar the Court from exercising review on the unusual facts of the case before it. Nor did the policy of avoidance preclude the court of appeals from deciding the merits issue before holding for the defendants on qualified immunity grounds. In response to a suggestion that the court's ruling could not have the intended law-settling effect, the Court pronounced that the merits ruling was "[n]o mere dictum". (Why not?)

(4) Although the Court held that it had jurisdiction to review the Ninth Circuit's decision, it expressly left open the question whether a court of appeals could review a district court decision in an appeal taken by a prevailing

defendant since "district court decisions—unlike those from courts of appeals— do not necessarily settle constitutional standards or prevent repeated claims of qualified immunity."

Justice Scalia, who cast a necessary fifth vote for the majority opinion, said that he did so because it "reasonably applies our precedents, strange though they may be". He added, however, that he would be willing to consider in an appropriate case whether it might be better "to end the extraordinary practice of ruling upon constitutional questions unnecessarily when the defendant possesses qualified immunity."

Justice Sotomayor, joined by Justice Breyer, agreed with the Court that the case was moot and that vacatur was the appropriate disposition but thought it improper to reach the "difficult" question of whether a prevailing party was entitled to seek review of a court of appeals decision.

Justice Kennedy, joined by Justice Thomas, dissented. In his view, review at the behest of a prevailing party violated the fundamental precept that judicial review will lie only to correct judgments, not to revise statements in lower court opinions. According to him, the precedents on which the Court relied were distinguishable. Obiter dictum was not a judgment in its own right, he added, and Camreta had no more standing to prosecute an appeal than would any other social worker or police officer. The Court, he concluded, had erred by providing the lower courts with "special permission to reach the merits" in qualified immunity cases when "settled principles of constitutional avoidance would [otherwise] apply."

Does the tangled skein of issue framed by the unusual posture of the Camreta case expose the Court's recent order-of-decision cases as resting on untenably shaky jurisprudential foundations?

In considering that question, note that less than one week after the decision in Camreta, the Court, in Ashcroft v. al-Kidd, 131 S.Ct. 2074 (2011)— in an opinion written by Justice Scalia and joined by Justices Kennedy and Thomas—accepted "that lower courts have discretion to decide which of the two prongs of qualified-immunity analysis to tackle first" and reasserted its own authority, when a court of appeals has ruled on both, to reverse erroneous rulings that a constitutional right exists even when upholding a defendant's entitlement to qualified immunity: "Although not necessary to reverse an erroneous judgment, doing so ensures that courts do not insulate constitutional decisions at the frontiers of the law from our review or inadvertently under-mine the values qualified immunity seeks to promote. The former occurs when the constitutional law question is wrongly decided; the latter when what is not clearly established is held to be so."

In al-Kidd, all eight participating Justices[a] agreed that the alleged actions of former Attorney General John Ashcroft in causing the detention of suspected terrorists as "material witnesses" to crimes (as authorized by a federal stat-ute), even in the absence of any intent actually to call them as witnesses, did not violate any clearly established constitutional rights. All participating Jus-tices also accepted that the Court had jurisdiction to decide whether any actual right was violated, even though it would suffice to hold that Ashcroft deserved to prevail on immunity grounds. Justices Ginsburg, Breyer, and Sotomayor nevertheless concurred in the judgment only. In their view, the merits issue

---

**a.**  Justice Kagan did not participate.

involved a number of complexities that the majority had not adequately reckoned with and that were better left for another case.

Following al-Kidd, would it be fair to say that the Justices view the problems presented in Camreta as limited to cases in which a defendant who has successfully asserted a qualified immunity defense seeks review of an adverse merits decision *and* the plaintiff does not seek review of the qualified immunity ruling? Some of the language in Justice Kennedy's dissenting opinion in Camreta seems to sweep more broadly, but how else could his joining of the majority opinion in al-Kidd be explained?[b]

**Page 1006.   Add to footnote 12:**

Recent studies disagree sharply about whether Saucier's order-of-decision rule had a significant impact in promoting the identification of new constitutional rights. Compare Leong, *The Saucier Qualified Immunity Experiment: An Empirical Analysis*, 36 Pepperdine L.Rev. 667, 670 (2009) (finding the "the decline in avoidance" mandated by Saucier "was accompanied only by a sharp increase in the percentage of cases in which courts explicitly held that no constitutional violation had occurred") and Healy, *The Rise of Unnecessary Constitutional Rulings*, 83 N.C.L.Rev. 847, 930 (2005) (reporting similar findings) with Note, *An Empirical Analysis of Section 1983 Qualified Immunity Actions and Implications of Pearson v. Callahan*, 62 Stan.L.Rev. 523 (2010) (concluding that the frequency of rights-affirming outcomes—in which courts found that the plaintiffs had alleged the violation of a constitutional right—"jumped from 34.2% of all pre-Saucier dispositions to 50.4% of all post-Saucier dispositions").

Examining circuit court practice in the wake of Pearson v. Callahan, Sampsell–Jones & Yauch, *Measuring Pearson in the Circuits*, 80 Fordham L.Rev. 623 (2011), conclude that circuit courts that ultimately held for the defendant and that thus had the option of ruling only on the immunity question instead followed the Saucier approach of deciding the merits question first in over 68 percent of all cases that cited Pearson in the calendar years 2009 and 2010.

See also Beermann, *Qualified Immunity and Constitutional Avoidance*, 2009 S.Ct.Rev. 139 (criticizing Pearson for giving lower courts "standardless, unreviewable discretion" about the order of decision in qualified immunity cases and urging a presumption in favor of ruling on the merits first); Jeffries, *Reversing the Order of Battle in Constitutional Torts*, 2009 S.Ct.Rev. 115 (arguing for a merits-first approach in cases involving constitutional rights that are difficult to enforce except through suits for money damages).

---

**b.** Pfander, *Resolving the Qualified Immunity Dilemma: Constitutional Tort Claims for Nominal Damages*, 111 Colum.L.Rev. 1601 (2011), argues that courts should allow plaintiffs in § 1983 and Bivens cases to avoid both the qualified immunity defense and worries about order-of-battle issues by seeking only nominal damages on the order of $1. Given the unavailability of significant attorneys' fees when a plaintiff recovers nominal damages only, how many parties could afford to pursue the type of action that Pfander proposes? With district court decisions generally having no binding precedential effect, and apparently being unable to create "clearly established" law, what incentives would defendants or their employers have to mount defenses against such suits as might be brought?

# CHAPTER X

# JUDICIAL FEDERALISM: LIMITATIONS ON DISTRICT COURT JURISDICTION OR ITS EXERCISE

———

INTRODUCTION: THE COORDINATION OF CONCURRENT JURISDICTION IN A FEDERAL SYSTEM

**Page 1016. Add to Paragraph (2)(c):**

See also Field, *Removal Reform: A Solution for Federal Question Jurisdiction, Forum Shopping, and Duplicative State Litigation,* 88 Ind.L.J. 611 (2013) (proposing to reduce duplicative litigation by authorizing removal to federal court of cases that involve federal defenses or are otherwise "likely to turn upon federal law").

———

## SECTION 1. STATUTORY LIMITATIONS ON FEDERAL COURT JURISDICTION

———

## SUBSECTION A: THE ANTI-INJUNCTION ACT

———

**Page 1036. Add to footnote 8:**

The American Law Institute's Principles of the Law of Aggregate Litigation (2010) § 3.14(a)(2) would limit collateral attacks to cases in which the court rendering a class action judgment lacked subject matter or personal jurisdiction, "failed to make the necessary findings of adequate representation, or failed to afford class members reasonable notice and an opportunity to be heard". For criticism of the ALI's proposal, and especially the narrowness of its definition of "adequacy of representation" exclusively in terms of "structural defects", *id.,* § 2.07 cmt. d, see Woolley, *Collateral Attack and the Role of Adequate Representation in Class Suits for Money Damages,* 58 U.Kan.L.Rev. 917 (2010).

**Page 1037. Add to footnote 11:**

The Court unanimously held the relitigation exception to the Anti–Injunction Act inapplicable in Smith v. Bayer Corp., 131 S.Ct. 2368 (2011). After a federal district court had denied class certification in a suit under a West Virginia consumer protection statute that was removed to federal court on the basis of diversity jurisdiction, the court, at the defendant Bayer's request, issued an injunction barring the named plaintiff in a parallel action in a West Virginia court from seeking class certification. In an opinion by Justice Kagan, the Supreme

Court found two flaws in the district court's conclusion that the relitigation exception applied. First, in holding that a class could not be certified under federal law, the district court had not determined whether a class could be certified under West Virginia law, which differs from federal law in some respects. Second, since no federal class action was ever certified, the named plaintiff in the West Virginia action was not a party to the federal suit and thus could not be bound by the district court's judgment. (Justice Thomas joined only in the first of these holdings, which the Court termed "little more than a rerun of Chick Kam Choo", but recorded no dissent from the second.) Twice in the course of its opinion, the Court quoted precedents establishing that "[a]ny doubts" in Anti–Injunction Act cases "should be resolved in favor of permitting the state courts to proceed."

----

## SUBSECTION B: OTHER STATUTORY RESTRICTIONS ON FEDERAL COURT JURISDICTION

----

### Page 1042.   Add to footnote 5:

See generally Solimine, *Congress, Ex parte Young, and the Fate of the Three–Judge District Court*, 70 U.Pitt.L.Rev. 101 (2008) (tracing the history of political support for three-judge district courts and attributing their near abolition in 1976 to considerations involving judicial workload).

### Page 1044.   Add a new footnote 5a at the end of Paragraph (1):

**5a**.  The Court both distinguished Hibbs v. Winn and appeared to limit its holding in Levin v. Commerce Energy, Inc., 560 U.S. 413 (2010). Levin involved a suit in federal court by one class of natural gas vendors seeking to enjoin the Ohio tax commissioner from granting statutorily authorized but allegedly unconstitutional tax exemptions to a different class (who delivered, as well as sold, natural gas). Writing for the Court, Justice Ginsburg found it unnecessary to determine whether the Tax Injunction Act (TIA) barred the action because the judge-made "comity doctrine", which commands federal judicial reluctance to interfere with functions better performed by state courts, furnished an adequate, alternative basis for dismissal. The TIA did not displace the comity doctrine, and neither did a Hibbs footnote that could be read to disparage comity concerns "recast" it. Moreover, Hibbs was distinguishable. Unlike in Hibbs, the challenged Ohio regulation addressed commercial matters and did "not involve a fundamental right or classification that attracts heightened judicial scrutiny." The plaintiffs were not true third-party challengers to an allegedly unconstitutional tax scheme, as were the Hibbs plaintiffs, but instead sought to improve their competitive position. Finally, if the plaintiffs should prevail on the merits, a state court would be better able than a federal court to determine whether the proper remedy would be to invalidate the exemptions granted to one class of natural gas vendors or to extend those exemptions to the plaintiffs. "Individually, these considerations may not compel forbearance * * *; in combination, however, they demand deference to the state adjudicative process."

Although the majority rested on the comity doctrine, a footnote suggested, without holding, that the TIA might have mandated the same result: "The District Court and Court of Appeals concluded that our decision in Hibbs placed the controversy outside the TIA's domain. That conclusion * * * bears reassessment in light of this opinion's discussion of the significant differences between Hibbs and this case."

Concurring in the judgment, Justice Thomas, joined by Justice Scalia, argued that the TIA forbade the exercise of federal jurisdiction and argued that "the 'proper course' is to dismiss this suit under the statute." Justice Alito also concurred in the judgment only.

By leaving the TIA's applicability uncertain and resting its comity holding on a "conjunction" of factors, the Levin majority rendered nearly as narrow a holding as it is possible to imagine, but also raised significant questions about the precedential force of Hibbs v. Winn. What might account for the Court's issuance of an opinion that unsettled more law than it clarified? Is it appropriate for the Court to rest on vague, judge-made notions of comity without deciding first whether a statute governs the case? *Cf.* Milwaukee v. Illinois, Sixth Edition p. 662.

---

# SECTION 2.  JUDICIALLY-DEVELOPED LIMITATIONS ON FEDERAL COURT JURISDICTION: DOCTRINES OF EQUITY, COMITY, AND FEDERALISM

**Page 1050: Delete the last three sentences from the second paragraph of Paragraph (1).**

---

## SUBSECTION A: EXHAUSTION OF STATE NONJUDICIAL REMEDIES

---

**Page 1062.  Add to footnote 4:**

For recent criticism of Professor Redish's thesis that abstention violates the separation of powers, see Marshall, *Abstention, Separation of Powers, and Recasting the Meaning of Judicial Restraint*, 107 Nw.U.L.Rev.881 (2013). Fallon, *Why Abstention Is Not Illegitimate: An Essay on the Distinction Between "Legitimate" and "Illegitimate" Statutory Interpretation and Judicial Lawmaking*, 107 Nw.U.L.Rev. 847 (2013), argues that if abstention involves an illegitimate judicial usurpation of congressional prerogatives, then so do a number of other federal courts doctrines, including many cited by Professors Shapiro and Friedman in the articles discussed on pp. 1061–62 of the Sixth Edition. Fallon relies heavily on stare decisis to reject any blanket condemnation of multiple doctrines as illegitimate, but he also rejects the view, which he ascribes to Professors Shapiro and Friedman, that past latitudinarian interpretations of jurisdictional statutes necessarily help to legitimate future claims of judicial prerogative.

**Page 1069.  Add a footnote 16a at the end of Paragraph (8):**

**16a.**  In Frost & Lindquist, *Countering the Majoritarian Difficulty*, 96 Va.L.Rev. 719 (2010), the authors cite evidence that state court judges who must run for reelection are sometimes under pressure to rule in accordance with majority preferences and argue that "federal courts should refuse to abstain in cases where it appears justice may be hard to find in state court". Do you agree that a federal court should decide a state law issue in a case otherwise fit for abstention because it believes that a state's court might decide a state law issue incorrectly due to electoral pressures—or for any other reason?

# CHAPTER XI

# FEDERAL HABEAS CORPUS

## SECTION 1.   INTRODUCTION

---

**Page 1153.   Add to footnote 2:**

A notable addition to the historical literature is Halliday, Habeas Corpus: From England to Empire (2010), whose rich account of the writ from 1500–1800 is not easily summarized. Among the themes with importance for the principal issues in this chapter are these: (1) by 1605, the writ had become "fundamentally an instrument of judicial power derived from the king's prerogative, a power more concerned with the wrongs of jailers than with the rights of prisoners"; (2) the King's Bench used procedural innovations in "transform[ing] habeas corpus from an instrument for moving around bodies as part of routine court business into an instrument for controlling other jurisdictions"; (3) the writ was not limited to detention of citizens but was available to aliens who came under the King's protection; (4) courts administering the writ had power over people, not places, and habeas corpus could follow those subject to the King's protection wherever they traveled, limited only by the practicalities created by distance; (5) though not strictly an equitable writ, habeas was administered equitably to do justice and redress wrongdoing; and (6) although a return's factual accuracy could not be challenged, judges evaded this limitation by looking to counsel, court officers, and affidavits to obtain additional information not contained in the return.

See also Freedman, *Habeas Corpus in Three Dimensions Dimension I: Habeas Corpus as a Common Law Writ*, 46 Harv.C.R.-C.L.L.Rev. 591 (2011) (arguing that in the colonial and early national period, demands for release from unlawful custody were made not merely through habeas corpus, but also through a variety of other common law writs, and that the full range of cases reflect a shared approach of treating a possibly wrongful detention as an emergency warranting swift and pragmatic resolution).

**Page 1159.   Add a new Paragraph (8):**

**(8) The Military Commissions Act of 2009.** In 2009, Congress enacted the Military Commissions Act of 2009, which amended the 2006 Act and provided greater procedural rights for defendants prosecuted before military commissions. See Title XVIII of the National Defense Authorization Act for Fiscal Year 2010, 123 Stat. 2190 (Oct. 29, 2009). The 2009 Act also established a new system of post-conviction review. A defendant who has been convicted by a military commission may first seek review before the Defense Department's Convening Authority, who has complete discretion to dismiss or reduce charges or to reduce the sentence. Thereafter, there is a right to appellate review— unusually, of fact as well as law—by the United States Court of Military Review, an Article I court. The appellate panels of that court have at least three military judges, but can have additional military or civilian judges; the latter are appointed by the President with the advice and consent of the Senate. Further review is available in the U.S. Court of Appeals for the D.C. Circuit, which has jurisdiction "only with respect to matters of law, including the sufficiency of the evidence to support the verdict". (Does the last phrase suggest more generally that the D.C. Circuit can review "mixed questions"—

that is, questions involving the application of law to fact?) Finally, there is certiorari review before the Supreme Court. Nothing in the 2009 Act addresses the availability or scope of habeas corpus.

---

## SECTION 2.    HABEAS CORPUS AND EXECUTIVE DETENTION

————

**Page 1180.    Add a new Subparagraph (2)(e):**

(e) In Al Maqaleh v. Gates, 605 F.3d 84 (D.C.Cir.2010), the court of appeals considered whether, in light of the Boumediene decision, the Suspension Clause grants a right to habeas review to detainees held not in Guatanámo but instead in Afghanistan. Three individuals suspected of being enemy combatants were seized outside of Afghanistan and then transported there for detention at the American-operated Bagram Theater Internment Facility outside Kabul. The district court denied the government's motion to dismiss for want of jurisdiction, viewing the degree of American control over the Bagram facility as little different from that at Guantánamo, and giving little weight to any practical barriers to the exercise of jurisdiction since the Executive had chosen to move petitioners there. The court thus concluded that, as in Boumediene, the statutory prohibition on the exercise of habeas jurisdiction was unconstitutional as applied to the petitioners.

On an interlocutory appeal, the D.C. Circuit reversed, applying the three factors that the Boumediene Court had found relevant: "(1) the citizenship and status of the detainee and the adequacy of the process through which that status determination was made; (2) the nature of the sites where apprehension and then detention took place; and (3) the practical obstacles inherent in resolving the prisoner's entitlement to the writ." As to the first factor, citizenship and status were no different from those in Boumediene, and given that the administrative hearing afforded the petitioners at Bagram was more rudimentary than the CSRT hearings afforded Guantánamo detainees,[2] the first factor weighed in the petitioners' favor. The second factor weighed in the government's favor, however, as the U.S. has no intention permanently to occupy Bagram and does not exercise the kind of de facto sovereignty present at Guantánamo. Most important, however, was the third factor, given Afghanistan's status as an active war zone and Bagram's exposure to all of the vagaries of war. The court acknowledged that a government transfer of detainees to an active theater of war for the purpose of evading habeas jurisdiction might in some cases be a factor relevant to jurisdiction, but found it unnecessary to assess the significance of that factor given the lack of evidence that the government had been so motivated in this case.

Consider the first factor set forth in Boumediene. Was the Supreme Court correct to treat the adequacy of procedures as bearing on the existence of

---

**2.**  By the time of the court of appeals' decision, the procedural and substantive protections afforded to those detained in Afghanistan were more robust than those that had been provided to the petitioners in Al Maqaleh, but the court decided the case based on the procedures afforded the petitioners. See Bovarnick, *Detainee Review Boards in Afghanistan: From Strategic Liability to Legitimacy*, Army Law., June 2010, at 9.

jurisdiction rather than on the appropriate scope of review when jurisdiction otherwise exists?

**Page 1189.  Add to Paragraph (5):**

For a powerful review of the history of the writ that supports Justice Scalia's position, see Tyler, *The Forgotten Core Meaning of the Suspension Clause*, 125 Harv.L.Rev. 901 (2012). Tyler reviews the history of the writ, and its suspension, from the Stuart period in Britain through the American Founding and up to the Civil War and Reconstruction. She concludes that persons owing allegiance to the government and thereby enjoying the protection of its law—most especially citizens—could not, absent suspension, be detained domestically except by the normal criminal process. That understanding extended, she argues, to persons suspected of aiding the enemy. She supports her argument by noting instances in which suspension was undertaken to permit the seizure and detention, outside of the criminal process, of persons accused of "adhering to the king's enemies" or taking up arms against the King. Although most of her evidence involves persons seized within a nation's sovereign territory, she contends that the extraterritorial seizure of Hamdi did not deprive him of protection and hence that he could not be detained outside of the criminal process absent suspension of the writ.

A quite different conclusion about the correctness of Justice Scalia's position is offered by Professor Harrison, in *The Habeas Corpus Suspension Clause and the Right to Natural Liberty* (forthcoming). Harrison argues that neither the text of the Suspension Clause nor historical practice places citizens outside the scope of permissible detention, noting in particular that during the Revolutionary War, both the British and the Americans held captured citizens as prisoners of war. He also contends, based on his review of English and early American history, that the Suspension Clause, despite its language, is not primarily about habeas corpus but rather about a substantive right to natural liberty. At the Founding, he argues, the central concept of a suspension was a law that conferred on the executive extremely broad discretion to detain— whether or not the judicial remedy of habeas corpus remained intact, and whether or not the detainee was a citizen.

**Page 1192.  Add to Paragraph (7)(b):**

The Supreme Court granted certiorari in the Al–Marri case, 555 U.S. 1066 (2008), but before oral argument, the newly installed Obama Administration decided to transfer Al–Marri out of military custody and indict him on federal civilian charges—a move for which the Justice Department sought the Court's permission, even though it maintained at the same time that the Court's permission was unnecessary. In March 2009, the Court, without opinion, granted permission for the transfer, vacated the Fourth Circuit's decision, and remanded the case with instructions to dismiss the appeal as moot. Al–Marri v. Spagone, 555 U.S. 1220 (2009). Al–Marri later agreed to plead guilty to a single count of conspiracy to provide material support to Al–Qaeda, in exchange for which the government dropped a second count. See Schwartz, *Plea Agreement Reached with Agent for Al Qaeda*, N.Y. Times, May 1, 2009, at A16.

**Page 1192.  Add a new footnote 7a at the end of Paragraph (8):**

**7a.**  For a review of the Supreme Court's habeas decisions arising out of the War on Terror up through Boumediene, see Fallon, *The Supreme Court, Habeas Corpus, and the War on Terror: An Essay on Law and Political Science,* 110 Colum.L.Rev. 352 (2010), which argues, *inter alia*, that the Court has grown more assertive in recognizing detainees' rights since the immediate aftermath of 9/11, partly in recognition of a changing political climate and a diminished sense of the urgency of the terrorist threat. Professor Fallon concludes, however, that doctrine involving the rights of persons who are identified as threats to national security is likely to be unusually volatile and that, "[s]hould the War on Terror become significantly more terrifying, all bets would be off." On this view, would you expect a post-Boumediene reduction in judicial assertiveness (because of events like the bombing attempts on Northwest Flight 253 on Christmas Day 2009 and in Times Square in 2010 and the Fort Hood shootings) or increased assertiveness (because of the more recent killing of Osama bin Laden)?

Compare Resnik, *Detention, the War on Terror, and the Federal Courts*, 110 Colum.L.Rev. 579 (2010), arguing that the challenges posed to federal courts by terrorism-related detention are continuous with those arising from other kinds of non-judicially authorized detentions, including solitary confinement of prison inmates in "supermax" facilities and immigration-related detention with only minimal procedural safeguards. According to Professor Resnik, post–9/11 jurisprudence illustrates the virtues of Article III judges, but judges are frequently unable to assure the fair treatment of detainees beyond the judicial gaze: "[I]f American law is to cherish human dignity, it will be because more than life-tenured judges make it do so."

### Page 1205.  Add a new footnote 2a after the first sentence of the first full paragraph:

**2a.** The study has been published. Denbeaux et al., *No Hearing Hearings: An Analysis of the Proceedings of the Combatant Status Review Tribunals at Guantánamo*, 41 Seton Hall L.Rev. 1231 (2011).

### Page 1208.  Add to Paragraph (4):

The federal courts in the District of Columbia, before which approximately 200 habeas petitions have been filed by Guantánamo detainees, have begun to address the kinds of procedural questions raised in the Sixth Edition.[a] In doing so, the courts presumably are implicitly, if not explicitly, determining what the Suspension Clause does, and does not, require when habeas courts review the detention of aliens, asserted to be subject to detention under the laws of war, who are held within the de facto but not de jure sovereignty of the United States.

**(a) Admissibility of Hearsay Evidence.** In Al–Bihani v. Obama, 590 F.3d 866, 879 (D.C.Cir.2010), the court held that hearsay is always admissible in these cases and that the only question is "what probative weight to ascribe to whatever indicia of reliability it exhibits."

**(b) Burden of Proof.** The Al–Bihani decision also ruled that the district court had permissibly adopted a preponderance of the evidence standard in reviewing the factual determinations of a CSRT. Thereafter, in Al–Adahi v. Obama, 613 F.3d 1102 (D.C.Cir.2010), the court of appeals requested supplemental briefing on the appropriate standard of proof, and the petitioner and the government agreed that the preponderance standard was appropriate. The court seemed unconvinced, citing cases from other contexts (review of deportation orders, selective service decisions, court martial convictions, and arrests) in which habeas courts applied a lesser standard—in the first two instances, a requirement only that there be "some evidence to support the order". Expressing doubt that the Suspension Clause requires the preponderance standard, the court nonetheless adhered to it arguendo, given the lack of adversary argument, in upholding the legality of the particular detention.

**a.** For discussion of a range of procedural and evidentiary issues arising in post-Boumediene habeas proceedings, see Azmy, *Executive Detention, Boumediene, and the New Common Law of Habeas,* 95 Iowa L.Rev. 445 (2010).

In at least some of the other settings noted by the court, an adversary hearing had been provided prior to the habeas proceeding. Isn't the difference between such a hearing and one before a CSRT a key factor in assessing the relevance of those precedents?

**(c) Presumption of Regularity**. In Latif v. Obama, 666 F.3d 746 (D.C.Cir.2011), the D.C. Circuit held that Government intelligence reports providing evidence against Guantánamo petitioners merit a presumption of regularity. This presumption " 'supports the official acts of public officers and, in the absence of clear evidence to the contrary, [allows] courts [to] presume that they have properly discharged their official duties' " (quoting Sussman v. U.S. Marshals Serv., 494 F.3d 1106, 1117 (D.C. Cir. 2007)). And the court noted that in Hamdi, the plurality had stated (albeit in dictum) that "once the Government puts forth credible evidence that the habeas petitioner meets the enemy-combatant criteria, the onus could shift to the petitioner to rebut that evidence with more persuasive evidence that he falls outside the criteria." The D.C. Circuit justified the presumption by arguing that "courts have no special expertise in evaluating the nature and reliability of * * * wartime records" and therefore should defer to the Executive Branch. The court stressed, however, that "[t]he presumption of regularity * * * presumes the government official accurately identified the source and accurately summarized his statement, but it implies nothing about the truth of the underlying non-government source's statement."

Judge Tatel's dissent argued that the presumption of regularity does not apply simply because an official action was performed, but only when government documents are the product of reliable and transparent processes, as is true with production of tax receipts, delivery of mail, and creation of business records. Here, however, the report was issued "in the fog of war by a clandestine method that we know almost nothing about," and he emphasized that it was, in the majority's own words, "prepared in stressful and chaotic conditions, filtered through interpreters, subject to transcription errors, and heavily redacted for national security purposes." He argued that Hamdi did not support the majority, because it justified a presumption only after the introduction of "credible" evidence, and he contended that requiring Latif to overcome the presumption of regularity would deny him a "meaningful opportunity" to contest the lawfulness of his detention, in contravention of Boumediene. Judge Tatel said he would apply a presumption of authenticity to the report, but would permit the factfinder to decide how much probative weight to accord the evidence.

**(d) Continuing Right to Counsel.** From 2004–12, an order issued by the United States District Court for the District of Columbia governed the access of Guantánamo detainees to counsel. In 2012, the government issued a new policy, under which access was significantly more restrictive, for detainees whose petitions had been dismissed or adjudicated on the merits. When that policy was challenged, the district court rejected the government's position that the court lacked power to determine the right of access to counsel when a detainee does not have an active or impending habeas petition and when it is only speculative whether a renewed petition will be filed. Appearing to rest its authority to regulate counsel on its understanding of its equitable power in exercising habeas corpus jurisdiction, the court ruled that access to counsel continued to be governed by the court order. In re Guantanamo Bay Detainee Continued Access to Counsel, 892 F.Supp.2d 8 (D.D.C.2012). The government did not appeal the ruling. For discussion, compare Kent, *Do Boumediene Rights Expire?*, 161 U.Pa.L.Rev. PENNumbra 20 (2012), with Vladeck, *Access to Counsel, Res Judicata, and the Future of Habeas at Guantanamo*, 161 U.Pa.L.Rev.PENNumbra 78 (2012).

**Pages 1208.   Add a new Paragraph (4a):**

**(4a)  Questions about the Substantive Scope of Detainability.** The habeas litigation in the District of Columbia courts has raised a range of questions about whether particular individuals may lawfully be detained. These questions of substantive authority reach beyond the existence of habeas corpus jurisdiction, the scope of habeas review, or the nature of the procedures followed. They turn on some combination of the scope of congressional authorization (in the Authorization for the Use of Military Force (AUMF)), the Constitution (which could be either a source of or a limit upon detention authority), and the content of international law to the extent that it is deemed relevant, itself a sharply-contested question. The Hamdi decision established, with respect to persons (including citizens) engaged in traditional combat in Afghanistan against the United States or its allies, that detention for the duration of the armed conflict in which they were captured is so fundamental and accepted an incident of war as to be within the "necessary and appropriate" force authorized by the AUMF. But Hamdi but did not establish the outer boundaries of detention authority.

**(a)  The Al–Bihani Decision.** The Al–Bihani decision, Paragraph (4), *supra*, addressed the scope of detention authority. The petitioner was a Yemeni citizen who accompanied and served as a cook in a paramilitary brigade that was allied with the Taliban and that included Al–Qaeda members within its command structure. Al–Bihani carried a brigade-issued weapon, which he never fired in combat. The brigade fought in Afghanistan against the Northern Alliance, a U.S. ally, to which the brigade ultimately surrendered. Eventually, Al–Bihani was transferred to U.S. custody and detained at Guantánamo Bay.

**(i)  The Government's Position.** In a court filing on March 13, 2009 in a different case, the Obama Administration set forth its view of the scope of the government's authority to detain those persons being held at Guantánamo Bay. See Respondents' Memorandum Regarding the Government's Detention Authority Relative to Detainees Held at Guantánamo Bay, In re Guantánamo Bay Detainee Litigation, Misc. Nos. 08–442, 05–0763, 05–1646, 05–2378 (D.D.C. 2009) The government rested its authority on the Authorization for the Use of Military Force (AUMF), which it said was "necessarily informed by principles of the laws of war", citing the Hamdi decision. It then offered this definitional framework:

> "The President has the authority to detain persons that the President determines planned, authorized, committed, or aided the terrorist attacks that occurred on September 11, 2001, and persons who harbored those responsible for those attacks. The President also has the authority to detain persons who were part of, or substantially supported, Taliban or al-Qaida forces or associated forces that are engaged in hostilities against the United States or its coalition partners, including any person who has committed a belligerent act, or has directly supported hostilities, in aid of such enemy armed forces."

The government stated that the laws of war are not well-defined with respect to an armed conflict against non-state actors like Al–Qaeda and the Taliban, and hence principles governing international armed conflicts must be adapted to this novel situation. In particular, the government noted that the terms "substantial support" and "associated forces" would require further development when applied to concrete facts in individual cases. Finally, the government stated that it rested its detention authority exclusively on the AUMF and not on a claim of inherent presidential authority under Article II (without, however, disclaiming such constitutional authority).

**(ii) The Panel Decision.** The Al–Bihani panel upheld the legality of detention, but viewed the government as having a broader detention authority than it had claimed in its March 13 definition. The majority rejected the premise that the laws of war limit detention authority, stating that nothing in the AUMF, the DTA, or the Military Commissions Acts of 2006 and of 2009 suggests "that Congress intended the laws of war to act as extra-textual limiting principles for the President's war powers under the AUMF". The majority added that the laws of war are not clearly defined and lack controlling legal force in the U.S. legal system. The court also looked to the jurisdictional provisions of the Military Commissions Acts of 2006 and 2009, which extend to persons who purposefully and materially support hostilities against the U.S. or its co-belligerents, and reasoned that detention authority under the AUMF "logically covers a category of persons no narrower than" the military commissions provision. (The majority did not mention that the Conference Report to the 2009 Military Commission Act declares that its jurisdictional provision "is included for the purpose of establishing persons subject to trial by military commission * * * and is not intended to address the scope of the authority of the United States to detain individuals in accordance with the laws of war".[b])

**(iii) Judge Williams' Concurrence.** Judge Williams, concurring in part and concurring in the judgment, reasoned that admissions made by Al–Bihani himself clearly established the lawfulness of his detention under the AUMF. He contended, however, that the majority's rejection of the laws of war as a limit on detention authority under the AUMF is difficult to square with the Hamdi decision, and added: "Curiously, the majority's dictum goes well beyond what even the *government* has argued in this case."

**(iv) The Denial of Rehearing En Banc.** The D.C. Circuit denied rehearing en banc in Al–Bihani without dissent, but several noteworthy opinions were written. 619 F.3d 1 (D.C.Cir.2010). Seven judges joined a brief opinion concurring in the denial, indicating that they declined "to en banc this case to determine the role of international law-of-war principles in interpreting the AUMF because, as the various opinions in the case indicate, the panel's discussion of that question is not necessary to the disposition of the merits." Judge Brown wrote separately to declare that the panel's view of the irrelevance of international law was not dictum but an alternative holding. She reiterated the argument in her panel opinion that international norms have no bearing on the scope of the AUMF and added that the government's position to the contrary warranted no deference.

Judge Kavanaugh agreed with the latter point. In a broad-ranging opinion arguing that international law imposes no limit on the scope of detention

**b.**  H.R. Rep. No. 111–288, at 862–63 (2009) (Conf. Rep.).

authority under the AUMF, he contended, *inter alia*, that (1) after the decision in Sosa v. Alvarez–Machain, Sixth Edition p. 680, customary international law has no force in the American legal system except to the extent that the political branches incorporate it in a statute or self-executing treaty; (2) the Charming Betsy canon,[c] under which ambiguous statutes should be construed in harmony with international law, should not apply in the post-Erie era, particularly when invoked to limit the scope of a congressional authorization of war; (3) it would be dangerous for judges to apply uncertain and shifting international-law norms to constrain the President; and (4) the Supreme Court has never invalidated presidential action on the ground that it violates the laws of war. In a separate opinion, Judge Williams disagreed with what he took to be Judge Kavanaugh's view that international law is a ratchet that can support expanding presidential authority (as in Hamdi) but not contracting it.

**(b) Key Issues About the Scope of Detention Authority.** According to Chesney, *Who May Be Held? Military Detention Through the Habeas Lens*, 52 B.C.L.Rev. 769 (2011), the decisions to date have "developed a consensus that membership in an AUMF-covered group is a sufficient condition for detention"; that operating within a command structure is a sufficient but not a necessary condition of membership; and that future dangerousness is not a necessary condition for detention. But questions remain about whether persons who are supporters but not "members" of Al–Qaeda or the Taliban may be detained— and if so, what kind of support must be established. In Hatim v. Gates, 632 F.3d 720 (D.C.Cir.2011), a panel reversed the district court's grant of the writ, citing the panel decision in Al–Bihani for the proposition that those who purposefully and materially support Al–Qaeda may be detained. But in the en banc proceedings in Al Bihani, seven judges were not ready to accept the broad reasoning of the panel decision in Al Bihani, at least in a case in which it was unnecessary to the decision.

**(c) Sources of Law.** The panel decision in Al–Bihani raised broad issues about whether the substantive scope of detainability is established by domestic law (*e.g.*, the AUMF), the laws of war, or other international norms (e.g., international humanitarian law).[d] Should detention be viewed as constitutionally unproblematic if properly authorized by Congress and permissible under the laws of war? What limit does the Constitution place on the class of individuals whom Congress may subject to military detention?

Similar questions arise with regard to the jurisdiction of military commissions to try individuals for war crimes. The Military Commissions Act of 2009 extends jurisdiction over an individual, not protected as a prisoner of war by the Geneva Convention, who (a) has engaged in hostilities against the United States or its coalition partners; (b) has purposefully and materially supported hostilities against the United States or its coalition partners; or (c) was a part of Al–Qaeda at the time of the alleged offense. Some scholars have argued that international law prohibits military jurisdiction over civilians unless they are direct participants in hostilities. In addition, the MCA sets forth certain offenses—notably conspiracy and providing material support for terrorism— that are not clearly recognized under the laws of war. What limits does the Constitution impose on the power of Congress to define offenses for trial before

---

**c.**  Murray v. Schooner Charming Betsy, 6 U.S. (2 Cranch) 64 (1804).

**d.**  For discussion of the bearing of international law on four questions that arise in detention cases—Who is subject to detention? What legal process is required? When does authority to detain terminate? And what

are a nation's repatriation obligations when detention ends?—see Bellinger & Padmanabhan, *Detention Operations in Contemporary Conflicts: Four Challenges for the Geneva Conventions and Other Existing Law*, 105 Am.J.Int'l.L. 201 (2011).

military commissions? See Vladeck, *The Laws of War as a Constitutional Limit on Military Jurisdiction*, 4 J.Nat'l Security L. & Pol'y 295 (2010).[e]

**(d) Express Conferral of Detention Authority.** Section 1021 of the National Defense Authorization Act for Fiscal Year 2012, 125 Stat. 1298 (2011) (the "NDAA"), declares that: "Congress affirms that the authority of the President to use all necessary and appropriate force pursuant to the Authorization for Use of Military Force * * * includes the authority * * * to detain covered persons (as defined in subsection (b)) pending disposition under the law of war." A covered person is defined as (1) "[a] person who planned, authorized, committed, or aided the terrorist attacks that occurred on September 11, 2001, or harbored those responsible for those attacks,", or "(2) [a] person who was a part of or substantially supported al-Qaeda, the Taliban, or associated forces that are engaged in hostilities against the United States or its coalition partners, including any person who has committed a belligerent act or has directly supported such hostilities in aid of such enemy forces." Section 1021 adds that "Nothing in this section is intended to limit or expand the authority of the President or the scope of the Authorization for Use of Military Force" or to "affect existing law or authorities relating to the detention of United States citizens, lawful resident aliens of the United States, or any other persons who are captured or arrested in the United States." But the new language codifies the Obama Administration's interpretation of the AUMF, as set forth above in Paragraph 4a(a)(i), and also (with respect to the question raised by the Al–Bihani decision, Paragraph 4a(a), *supra*) refers to detention "under the law of war".

**Page 1208.   Substitute the following for Paragraph (5):**

**(5) The End of DTA Review.** Whatever worries the Boumediene majority might have had about the quality of the DTA review process, the opinion stated that DTA review remained intact. See 553 U.S. at 795. But the D.C. Circuit has subsequently held that DTA review is no longer available. The court reasoned that the DTA's provision for review in the D.C. Circuit could not be severed from the provision purporting to preclude habeas jurisdiction that Boumediene had invalidated. The court did not view the Supreme Court's statement that the DTA remained intact as a barrier to its ruling, reasoning that Boumediene had not addressed the issue of severability. Bismullah v. Gates, 551 F.3d 1068 (D.C.Cir. 2009).

---

# SECTION 3.   COLLATERAL ATTACK ON CRIMINAL CONVICTIONS

---

**e.** For more on developments in the D.C. federal courts, see Wittes, Chesney, and Reynolds, The Emerging Law of Detention 2.0: The Guantánamo Habeas Cases as Lawmaking (2011), http://www.brookings.edu/papers/2011/05_guantanamo_wittes.aspx; Hafetz, *Calling the Government to Account: Habeas Corpus after Boumediene*, 57 Wayne L.Rev. 99 (2011); Vladeck, *The D.C. Circuit After Boumediene*, 41 Seton Hall L.Rev. 1451 (2011).

# SUBSECTION A: COLLATERAL ATTACK ON STATE CONVICTIONS

**Page 1215.   Add to Paragraph (3):**

In two decisions of limited reach, the Court has indicated that petitioners who file more than one year after the dates specified in § 2244(d) would nonetheless not be time barred if they can show either that their claim falls within the doctrine of equitable tolling or that they are actually innocent (under an exacting standard of actual innocence).[f]

**Page 1215.   Add to footnote 6:**

In Wood v. Milyard, 132 S.Ct. 1826 (2012), the Court unanimously held that when the state has not merely failed to raise a limitations defense, as in Day v. McDonough, but has expressly disclaimed reliance on a defense of which it was aware, the court of appeals abused its discretion by resurrecting the limitations issue.

**Page 1217.   Add to footnote 17:**

For a detailed empirical study of non-capital habeas cases on appeal, see King, *Non-Capital Habeas Cases after Appellate Review: An Empirical Analysis*, 24 Fed. Sent'g Rep. 308 (2012).

**Page 1219.   Add to Paragraph (2):**

A continuation of the study of petitions filed in 2003–04, focusing on appeals from the district court, found a somewhat higher overall success rate in non-capital cases. First, seven of the cases that had not been resolved when the original study was published later resulted in a grant of relief by the district court, raising the total number of cases in which the district court initially granted relief from seven (0.3%) to fourteen (0.6%). Second, another six

---

**f.** In Holland v. Florida, 130 S.Ct. 2549 (2010) (7–2), the Court held that § 2244(d)'s statute of limitations is subject to equitable tolling. The Court reasoned that § 2244(d) does not inflexibly require dismissal upon the running of the limitations period and is properly considered "nonjurisdictional". The Court added that substantive habeas corpus law has traditionally been governed by equitable principles and that § 2244(d) lacks many of the characteristics—such as emphatic wording, detailed provisions, a subject matter particularly calling for repose, or an unusually long limitations period—on which prior decisions had relied when holding that a limitations period is *not* subject to equitable tolling. Finally, the Court concluded that equitable tolling would not undermine the AEDPA's purposes.

In McQuiggin v. Perkins, 133 S.Ct. 1924 (2013) (5–4), the Court held that a petitioner who can demonstrate "actual innocence"—that in light of new evidence, no juror, acting reasonably, would have found the petitioner

guilty beyond a reasonable doubt—is not time-barred under § 2244(d). The Court noted that prior to 1996, actual innocence was a recognized exception to judge-made procedural limits to the exercise of habeas jurisdiction, and reasoned that in enacting § 2244(d) in 1996, Congress legislated in light of that exception. Accordingly, the Court held that § 2244(d) did not foreclose access to a habeas court by a petitioner who can make such a showing—even if, as in this case, the petitioner could not show due diligence in presenting a claim based on newly-discovered evidence. The Court stressed, however, that the standard for showing actual innocence is a demanding one.

In both cases, Justice Scalia dissented, contending that Congress, in § 2244(d), had spelled out the manner in which equitable considerations bore on the timeliness of a petition and that the Court lacked authority to create additional qualifications or exceptions to the limitations period.

petitioners obtained relief after the court of appeals reversed the district court's initial denial of relief. Third, the government appealed in six of the fourteen cases in which the district court initially granted relief and prevailed in two of those cases. Thus, a total of eighteen petitioners, or 0.8%, ultimately obtained relief. See King, *Non-Capital Habeas Cases after Appellate Review: An Empirical Analysis*, 24 Fed. Sent'g Rep. 308 (2012).

**Page 1232.   Add to Paragraph (2):**

King and Hoffman's argument is included in their book, Habeas for the Twenty–First Century (2011). They attribute part of the decline in the percentage of criminal convictions resulting in habeas petitions to improved litigation prospects in state courts (including state postconviction review) and to the increase in the percentage of dispositions by guilty plea. Their analysis leads them to propose limiting postconviction review for state prisoners in noncapital cases to claims that (1) rely on new rules of constitutional law, made retroactive on collateral review, or (2) the petitioner is in custody in violation of federal law and "has established by clear and convincing new evidence, not previously discoverable through the exercise of due diligence, that * * * no reasonable fact finder would have found him guilty of the underlying offense".

For a critical response to King and Hoffman's 2009 article, see Blume, Johnson & Weyble, *In Defense of Noncapital Habeas: A Response to Hoffman and King*, 96 Cornell L.Rev. 435 (2011). The authors argue, among other things, that in many state court systems there are impediments to meaningful appellate and postconviction review; that review by a tenured Article III judge is important; that it is mistaken to assume that racial discrimination, so egregious in the 1950s and 1960s, has ended; that the prospect of habeas review affects state court behavior, which would change under Hoffman and King's proposal; and that the proposed reallocation of resources to criminal defense is at once politically unrealistic and financially inadequate.

**Page 1237.   Add a new Subparagraph (3)(c):**

(c) In In re Davis, 130 S.Ct. 1 (2009), the Court transferred an original petition for habeas corpus to a district court, with instructions that it should hold an evidentiary hearing on a freestanding innocence claim raised in the petition. Dissenting from the order, Justice Scalia, joined by Justice Thomas, emphasized that the Court had never held, and indeed had expressed considerable doubt, that a freestanding innocence claim is constitutionally cognizable. For further discussion of Davis, see p. 37, *supra*.[g]

**Page 1238.   Add a new footnote 17 at the end of Paragraph (5):**

**17.**   In 2006, North Carolina established a commission to review postconviction claims of actual innocence. Drawing in part on a British model, the North Carolina Innocence Inquiry Commission hears claims of factual innocence by living felons. Applicants must offer evidence that was not presented at trial or on postconviction review and must waive all evidentiary privileges. The Commission operates non-adversarially, with power to investigate. If a majority find clear and convincing evidence that the applicant is factually innocent, the case is referred

**g.**   After the transfer, the district court reasoned that it would violate the Eighth Amendment to execute a prisoner who could show by clear and convincing evidence that no reasonable juror would have convicted him in light of the new evidence, but ruled that the petitioner had not made that showing. See 2010 WL 3385081 (S.D.Ga. 2010). Thereafter, the Supreme Court denied Davis' petition for a writ of habeas corpus. 131 S.Ct. 1808 (2011).

to a special three-judge panel that can exonerate the applicant only by unanimous decision. See Wolitz, *Innocence Commissions and the Future of Post–Conviction Review*, 52 Ariz.L.Rev. 1027 (2010).

**Page 1242.   Add a new footnote a at the end of Paragraph (4):**

a.   In Davis v. United States, 131 S.Ct. 2419 (2011), the dissent accused the majority of rendering a decision that was not compatible with the approach set forth in Griffith v. Kentucky. In the Davis case, a police officer conducted a search that was lawful under the decisions of the federal circuit in question. Accordingly, evidence obtained in the search was admitted at trial. After Davis appealed his conviction, the Supreme Court decided, in a different case, that a search like the one in Davis' case violated the Fourth Amendment. When Davis' case reached the Supreme Court, Justice Alito, writing for a six Justice majority, first ruled that under Griffith, the search must be found to be unlawful. But the Court went on to say that the question whether that violation required suppression of evidence was one of the appropriate remedy, and the remedial question was distinct from the constitutionality of the officer's conduct. The decision whether to apply the Fourth Amendment's exclusionary remedy turns on the balance of the deterrent value and the social cost of exclusion. Here, the officer had acted in accordance with binding judicial precedent, so there was no police misconduct; accordingly, suppression would serve no useful deterrent purpose. In dissent, Justice Breyer (joined by Justice Ginsburg) said that the distinction between application of a new rule and the availability of a remedy was highly artificial and "recreates the very problems that led the Court to abandon Linkletter's approach to retroactivity in favor of Griffith's." In many cases (unlike the present one) the question whether the officer's conduct was consistent with precedent will be unclear and contested, and the majority's approach creates the risk that similarly situated defendants will be treated differently on direct review.

The Davis decision appears to depend on the distinctive nature of the Fourth Amendment's exclusionary remedy, which the Supreme Court has repeatedly held not to be a right of the particular defendant but rather a deterrent remedy. As a result, any tension with Griffith is likely to be confined to the search and seizure area.

**Page 1245.   Add a new Paragraph (3a):**

**(3a) Threshold Issues vs. Routine Applications of Law to Fact.** In Chaidez v. United States, 133 S.Ct. 1103 (2013), the Court resolved the question whether its decision in Padilla v. Kentucky, 559 U.S. 356 (2010), announced a new rule. In doing so, it articulated a new distinction between "threshold issues" about whether a constitutional right applies and "garden variety" applications of established law to new facts.

In Padilla, the Court held that an attorney's failure to provide competent advice about the risk of deportation resulting from a guilty plea denies a defendant the effective assistance of counsel, in violation of the Sixth Amendment. Relying on Padilla, Chaidez, a *federal* prisoner, filed a collateral attack on her conviction. Assuming that the matter was governed by the principles of Teague v. Lane, the Supreme Court ruled that the Padilla decision did not apply retroactively. In an opinion joined by five other Justices, Justice Kagan acknowledged that a decision does not announce a new rule when it merely applies a governing principle to a new set of facts. Accordingly, "garden variety" application of the standards of ineffective assistance of counsel set forth in Strickland v. Washington "do not produce new rules." But the Court found that "Padilla did something more." It "considered a threshold question: Was advice about deportation 'categorically removed' from the scope of the Sixth Amendment right to counsel because it involved only a 'collateral consequence' of a conviction, rather than a component of the criminal sentence?" Before the Padilla decision, the Supreme Court had explicitly left open the question whether the Sixth Amendment governed the competence of advice to a defendant concerning a collateral consequence of conviction. And all ten federal courts of appeals and 27 of the 29 state appellate courts to consider the question had decided that a failure to inform a defendant of the collateral consequences of a guilty plea is never a violation of the Sixth Amendment. Padilla held otherwise, but, Justice Kagan said, "[i]f that does not count as 'break[ing] new ground' or 'impos[ing] a new obligation,' we are hard pressed to know what would." Although Padilla refused to recognize a sharp distinction between advice about direct and collateral consequences, "it is the very premise of Teague that a decision can be right and also be novel."

Justice Sotomayor's dissent (joined by Justice Ginsburg) viewed Padilla as a more straightforward application of the Strickland standard. She noted that the Padilla decision suggested that for at least fifteen years, "professional norms have generally imposed an obligation on counsel to provide advice on the deportation consequences of a client's plea," and had reasoned that a distinction between direct and collateral consequences of conviction was ill-suited to the issue involved there, given the "close connection to the criminal process" of deportation. Nearly half of the state and lower federal cases on which the majority relied predated the 1996 amendments to the immigration laws, which eliminated the Attorney General's authority to grant discretionary relief from removal in all but a small set of cases. Moreover, all but two of the federal appellate cases cited by the majority predated the Supreme Court's decision in INS v. St. Cyr (2001), Sixth Edition pp. 315, 1192, which although not involving a Sixth Amendment question, had stated that a reasonably competent lawyer will inform a non-citizen client about the deportation consequences of a plea, given that avoiding deportation may be more important to the client than any potential jail sentence. Lower federal court decisions following those developments had concluded that a lawyer's affirmative misrepresentations about immigration consequences of a guilty plea can violate Strickland, and both federal courts of appeals to address that question after St Cyr so held. The Teague standard, Justice Sotomayor said, is objective, and the mere existence of some contrary authority does not establish that a rule is new. In responding to Justice Sotomayor, the majority noted, *inter alia,* that "[i]n the years following St. Cyr, not a single state or lower federal court considering a lawyer's failure to provide deportation advice abandoned the distinction between direct and collateral consequences, and several courts reaffirmed that divide."[h]

The majority's emphasis on the "threshold" nature of the Sixth Amendment issue seems designed to leave intact the principle that the application of the Strickland standard—or more generally, the application of established constitutional principles—to a distinctive set of facts is not "new". Could one have characterized other Sixth Amendment questions—*e.g.*, does the Sixth Amendment apply to capital sentencing hearings—as "threshold" issues when they first reached the Supreme Court? Would such a characterization alone show that the question was new within the meaning of Teague, or does the force of the "threshold" argument depend upon the state of precedent in the Supreme Court and courts below?

**Page 1262. Add a new footnote 1a at the end of the penultimate paragraph in Paragraph (1):**

**1a.** In Knowles v. Mirzayance, 556 U.S. 111 (2009), the Court applied the Yarborough principle to the evaluation of a Sixth Amendment claim of ineffective assistance of counsel

---

**h.** Justice Thomas concurred in the judgment on the ground that he continued to believe that Padilla was wrongly decided.

under the standards of 28 U.S.C. § 2254(d)(1). Under Strickland v. Washington, 466 U.S. 668, 687–88, 691 (1984), a defendant seeking to establish ineffective assistance of counsel must prove that defense counsel's representation fell below "objective standard[s] of reasonableness" and that the deficiency gave rise to the "reasonable probability" of a different result. In his opinion for the Court in Knowles, Justice Thomas concluded that when a federal court considering a habeas petition assesses such a claim under § 2254(d)(1), the habeas petitioner faces "doubly deferential judicial review". Citing Yarborough, the Court noted that "because the Strickland standard is a general standard, a state court has even more latitude to reasonably determine that a defendant has not satisfied that standard." At the same time, the Knowles Court made clear that where its common law elaboration of the Strickland standard has established "a specific legal rule" to govern a recurring fact pattern, a state court decision will run afoul of § 2254(d)(1) if it fails to apply that rule.

For other decisions stressing the double deference due state court resolutions of claims of ineffective assistance of counsel, see Premo v. Moore, 131 S.Ct. 733 (2011); Harrington v. Richter, p. 137, *infra.*

In Renico v. Lett, 559 U.S. 766 (2010), the Court reaffirmed the difficulty habeas petitioners face under 28 U.S.C. § 2254(d)(1) when the underlying constitutional standard is framed in general terms. At issue was whether the Double Jeopardy Clause barred retrying Lett for first-degree murder after the state trial judge had announced a mistrial on the basis of her finding that the jury had deadlocked. Under established Supreme Court case law, double jeopardy principles do not bar retrial if the trial judge announces a mistrial based on "manifest necessity" (later refined to a "high degree" of necessity), and a reviewing court must defer to that determination unless the record reveals that the trial judge failed to exercise " 'sound discretion' " (quoting Arizona v. Washington, 434 U.S. 497, 506, 510 n.28 (1978)). The Court, per Chief Justice Roberts, held that the habeas petitioner, who had attempted to establish double jeopardy on the ground that the trial judge's grant of a mistrial was an abuse of discretion, failed to satisfy § 2254(d)(1)'s requirement of "an unreasonable application * * * of clearly established federal law". The Chief Justice emphasized that " '[t]he more general the rule' at issue—and thus the greater the potential for reasoned disagreement among fair-minded judges—'the more leeway [state] courts have in reaching outcomes in case-by-case determinations' " (quoting Yarborough v. Alvarado, Sixth Edition p. 1262). Justice Stevens, joined by Justice Sotomayor and joined in part by Justice Breyer, dissented.

If the constitutionally mandated standard of review asks whether the trial court abused its discretion in determining that the jury deadlocked, under what circumstances might the Court find that the state appellate court unreasonably applied the abuse of discretion standard? The Court suggested that if the trial court has considered factors " 'completely unrelated' " to the grounds for mistrial or has acted " 'irrationally or irresponsibly' ", review would be appropriate. How frequently could one expect to see such a course of action by a trial judge? Does the Court's position effectively insulate from habeas review state court determinations about whether there was manifest necessity for a mistrial?

**Page 1262.   Add to Paragraph (2):**

In Greene v. Fisher, 132 S.Ct. 38 (2011), the Supreme Court ruled unanimously, in an opinion by Justice Scalia, that "clearly established law", for purposes of § 2254, does not include Supreme Court decisions announced after the last adjudication on the merits in state court but before the defendant's conviction became final on direct review. The petitioner had argued that § 2254(d) should be interpreted in line with Teague v. Lane, under which a habeas corpus court may rely on new rules of constitutional criminal procedure announced before the conviction became final on direct review. But citing Horn v. Banks, Sixth Edition p. 1262, the Court stressed that the inquiries under § 2254(d) and Teague are distinct and relied upon what it viewed as the plain meaning of § 2254(d).[i]

The Court added that it need not decide the question whether § 2254(d)(1) bars a habeas court from relying upon a Supreme Court decision that was rendered after the last state-court decision on the merits when the case falls within one of the two Teague exceptions. Is it consistent with the thrust of the decision—that the inquiries under Teague and § 2254(d) are distinct and that the language of § 2254(d) is plain about the timing issue—to suggest that that question is open?

**Page 1263. Add to Paragraph (3):**

In Harrington v. Richter, 131 S.Ct. 770 (2011), the Supreme Court considered the application of § 2254(d) to summary state court decisions that deny federal constitutional claims on the merits without any explanation. After Richter's state court conviction became final on direct review, he petitioned directly to the California Supreme Court for a writ of habeas corpus. That court denied the petition in a one sentence summary order that provided no explanation. When Richter's federal habeas corpus case reached the Supreme Court, it ruled, without dissent, that the California Supreme Court's order was an adjudication on the merits within the meaning of § 2254(d). Justice Kennedy's opinion stressed that if § 2254(d) came into play only when the state court provided a statement of reasons, state judiciaries could be prevented from concentrating resources on cases where opinions are most needed. He noted that the California Supreme Court disposes of nearly 10,000 cases annually, including more than 3400 original habeas petitions.

Proceeding to apply § 2254(d), the Supreme Court said that a habeas court must determine what arguments or theories supported or, as here, could have supported the state court's decision, and then ask whether fair-minded jurists could disagree about whether those arguments or theories are inconsistent with the holding in a prior decision of the Court. The Court added: "If this standard is difficult to meet, that is because it was meant to be," as § 2254(d) was designed to be a " 'guard against extreme malfunctions in the state criminal justice systems,' not a substitute for ordinary error correction through appeal" (quoting Jackson v. Virginia, 443 U.S. 307, 332 n.5 (1979)) (Stevens, J., concurring in judgment). The Court added that to obtain relief, a prisoner must show that the state court ruling "was so lacking in justification that there was an error well understood and comprehended in existing law beyond any possibility for fairminded disagreement."

---

**i.** The Court said that the petitioner's predicament was one of his own creation, because he could have sought certiorari in the U.S. Supreme Court—which surely would have granted the petition and vacated the state court's judgment—or could have filed a state postconviction petition. Note, however, that defendants have no constitutional right to counsel before the U.S. Supreme Court or in state postconviction proceedings. Thus, most commonly the rule of Greene v. Fisher will affect prisoners who, while incarcerated, fail to read a recent Supreme Court slip opinion, understand its relevance, and prepare pro se a timely petition for certiorari or for postconviction relief.

Two Terms later, in Johnson v. Williams, 133 S.Ct. 1088 (2013), the Court extended Harrington v. Richter. In Williams, the defendant had argued, when appealing her state court conviction, that the trial court's discharge of a particular juror violated both a California statute and the Sixth Amendment's right to jury trial. The state intermediate appellate court's extended discussion of the dismissal never expressly stated that the court was deciding the Sixth Amendment issue. On habeas review, the Court of Appeals for the Ninth Circuit held that § 2254(d) did not apply, deeming it "obvious" that the state appellate court had "overlooked or disregarded" the Sixth Amendment claim; the Ninth Circuit proceeded to review that claim de novo and found a constitutional violation. The Supreme Court unanimously reversed. After noting that "Richter itself concerned a state-court order that did not address *any* of the defendant's claims," the Court said that there was "no reason why the *Richter* presumption should not also apply when a state-court opinion addresses some but not all of a defendant's claims." For the Court, Justice Alito noted several reasons why a state court may not expressly address one of many claims raised on appeal: the state law standard may incorporate a federal constitutional standard; the state court may view a "fleeting reference" to federal law as insufficient to raise a federal claim; or a state court may view a claim as too insubstantial to warrant discussion. He also noted that many state appellate courts have heavy caseloads and stated that federal courts have no authority to impose on them standards concerning the writing of opinions.

The Court rejected, however, the warden's submission that the presumption that a state court resolved the merits of a federal issue presented to it should be irrebuttable. Justice Alito suggested that if the state standard is less protective than, or very different from, the federal standard, the presumption may be rebutted, either by the petitioner (in order to obtain de novo federal review) or by the state (in order to show that the claim was not decided on the merits at all and hence might have been forfeited). Section 2254(d) does not apply, he stressed, if the federal claim was rejected because of "sheer inadvertence."

Turning to Williams' case, Justice Alito noted that the California Supreme Court had decided a case on the exclusion of jurors while Williams' appeal from the state intermediate appellate court to the state supreme court was pending; thereafter, the intermediate court of appeals' decision was vacated and the case remanded for reconsideration in light of the state supreme court's intervening decision. The state supreme court had clearly been aware, Justice Alito remarked, that it was deciding a question of federal constitutional dimension, as its decision had referred to, although it had not followed, three federal court of appeals decisions. Indeed, Justice Alito added, it was hard to imagine that a state court would interpret a state statute to provide less protection than the U.S. Constitution, as the statute would then provide little guidance. It was also hard to imagine, he added, that the state intermediate court of appeals, after reading the state supreme court's decision, could on remand have resolved the statutory issue without realizing that the discharge of the juror potentially implicated the Sixth Amendment. Given those circumstances, the Ninth Circuit's conclusion that the state court had overlooked the Sixth Amendment issue could not be sustained.[j]

---

**j.** Concurring in the judgment, Justice Scalia emphasized that a state court judgment denying relief necessarily adjudicates all claims that a prisoner has raised. As a result, he argued that to overcome the presumption that an issue was decided on the

**Page 1264.   Add to Paragraph 5:**

See also the discussion above of Greene v. Fisher, leaving open the status of the Teague exceptions under § 2254(d)(1).

**Page 1266.   Add a new Paragraph (8):**

**(8) De Novo Review Under the AEDPA?** In Berghuis v. Thompkins, 560 U.S. 370 (2010), the Supreme Court encountered the question whether, when § 2254(d)(1) clearly preludes relief, it is appropriate for a federal court also to address the question whether the state court's decision was correct. The federal court of appeals ruled that Thompkins was entitled to habeas relief, finding, *inter alia*, that the state court had unreasonably applied Miranda v. Arizona, 384 U.S. 436 (1966), and that Thompkins was therefore entitled to relief under 28 U.S.C. § 2254(d)(1). In reversing, the Supreme Court held that "[t]he state court's decision rejecting Thompkins' Miranda claim was * * * correct under *de novo* review and therefore necessarily reasonable under the more deferential AEDPA standards of review" (citing 28 U.S.C. § 2254(d)(1)).

Quite apart from disagreeing with the Court's understanding of Miranda, Justice Sotomayor's dissent (joined by Justices Stevens, Ginsburg, and Breyer) complained that "[t]he broad rules the Court announces today are also troubling because they are unnecessary to decide this case, which is governed by the deferential standard of review set forth in the [AEDPA]." Certainly, Justice Sotomayor is correct in stating that the Court needed only to decide whether the state court had made an "unreasonable application * * * of clearly established Federal law, as determined by the Supreme Court of the United States." Does that mean that any determination beyond finding that the state court had *reasonably* applied existing law constitutes dictum? Or is there a systemic interest in having the Court resolve unsettled legal questions *de novo* in § 2254(d)(1) cases? Should the Court ever exercise that authority in a 5–4 case? For a discussion of similar issues in the context of determining whether an officer violated "clearly established" constitutional rights for qualified immunity purposes, see pp. 115–118, *supra*, and Sixth Edition pp. 1004–06.

**Page 1269.   Add a new Paragraph (4):**

**(4) The Relationship Between §§ 2254(d)(1) and 2254(e)(2).** In Cullen v. Pinholster, 131 S.Ct. 1388 (2011), the Court considered whether, when determining if § 2254(d)(1) bars habeas relief, the habeas court may take account of evidence introduced in an evidentiary hearing otherwise authorized by the § 2254(e)(2). In this case, a prisoner claimed a denial of the effective assistance of counsel at his capital sentencing hearing. After that claim was rejected on the merits in state postconviction proceedings, he filed a federal habeas corpus action. The district court held an evidentiary hearing and granted relief. In affirming, the Ninth Circuit en banc ruled that a habeas court could consider new evidence adduced in an evidentiary hearing when determining under § 2254(d)(1) whether the state court's rejection of a constitutional claim was

merits, a prisoner could not rely on a claim of "sheer inadvertence," but instead must show, "based on the explicit text of the court's order, or upon standard practice and understanding in the jurisdiction with regard to the meaning of an ambiguous text, that the judgment *did not purport* to decide the federal question." And he stressed that under § 2254(d) as interpreted in Richter, "what is accorded deference is not the state court's reasoning but the state court's judgment, which is presumed to be supported by whatever valid support was available."

contrary to, or an unreasonable application of, clearly established federal law. The Supreme Court reversed the grant of the writ, 5–4, and only Justices Alito and Sotomayor agreed with the Ninth Circuit that when applying § 2254(d)(1), a habeas court may consider new evidence adduced in an evidentiary hearing.

Justice Thomas' majority opinion reasoned that § 2254(d)(1)'s use of the past tense—in referring to a state court determination that "resulted" in a decision that was contrary to, or "involved" an unreasonable application of, clearly established law—was backward looking and required an examination of the record when the decision was made. To permit consideration of new evidence would conflict with the purpose of the exhaustion requirement. "It would be strange to ask federal courts to analyze whether a state court's adjudication resulted in a decision that unreasonably applied federal law to facts not before the state court." Justice Thomas asserted that this approach did not render superfluous § 2254(e)(2), which sharply limits the authority of a district court to conduct a hearing; that section continues to have force where § 2254(d)(1) does not bar federal habeas relief.

Justice Sotomayor's dissent stressed that evidentiary hearings are held in only 4 of every 1000 non-capital cases and 9.5 of every 100 capital cases and are permitted by § 2254(e)(2) only when the prisoner was diligent or when very restrictive requirements are satisfied. In these limited circumstances, permitting consideration of new evidence does not upset the balance established by AEDPA. She contested the majority's linguistic argument by noting that § 2254(d) expressly requires district courts to base their review on the state court record—a direction that would be unnecessary if the use of the past tense in § 2254(d)(1) and § 2254(d)(2) required the same result. When § 2254(e)(2) permits a hearing, some courts of appeals had held (incorrectly, she declared) that § 2254(d)(1) simply does not apply; others had followed the approach of the Ninth Circuit. No court of appeals, however, had followed the majority's approach, which, she said, gave § 2254(e)(2) an unnaturally cramped reading and prevented diligent petitioners from having any court available to resolve their claims based on the relevant evidence available.

Justice Alito's separate opinion agreed with Justice Sotomayor's conclusion, although he would add a gloss to § 2254(e)(2) by precluding an evidentiary hearing in all cases unless the evidence was not and could not have been introduced in state court—a standard that, in his view, made the evidentiary hearing inappropriate in this case.

Under the majority's view, isn't the next logical step to bar evidentiary hearings until the habeas court has first determined that § 2254(d)(1) does not preclude relief?

After this decision, how much remains of the federal evidentiary hearing? The rare case in which § 2254(d)(1) is not a barrier is likely to be one in which (a) the state court determination is plainly wrong on the merits, or (b) no state court determination was rendered on the claim. In the first instance, no evidentiary hearing is likely to be needed; in the second, it is likely that the petitioner did not properly raise the claim in state court and the habeas claim will be barred by either the exhaustion or the procedural default doctrine.

### Page 1285.   Add to Paragraph (4), after subparagraph (b):

In Martinez v. Ryan, 132 S.Ct. 1309 (2012), the Court addressed the situation raised in Paragraph (4)(b) of the Sixth Edition. Arizona requires that ineffective assistance of counsel claims be litigated in state collateral proceedings rather than on direct review. After Martinez's conviction became final on direct review, his lawyer filed a state postconviction proceeding but made no claim that Martinez's trial counsel had been ineffective, instead stating that she could not identify any colorable claim to raise on Martinez's behalf. Martinez did not respond to the trial court's invitation to raise any claims he felt his lawyer had overlooked, and postconviction relief was denied.

Later, a still different lawyer filed a second state postconviction proceeding, alleging that Martinez's trial counsel had been ineffective. The state courts dismissed the petition on the basis of a state rule barring a claim that could have been raised in a prior state postconviction proceeding. Martinez then filed a federal habeas corpus petition asserting the ineffectiveness of both his trial counsel and his counsel in the first state postconviction proceeding.

When the case reached the Supreme Court, it ruled, 7–2, that the lower federal courts had erred in ruling that Martinez had procedurally defaulted. Justice Kennedy's majority opinion declined to decide whether the Sixth Amendment guarantees the assistance of counsel in state postconviction proceedings that constitute the first opportunity for a defendant to allege the ineffectiveness of trial counsel. Instead, the Court qualified its general rule that attorney ignorance or inadvertence is cause for a procedural default only where it deprives the defendant of the *constitutional* right to counsel, by holding that "[i]nadequate assistance of counsel [in a state collateral proceeding that provides the first occasion at which the ineffectiveness of trial counsel may be litigated] may establish cause for a prisoner's procedural default of a claim of ineffective assistance at trial." If attorney error in a postconviction proceeding could bar a claim that trial counsel was ineffective, the Court reasoned that no state court—and hence neither the Supreme Court on direct review nor a federal habeas court—could hear the claim.

The procedural default rules on habeas, the Court stated, "are elaborated in the exercise of the Court's discretion". Although it declined to decide the Sixth Amendment question, the Court borrowed from Sixth Amendment jurisprudence in ruling that cause can be established "in two circumstances. The first is where the state courts did not appoint counsel in the initial-review collateral proceeding for a claim of ineffective assistance at trial. The second is where appointed counsel in the initial-review collateral proceeding, where the claim should have been raised, was ineffective under the standards of Strickland v. Washington, 466 U.S. 668 (1984). To overcome the default, a prisoner must also demonstrate that the underlying ineffective-assistance-of-trial-counsel claim is a substantial one, which is to say that the prisoner must demonstrate that the claim has some merit."

AEDPA includes a provision, 28 U.S.C. § 2254(i), that states that "the ineffectiveness ... of counsel during Federal or State collateral post-conviction proceedings shall not be a ground for relief." The Court said that recognizing ineffectiveness as "cause" to excuse a default differed from recognizing it as a ground for relief.

Justice Scalia's dissent (joined by Justice Thomas) objected that the result of the Court's decision was no different from the recognition of a constitutional right to counsel in this postconviction setting. The Court, he claimed, may not have called into question the "legality" of denying counsel in postconviction proceedings, only its "sanity", for if counsel is denied, the state risks having to defend the adequacy of trial counsel in a federal habeas corpus proceeding, many years later. (But might not a state rationally choose that option, given that some prisoners will never file a federal habeas petition, while others will find their petitions blocked by other procedural rules limiting the exercise of habeas jurisdiction?) Justice Scalia also accused the Court of giving insufficient weight to the value of finality and of ignoring the frequency with which claims of ineffective assistance of counsel can be made. Noting the potential of a habeas corpus petition to delay carrying out capital sentences, he predicted that all capital prisoners will claim that trial counsel was ineffective.

Justice Scalia's dissent also objected that the Court's limitation of its holding to cases in which the State has barred litigation on direct appeal of the ineffectiveness of trial counsel "lacks any principled basis, and will not last. Is there any relevant difference between cases in which the State says that certain claims can only be brought on collateral review and cases in which those claims by their nature can only be brought on collateral review, since they do not manifest themselves until the appellate process is complete?" His fear was realized the following Term in Trevino v. Thaler, 133 S.Ct. 1911 (2013). There too, a prisoner sought to raise in a federal habeas proceeding a claim of ineffective trial counsel that he had not raised in state postconviction proceedings or on direct review of his conviction. Texas law did not bar the litigation on direct review of ineffective assistance of counsel claims. But the state courts had expressed a preference for litigating such claims in state collateral proceedings and had acknowledged that it was "virtually impossible for appellate counsel to adequately present an ineffective assistance [of trial counsel] claim."

In Trevino, the Court, with Justice Breyer writing for the majority, held, 5–4, that "where, as here, state procedural framework [sic], by reason of its design and operation, makes it highly unlikely in a typical case that a defendant will have a meaningful opportunity to raise a claim of ineffective assistance of trial counsel on direct review, our holding in Martinez applies." In a dissent joined by Justice Alito, Chief Justice Roberts objected that the narrow holding in Martinez was being greatly expanded. He complained that the Court's opinion was unclear about "how meaningful is meaningful enough, how meaningful-ness is to be measured, how unlikely highly unlikely is, * * * or what case qualifies as the 'typical' case." Justices Scalia and Thomas also dissented.

In considering how broadly the Trevino decision permits collateral litigation of ineffective assistance of counsel claims, note that Justice Breyer's opinion in the case detailed some of the difficulties facing any effort in Texas to raise such a claim on direct review. But one of the key problems—that the trial record often does not contain the information necessary to assess a claim of ineffectiveness—would commonly exist in any state system.

Consider also whether the Court's approach in Martinez and Trevino can be limited to the right to effective assistance of counsel. In Martinez, the Court stressed that that right is a "bedrock principle" of the criminal justice system. But could a federal habeas court refuse to excuse an attorney's error in failing to raise, in state postconviction proceedings, a claim (not discoverable earlier) that the prosecutor failed to disclose exculpatory evidence? What if the failure was that of a prisoner appearing pro se?

Finally, consider the majority's requirement in Martinez, reiterated in Trevino, that in order to establish cause, the petitioner must show that the claim of ineffective assistance at trial is substantial. That requirement quite evidently was developed to try to reduce the burdens on the state. But even where a substantial claim does exist, won't it often be difficult for a petitioner, who is likely to lack counsel and access to relevant materials, to prepare a habeas petition whose allegations satisfy the Court's requirement?

**Page 1286.  Add a new Paragraph (4a):**

**(4a) Abandonment by Counsel.** In Maples v. Thomas, 132 S.Ct. 912 (2012), a death row inmate was represented in state postconviction proceedings by two volunteers, both associates at Sullivan & Cromwell in New York City, as well as by local counsel as then required by Alabama law. Although state rules prescribed that local counsel was jointly responsible for representation, the Alabama lawyer told the Sullivan & Cromwell associates that he would serve only for the purpose of permitting them to appear *pro hac vice* on the petitioner's behalf.

While the state post-conviction petition was pending, both associates left Sullivan & Cromwell to take government positions in which they could no longer represent the petitioner. Neither moved to withdraw or in any way informed the court, the petitioner, or local counsel.

Thereafter, the state trial court denied the postconviction petition. The court sent notices to the two lawyers at their former address at Sullivan & Cromwell, whose mailroom returned the unopened envelopes to the court with an indication that they could not be delivered at that address. The court clerk took no action in response to the returned mail. Local counsel also received a notice of the petition's denial but took no action, assuming that the out-of-state lawyers would continue to take responsibility for the matter. No notice was sent to the petitioner, and no appeal was filed.

Petitioner's subsequent federal habeas corpus petition was dismissed by the lower courts on the ground that the failure to appeal in the state post-conviction proceeding was a procedural default. The Supreme Court reversed, 7–2. Justice Ginsburg's opinion for the Court said that the holding of Coleman v. Thompson, Sixth Edition p. 1285, that the negligence of a postconviction attorney does not constitute cause rests on the principle of agency law that a principal bears the risk of negligent conduct by his agent. Here, by contrast, petitioner's attorneys had abandoned their client, severing the agency relationship whose existence was critical to the reasoning of Coleman. Nor could petitioner be faulted for failing to act pro se when he had no reason to believe that his attorneys were no longer representing him. And given local counsel's failure even to call the two out-of-state lawyers when the notice of the decision arrived, the Court concluded that at that time, he was not "serving as [petitioner's] agent 'in any meaningful sense of that word'" (quoting Holland v. Florida, 130 S.Ct. 2549, 2568 (2010) (opinion of Alito, J)).

In dissent, Justice Scalia, joined by Justice Thomas, agreed that a petitioner's default "may be excused when it is attributable to abandonment by his attorney." However, he believed that other lawyers at Sullivan & Cromwell who had done some work on the petitioner's case were still representing him when the state trial court denied the petition. (To this, Justice Ginsburg responded that any such lawyers were not counsel of record and had not been admitted in Alabama and thus had no authority to represent the petitioner.) Justice Scalia also argued that the petitioner was represented by his local counsel, and that to treat his failure to call the lawyers in New York as a disclaimer of "any genuinely representative role" mistakenly equated attorney error with termination of the agency relationship.

What exactly distinguishes abandonment from attorney error? Is it critical to the Maples decision that both of the former Sullivan & Cromwell lawyers, in their new government jobs, were barred from representing private clients?

**Page 1291.   Add a new Paragraph (4) before Subsection E:**

**(4) The State Court's Failure to Decide a Properly Presented Issue.** In Cone v. Bell, 556 U.S. 449 (2009), the Court addressed unusual circumstances in which a claim raised in state proceedings had been neither waived by the defendant nor decided by the state court, leaving a federal habeas court free to decide the question *de novo*. The habeas petitioner, Cone, sought review of a Brady claim that the state at trial had withheld material evidence bearing directly upon an insanity defense. The state proceedings had been complex and circuitous, and Cone had raised several versions of the claim of prosecutorial nondisclosure: a state-law claim on direct appeal and in the first state postconviction proceeding; a federal Brady claim in his second state postconviction petition; and a new Brady claim in his second amended state postconviction petition, this one based on the state's disclosure of new evidence following another state court's novel ruling that prosecution files could be obtained under the Tennessee Public Records Act. With respect to the second amended petition, the state court dismissed some claims on the ground that Cone had waived them by not raising them in earlier proceedings and others, including his Brady claim, on the ground that they had been previously determined on direct appeal or in the first petition for state postconviction relief. The Tennessee Court of Criminal Appeals affirmed.

In a federal habeas petition that ultimately went up to the Supreme Court and down on remand three times, Cone sought to assert his Brady claim. After rejecting the state's contention that Cone had waived his Brady claim,[15] the Court, per Justice Stevens, turned to the state court's finding that Cone's Brady claim had received a full and fair determination in a prior state proceeding. Justice Stevens concluded that "[w]hen a state court declines to review the merits of a petitioner's claim on the ground that it has done so already, it creates no bar to federal habeas review." On the contrary, he wrote, such a determination "provides strong evidence that the claim has already been given full consideration by the state courts and thus is *ripe* for federal adjudication."

Cone's petition, however, presented a further procedural twist. The Court held that Cone's Brady claim was not limited to review under the deferential standards prescribed by 28 U.S.C. § 2254(d)(1). Justice Stevens reasoned that the state court had erred in concluding that his Brady claims had been adjudicated in a prior state proceeding. In fact, Cone's second amended petition presented a novel Brady claim premised on new evidence just released pursuant to the new state court interpretation of the Tennessee Public Records Act. Because § 2254(d) applies only to a "claim that was adjudicated on the merits in State court proceedings", Justice Stevens found that the predicate for applying that provision had not been satisfied. The Court thus reviewed Cone's

**15.** Although the state argued that Cone had in fact waived his Brady claim under state law, the Supreme Court treated the state courts' determination to the contrary as conclusive. Justice Stevens thus noted that "[a]lthough we have an independent duty to scrutinize the application of state rules that bar our review of federal claims, we have no concomitant duty to apply state procedural bars where state courts have themselves declined to do so" (internal citation omitted).

Brady claim *de novo*. Finding a Brady violation, the Court remanded to the district court to determine if the suppressed evidence might have affected one or more jurors' decision to impose a capital sentence.

How frequently can one expect to see a claim that is properly presented by the defendant but simply left undecided by a state court? Consider Chief Justice Roberts' separate opinion, which emphasized that "[t]he Court's decision is grounded in unusual facts that necessarily limit its reach."[16]

---

# SUBSECTION B: COLLATERAL ATTACK ON FEDERAL CONVICTIONS

---

**Page 1310.   Add to the end of Paragraph (8):**

For a decision refusing to provide relief under § 2241 in these circumstances, see Prost v. Anderson, 636 F.3d 578 (10th Cir.2011) (2–1).

---

**16.**   Justice Alito concurred in part and dissented in part. After reviewing the complex state court record, he concluded that Cone never raised his Brady claim before the Tennessee Court of Appeals and that his claim was thus "either unexhausted or procedurally barred". Justice Thomas, joined by Justice Scalia, dissented on the ground that Cone could not establish a "reasonable probability" that the suppressed evidence would have caused the jury to impose a different sentence.

# CHAPTER XII

# ADVANCED PROBLEMS IN JUDICIAL FEDERALISM

## SECTION 1. PROBLEMS OF RES JUDICATA

---

## SUBSECTION B: THE PRECLUSIVE EFFECTS OF STATE COURT JUDGMENTS IN FEDERAL COURT

---

**Page 1331. Add a new footnote 4a at the end of the penultimate paragraph of Paragraph (6):**

**4a.** Although the Supreme Court has not yet ruled on the question, and the courts of appeals are not unanimous, several of those courts have held that the Elliott decision (giving issue preclusive effect to a state administrative finding in a subsequent federal question suit in a federal court) does not require giving *claim* preclusive effect to a state administrative proceeding, at least in the context of a § 1983 action. See, *e.g.*, Gjellum v. City of Birmingham, 829 F.2d 1056 (11th Cir. 1987); Dionne v. Mayor and City Council of Baltimore, 40 F.3d 677 (4th Cir. 1994).

**Page 1334. Add a new Subparagraph (7)(c):**

**(c) Dicta in Gunn v. Minton.** In Gunn v. Minton, 133 S.Ct. 1059 (2013), also discussed at p. 95, *supra*, the Court held that the provision for exclusive federal jurisdiction over cases arising under the patent laws did not bar a state court from adjudicating a state legal malpractice claim based on the conduct of an attorney in a prior federal patent action. In responding to the argument that an important federal interest could be found in the possible issue preclusive effect of a state court ruling on the scope of the relevant patent, the Court said: "It is unclear whether this [i.e., the possibility of issue preclusive effect] is true. * * * In fact, Minton has not identified any case finding such preclusive effect based on a state court decision. But even assuming that state court's case-within-a-case adjudication may be preclusive under some circumstances, the result would be limited to the parties and patents that had been before the state court. Such 'fact-bound and situation-specific' effects are not sufficient to establish federal arising under jurisdiction."

Is the Court saying that even if the state court decision would have issue preclusive effect as between the parties in subsequent federal patent litigation, it could not be accorded *non-mutual* issue preclusive effect?

## SECTION 2.   OTHER ASPECTS OF CONCURRENT OR SUCCESSIVE JURISDICTION

**Page 1342.   Add to Paragraph (1)(a):**

In Skinner v. Switzer, 131 S.Ct. 1289 (2011), the Court, in phrasing the question presented, asked: "May a convicted state prisoner seeking DNA testing of crime scene evidence assert that claim [under § 1983] or is such a claim cognizable in federal court only * * * in a petition for a writ of habeas corpus * * *?" After Skinner's conviction in a Texas state court, Texas enacted a law allowing postconviction DNA testing in certain circumstances, but the state court rejected Skinner's efforts to obtain such testing under the new law. Claiming that the state's law, as interpreted by the decisions rejecting his requests for testing, constituted a denial of procedural due process, Skinner filed a federal court action under § 1983 seeking an order that the testing be performed. Reversing the judgment of the court below that the action was one that could only be brought in habeas, the Supreme Court held that the action could be maintained under § 1983.

For Justice Ginsburg, writing for the majority, it was crucial that "[s]uccess in [Skinner's] suit for DNA testing would not 'necessarily imply' [quoting Heck] the invalidity of his conviction." The test might well prove inconclusive or even further incriminate him. In no case, she observed, has the Court recognized habeas as the sole remedy—"or even an available one"—where the relief sought would not either terminate custody, reduce the level of custody, or accelerate release. And allowing such an action to be brought under § 1983 was not likely to result in a flood of litigation, since no such flood had occurred in the circuits that already allowed such an action and since the decision would not "spill over" to claims (under Brady v. Maryland, 373 U.S. 83 (1963)) that the prosecution had withheld exculpatory evidence to the prejudice of the defendant. Such evidence is, "by definition, always favorable to the defendant and material to his guilt or punishment."

Justice Thomas, joined by Justices Kennedy and Alito, dissented. While accepting *arguendo* the majority's conclusion that the specific relief sought, if obtained, would not necessarily imply the invalidity of Skinner's conviction, Justice Thomas argued for an extension of the Preiser–Heck rule "to all constitutional challenges to procedures concerning the validity of a conviction." Failure to do so, he contended, would undermine federal-state comity as evidenced by the judicial and legislative restrictions that had in recent decades been imposed on the availability of the habeas remedy. (He distinguished language in Wilkinson v. Dotson (Sixth Edition p. 1345), relied on by the majority, on the ground that the case related only to parole proceedings and did not involve the validity of a conviction.)

Should the Preiser–Heck doctrine have been extended as Justice Thomas urged? Isn't there a problem in holding that the existence of the habeas remedy is preemptive of other avenues of relief when the relief sought falls so far outside the core of the traditional habeas remedy that, as Justice Ginsburg noted, it is not even clear that habeas would lie?

**Page 1353.  Add to footnote 2:**

Rooker–Feldman continued to fare badly in the Supreme Court in the 2010 Term. In Skinner v. Switzer, discussed *supra*, the Court agreed unanimously that Rooker–Feldman did not bar the § 1983 action because Skinner "[did] not challenge the adverse [state court] decisions themselves; instead he target[ed] as unconstitutional the Texas statute they authoritatively construed."

**Page 1353.  Add to Paragraph (3):**

Consider a case in which a state allows a person whose property has been condemned by a municipality in a judicial proceeding to collaterally attack the judgment in that proceeding on the ground that the notice given was constitutionally inadequate. Should a federal court have jurisdiction to entertain a § 1983 action brought by that person against the municipality for damages allegedly resulting from the failure to give constitutionally adequate notice? See Ritter v. Ross, 992 F.2d 750 (7th Cir.1993) (holding that Rooker–Feldman barred such an action).[a]

Assume a case in which state preclusion doctrine—applied in the federal courts through 28 U.S.C. § 1738—does not bar a federal court from proceeding with an independent action after a state court judgment has become final. Should there be an exception to Rooker–Feldman if the federal plaintiff can show that the challenged state court judgment was obtained by fraud? The question has arisen in the context of federal attacks on state court mortgage foreclosure judgments, and a number of circuits have disagreed on the answer. See Baker, *The Fraud Exception to Rooker–Feldman: How It Almost Wasn't (and Probably Shouldn't Be)*, 5 Fed.Cts.L. Rev. 139 (2011).

[a]. See Buehler, *Jurisdiction, Abstention, and Finality: Articulating a Unique Role for the Rooker–Feldman Doctrine*, 42 Seton Hall L.Rev. 553, 597 (2012). Buehler argues that Rooker–Feldman has a distinct and valuable role in addition to those played by preclusion and the Younger abstention doctrines. First, it is "the only doctrine that bars federal claims complaining of injuries caused by final state court judgments." And second, at least under an expansive interpretation, it "bars collateral attacks on non-final state court judgments in civil cases lacking important state interests or where plaintiff seeks monetary relief." Is the Ritter case an example of the first category? Should an action in either category be barred if it otherwise meets all federal jurisdictional requirements and is not barred either by doctrines of preclusion or abstention?

# CHAPTER XIII

# THE DIVERSITY JURISDICTION OF THE FEDERAL DISTRICT COURTS

## SECTION 1. INTRODUCTION

**Page 1356. Insert the following after the fourth paragraph on this page:**

In 2011, Congress enacted the Federal Courts Jurisdiction and Venue Clarification Act of 2011, Pub.L. 112–63, 125 Stat. 758, making a number of changes discussed here and in Chapter 14 of this Supplement. With respect to diversity jurisdiction, the Act substituted for the 1988 change relating to resident aliens (discussed in this Paragraph of the Sixth Edition) the following language: "except that the district courts shall not have jurisdiction under this subsection [1332(a)] of an action between citizens of a State and citizens or subjects of a foreign state who are lawfully admitted for permanent residence in the United States and are domiciled in the same State." (For further discussion of this provision, see addition to Sixth Edition p. 1363, *infra.*)

The 2011 Act also changed the words "any State" in § 1332(c)(1) to "every State and foreign state". As a result of this change (part of which was suggested in the Sixth Edition p. 1373), Congress made it even clearer that diversity jurisdiction does not exist when, for example, a citizen of state A sues a corporation incorporated in states A and B. The change, along with corresponding changes in the "direct action" provision of this subsection (discussed at Sixth Edition p. 1356), also extended the reach of the subsection to corporations incorporated in other countries.

**Page 1361. Add at the end of Paragraph (4):**

Since fiscal 2006, the number of diversity cases filed, and their ratio to the number of all civil cases filed, has continued to rise. In fiscal 2011, 101,366 diversity cases were filed—slightly more than 35% of all civil cases filed during that period. See Table 4 of the most recent annual report of the Administrative Office, available at www.uscourts.gov.

## SECTION 2. ELEMENTS OF DIVERSITY JURISDICTION

**Page 1363: Add a new paragraph at the end of footnote 3:**

The constitutional issue raised in text and in this footnote (whether Article III permits a federal court suit on a non-federal question brought by one alien against another) has been mooted by the 2011 statutory amendment to § 1332(a), discussed above.

**Page 1367.   Add a new footnote 1a at the end of Paragraph (2):**

**1a.**  In Sherkow, *A Call for the End of the Doctrine of Realignment*, 107 Mich.L.Rev. 525 (2008), the author notes a division among the circuits on the proper test for applying the realignment doctrine laid down by the Supreme Court, argues that any test would be undesirable because it would necessarily force federal courts to examine the merits of jurisdictionally doubtful cases, and urges that the doctrine be abandoned altogether. Such provisions as 28 U.S.C. § 1359 (dealing with improper joinder) and § 1332(c)(1) (dealing with "direct actions"), he contends, are available to take up any slack.

**Page 1370.   Add to footnote 3:**

See also Cabraser, *Just Choose: The Jurisprudential Necessity To Select a Single Governing Law for Mass Claims Arising from Nationally Marketed Consumer Goods and Services*, 14 Roger Williams U.L.Rev. 29 (2009); Richardson, *Class Dismissed, Now What? Exploring the Exercise of CAFA Jurisdiction After the Denial of Class Certification*, 39 N.M.L.Rev. 121 (2009) (contending, after discussing the confusion in the decided cases, that a federal court's denial of class certification in a CAFA case does not obviate jurisdiction already acquired, but that federal courts should have the ability to abstain in such cases); Silberman, *Choice of Law in National Class Actions: Should CAFA Make a Difference?*, 14 Roger Williams U.L.Rev. 54 (2009) (stating that "if one views CAFA as designating specific types of class actions appropriate for 'national treatment'—that is, in need of federal jurisdiction to ensure neutral and non-parochial assessment with respect to class viability—it follows that such cases are also deserving of independent 'federal' choice of law rules"); Wood, *The Changing Face of Diversity Jurisdiction*, 82 Temp.L.Rev. 593, 605 (2009) (commending Congress' adoption of "a more robust form of minimal diversity", particularly in CAFA, as a useful "tool for assuring a national approach to national problems that happen to be governed by state law").

For an analysis addressing the questions posed in the final sentences of this Paragraph and persuasively contending that, despite the holdings of several appellate courts, a case removed under CAFA must be remanded if class certification is denied and federal jurisdiction depends solely on CAFA, see Note, *Class Certification as a Prerequisite for CAFA Jurisdiction*, 96 Minn.L.Rev. 1151 (2012) (also contending that upon remand, certification of a class in state court is not foreclosed). The Note argues that the lack of federal jurisdiction after denial is consistent with the principle that jurisdiction properly invoked is not ousted by later events because certification is itself an essential element of CAFA jurisdiction. Do you agree?

**Page 1373.   Add to Paragraph (3):**

Addressing the question of a corporation's "principal place of business" for the first time, the Court held unanimously that the "nerve center" test should apply in *all* cases. Hertz Corp. v. Friend, 130 S.Ct. 1181 (2010). Conceding that there is probably no ideal test, the Court concluded that this approach was not only supported by the text and history of 28 U.S.C. § 1332 (c)(1), but was easier to apply than any of the other tests that the lower courts had developed.

**Page 1374.   Substitute the following for footnote 2:**

**2.**  In Wachovia Bank Nat'l Assn. v. Schmidt, 546 U.S. 303 (2006), a unanimous Supreme Court held that for purposes of determining the state citizenship of a national bank, the word "located" in § 1348 refers to the state in which the bank has its main office and does not include states in which the bank has only branch offices. *Cf.* Note, *Determining Diversity Jurisdiction of National Banks After Wachovia Bank v. Schmidt*, 81 Fordham L.Rev. 1447 (2012) (arguing that the statute can and should be read to make a national bank a citizen of *both* the state of location of its main office and the state of its principal place of business, when the two states are not the same).

**Page 1374.  Add a new footnote 2a at the end of Paragraph (5):**

**2a.**  See Lund, *Federally Chartered Corporations and Federal Jurisdiction*, 36 Fla.St. U.L.Rev. 317 (2009) (questioning the judicial recognition of a "localization" rule for federally chartered corporations and urging Congress to enact a statute defining the citizenship (for diversity purposes) of all such corporations).

---

# SECTION 4.  SUPPLEMENTAL JURISDICTION

**Page 1400.  Add a new footnote 2a at the end of Paragraph (2):**

**2a.**  In a critique of the rationale of Exxon Mobil, Steinman, *Claims, Civil Actions, Congress & the Court: Limiting the Reasoning of Cases Construing Poorly Drawn Statutes*, 65 Wash. & Lee L.Rev. 1593 (2008), contends that the Court has redefined the terms "claim" and "civil action" by sometimes conflating them. Noting that the lower courts have not extended this redefinition to other statutory contexts though they may have a duty to do so under accepted notions of the effects of a binding Supreme Court precedent, Steinman argues that such an extension would have undesirable consequences, particularly in cases removed from state courts. She concludes by urging congressional action to clarify the law and to prevent such consequences from occurring.

# CHAPTER XIV

# ADDITIONAL PROBLEMS OF DIS-
# TRICT COURT AUTHORITY
# TO ADJUDICATE

## SECTION 1. CHALLENGES TO JURISDICTION

**Page 1412. Add a new footnote 3a at the end of Paragraph (1):**

**3a.** In an interesting article, Professor Vladeck argues that the rejection of the notion of "hypothetical jurisdiction" in the Steel Co. Case has had an effect on the precedential force of earlier decisions. Vladeck, *The Problem of Jurisdictional Non–Precedent*, 44 Tulsa L.Rev. 587 (2009). In particular, he contends that such World War II-era precedents as Hirota v. MacArthur (Sixth Edition pp. 272, 1182) and Eisentrager v, Forrestal (Sixth Edition pp. 272, 1173–74) proved "so easy to distinguish" in the post-Steel Co. decisions in Munaf v. Geren (Sixth Edition p. 1182) and Boumediene v. Bush (Sixth Edition p. 1168) because the earlier decisions, in denying jurisdiction, relied in significant part on "the Justices' conclusion that the detainees were bound to lose on the merits."

**Page 1415. Add to footnote 4:**

See also Clermont, *Sequencing the Issues for Judicial Decisionmaking: Limitations from Jurisdictional Primacy and Intrasuit Preclusion*, 63 Fla.L.Rev. 301, 321–32 (2011) (arguing that a federal court should be able to bypass the question of subject matter jurisdiction only when its dismissal on another ground is based on a threshold defect that the plaintiff can correct in a second suit).

**Page 1417. Add a new footnote 5a at the end of Paragraph (3)(f):**

**5a.** Professor Sisk uses the John R. Sand & Gravel case as an example of the unfortunate consequences of a congressional decision (appearing in the Act of June 25, 1948, ch. 646, § 33, 62 Stat. 869, 991) prohibiting the drawing of any inferences from the placement of a provision in a particular chapter of Title 28. Sisk, *Lifting the Blindfold from Lady Justice: Allowing Judges To See the Structure in the Judicial Code*, 62 Fla.L.Rev. 457 (2010). Since the time limit involved in the case appears in a chapter of Title 28 other than those dealing with "Jurisdiction and Venue", the placement of the provision would have lent additional force to the argument, rejected by the majority, that the time limit was subject to waiver. (Sisk goes on to question the constitutionality of § 33, and to urge its repeal.)

**Page 1417. Add at the end of Paragraph (3)(h):**

The Arbaugh decision was followed, and its significance reinforced, in Reed Elsevier, Inc. v. Muchnick, 130 S.Ct. 1237 (2010). The issue in Reed was whether a provision of the Copyright Act—which generally requires copyright holders to register their works before suing for infringement—was "jurisdictional." On appeal from the district court's approval of a settlement of a class action for copyright infringement, the court of appeals, acting *sua sponte*, concluded that the failure of some plaintiff class members to register deprived the district court of jurisdiction to certify the class and to approve the settlement. The Supreme Court unanimously reversed.

Justice Thomas, writing for the Court, quoted Arbaugh's statement that a limitation on a statute's coverage should be treated as non-jurisdictional "when Congress does not rank [that limitation] as jurisdictional". Applying that standard to the case at bar, he said that (a) the registration requirement was not stated in jurisdictional terms, and (b) there were no other factors suggesting that the requirement referred to the existence of jurisdiction. Bowles v. Russell, Paragraph (3)(f), Sixth Edition p. 1417, holding that the statutory time limit for seeking appellate review was "jurisdictional", was distinguished on the basis of its "context, including this Court's interpretation of similar provisions in many years past".

Justice Ginsburg, concurring for herself and Justices Stevens and Breyer, noted the "undeniable tension" between the ruling in Bowles and those in Arbaugh and Reed. She then distinguished Bowles—as well John R. Sand & Gravel Co, Sixth Edition p. 1416—on the ground that both relied "on longstanding decisions of *this Court* typing the relevant provisions 'jurisdictional' ", whereas the precedents relied on in Reed were lower court decisions, many of which were " 'drive-by' " jurisdictional rulings that should be accorded " 'no precedential effect' " (quoting Arbaugh).[a]

To return to, and rephrase, the questions at the outset of this Paragraph (Sixth Edition p. 1416), how important is it to determine whether or not a particular aspect of a statute's coverage, a particular condition on the ability to sue or appeal, or a particular defense is "jurisdictional", and how clear is (or should be) the line between what is jurisdictional and what is not? In what has become a substantial body of work in the area, Professor Dodson has argued, inter alia, that while there is a significant and useful distinction between issues of subject matter jurisdiction and other issues, the distinction is not one that must always be sharp and precise; moreover, jurisdictional rules often contain non-jurisdictional aspects, such as considerations calling for pragmatic judgments, while non-jurisdictional rules may contain such jurisdictional aspects as non-waivability. See, *e.g.*, *Hybridizing Jurisdiction*, 99 Cal.L.Rev. 1439 (2011); *The Complexity of Jurisdictional Clarity*, 97 Va.L.Rev. 1 (2011); *Mandatory Rules*, 61 Stan.L.Rev. 1 (2008). See also Bloom, *Jurisdiction's Noble Lie*, 61 Stan.L.Rev. 971 (2009) (contending that the "jurisdictional rhetoric" of firm inflexibility breaks with the "jurisdictional reality" of flexibility and suggesting, in support of the continued existence of this gap, that it "focuses adjudicative energy, encourages judicial caution, constrains jurisdictional discretion, and eases structural tension").[b]

---

**a.** Reed Elsevier was cited, and followed, by a unanimous Court in Henderson v. Shinseki, 131 S.Ct. 1197 (2011) (holding that the deadline for filing a notice of appeal with the Veterans Court—an Article I tribunal—did not constitute a jurisdictional requirement for appeal). See also Gonzalez v. Thaler, 132 S.Ct. 641 (2012) (holding, 8–1, that the provision of 28 U.S.C. § 2253(c)(3), requiring that a certificate of appealability granted to a habeas corpus petitioner by a district court shall contain a statement of the specific constitutional issue(s) in the case is "mandatory" but not "jurisdictional"; thus the failure to include such a statement in a certificate does not deprive the appellate court of jurisdiction over the appeal).

**b.** In an administrative law case, City of Arlington, Texas v. FCC, 133 S.Ct. 1863 (2013), the Court held that the FCC was entitled to deference, under the Chevron doctrine, on the question whether the agency had the power to take the particular action

# SECTION 2. PROCESS AND VENUE IN ORIGINAL ACTIONS

**Page 1423. Add at the end of Paragraph (1):**

In 2011, Congress substantially overhauled Title 28's general venue and related provisions in the Federal Courts Jurisdiction and Venue Clarification Act of 2011 (the "Clarification Act"), Pub.L. 112–63, 125 Stat. 758. Among the provisions is a new § 1390, which, in subsection (a) defines "venue" as the "geographic specification of the proper court or courts of a civil action that is within the subject-matter jurisdiction of the district courts in general", and in succeeding subsections excludes from the general venue provisions (except those relating to transfer) both removed cases and cases arising under § 1333 (admiralty, maritime, and prize cases). This section was designed to codify and clarify, not to change, existing law. But Congress went on to make other changes, including a revised version of the general venue provision, § 1391. The changes in this provision include:

● Elimination of what appeared to be a purely verbal distinction (discussed in this Paragraph of the Sixth Edition) between the catch-all venue provisions in diversity cases and in other cases (new subsection (b)(3)).

● A new definition, in subsection (c), of residency for purposes of the venue statutes. Under this definition, a natural person, *whether citizen or alien*, is a resident of the district in which he or she is *domiciled* (compare the discussion in Paragraphs (2) and (3) of this Note in the Sixth Edition); a non-resident of the United States, *whether citizen or alien*, may be sued in any district (compare the discussion in Paragraph (3) of this Note in the Sixth Edition); and a corporation *or unincorporated entity* with capacity to sue in its own name, if a defendant, is deemed a resident of any district in which it is subject to the court's jurisdiction with respect to the civil action in question, but, if a plaintiff, is deemed a resident only of the district in which it has its principal place of business (compare the discussion in Paragraphs (8) and (9) of this Note in the Sixth Edition). With respect to the last of these revisions, when would the residence of a corporate or unincorporated *plaintiff* be relevant for venue purposes?

**Page 1425. Add at the end of Paragraph (7):**

Ending some 200 years of confusion about the nature and significance of the concept of a "local action", Congress in the Clarification Act, *supra*, repealed § 1392. Of course, the location of land may still serve as basis for laying venue, for example, under new § 1391(a)(2) in a dispute over the ownership of the land.

under review. In response to the argument that the agency decision was not entitled to deference because the question of the agency's power to act was "jurisdictional", the Court said that in the administrative (as op-posed to the judicial) context: "[T]he distinction between 'jurisdictional' and 'nonjurisdictional' determinations is a mirage * * * [,] a false dichotomy".

**Page 1427.   Add at the end of Paragraph (3):**

In the Clarification Act, *supra*, Congress modified the result in Hoffman v. Blaski, discussed in this Paragraph, by amending § 1404 to allow transfer to a district (or division) in which the action could not have been brought if, *but only if*, all parties have consented. By limiting the change in this way, has Congress implicitly recognized the argument made in this Paragraph—that the venue provisions are designed for the protection of plaintiffs as well as defendants and thus a plaintiff may have a reasonable objection to transfer on a defendant's motion to a district that plaintiff has not chosen and in which venue does not lie under the general venue provisions?

---

# SECTION 3.   REMOVAL JURISDICTION AND PROCEDURE

**Page 1433.   Add at the end of Paragraph (1):**

In the Clarification Act, p. 157, *supra*, Congress made some significant changes in the provisions for removal. Among the changes are the following:

• The provisions for removal of civil and criminal actions are now dealt with in separate sections (§ 1446 for civil and § 1455 for criminal).

• Section 1446 makes clear that (as has been held) removal is ordinarily available only when *all* defendants properly joined and served agree to the removal; at the same time it resolves a conflict among the circuits by starting the time limit for removal for each defendant from the date on which that defendant is served (subsections (2)(A) and (B)); continues the overall one-year time limit for removal of diversity cases, but includes an exception if the district court finds that "the plaintiff has acted in bad faith" in order to prevent removal (subsections (c)(1) and (c)(3)(B)) (see the discussion of the bad faith problem on p. 1433, note 3 of the Sixth Edition); and provides that the sum demanded in good faith in the state court pleading shall be deemed to be the amount in controversy, subject to certain exceptions (*e.g.*, the notice of removal may assert the amount in controversy if non-monetary relief is sought or if state law does not permit demand for a specific sum or allows recovery of a larger amount than that demanded (subsections (c)(2) and (c)(3)(A)) (compare the discussion of prior law in Paragraph (5)(b) of this Note in the Sixth Edition).

**Page 1433.   Add a new footnote 1a at the end of Paragraph (1):**

**1a.**   Professor Field has made a comprehensive argument in favor of two major changes in removal jurisdiction: "reforming removal [1] so that resident defendants also could remove in diversity suits, and [2] so that in federal question cases, either party could opt for federal court on the basis of a federal cause of action or because the case otherwise appeared to turn on federal law, based not only on the complaint but also on the defendant's answer and the plaintiff's reply". Field, *Removal Reform: A Solution for Federal Question Jurisdiction, Forum–Shopping, and Duplicative State–Federal Litigation*, 88 Ind.L.J. 611, 666 (2013).

**Page 1433.   Add to Paragraph (3):**

As noted at p. 92, *supra*, Congress in 2011 overruled the specific holding of the Holmes Group decision and its implications for the removal of counterclaims arising under § 1338, but in doing so, made no change in the law affecting removal based on other counterclaims arising under federal law.

### Page 1433.   Add a new footnote 3a at the end of Paragraph (5)(a):

**3a.**   In *The Roots of Removal*, 77 Brook.L.Rev. 1 (2011) Professors Bassett and Perschbaker argue that the tension between the notion that the plaintiff is the master of the complaint and the defendant;'s right of removal is highlighted by several issues that arise when removal is allowed after the 30–day limit applicable in most cases under § 1446. One of these issues is that discussed in the text of this Paragraph: the judicially imposed requirement that the event making the case removable after the 30–day period must have been the result of a "voluntary" act of the plaintiff.

### Page 1435.   Add a new footnote 5a at the end of the first paragraph of Paragraph (8):

**5a.**   In 2009, Congress corrected its drafting error with regard to the time for appealing a remand order in a case removed under CAFA. Pub.L. 111–16, 123 Stat. 1607, changed the time for appeal from "not less than 7 days after entry of the order" to "not more than 10 days after entry of the order".

### Page 1435.   Add a new footnote 5b at the end of the first paragraph of Paragraph (8):

**5b.**   In Standard Fire Ins. Co. v. Knowles, 133 S.Ct. 1345 (2013), the Supreme Court held that a state court stipulation by the class representative that he and absent class members would seek less than 5 million dollars in damages (the amount threshold for removal under CAFA) does not prevent CAFA removal because the stipulation cannot bind absent members.

### Page 1435.   Add to footnote 6:

As part of a minor revision in the provisions of § 1442 (removal by federal officers or agencies), Congress in 2011 (Pub.L. 112–51, 125 Stat. 745) included cases removed under that section in its short list of exceptions to § 1447(d)'s prohibition of review of remand orders.

### Page 1437.   Substitute the following for footnote 8:

**8.**   In Carlsbad Technology, Inc. v. HIF BIO, Inc., 129 S.Ct. 1862 (2009), the Court followed existing precedent in allowing appellate review of a remand order despite the prohibition of § 1447(d). It ruled unanimously that, because the remand of a state claim following dismissal of an accompanying federal claim was "discretionary" under § 1367(c) and not based on lack of subject matter jurisdiction, the rule of the Thermtron case applied and thus appeal was not barred. But the skepticism about the results in Thermtron and subsequent cases expressed in the Sixth Edition (at pp. 1435–37) was evident in all the opinions. The Court (per Justice Thomas) explicitly stated that it was not considering whether Thermtron had been correctly decided because the question had not been raised by the parties. And in three separate concurring opinions, Justices Stevens, Scalia, and Breyer (joined by Justice Souter) all indicated their dissatisfaction with the Thermtron rule. (Justice Scalia compared the statute's "clear bar on appellate review" to the "hodgepodge of jurisdictional rules" that was "entirely of our own making", and Justice Breyer, after noting that the existing rules appeared to prohibit review of important legal issues while permitting review of matters of district court discretion, suggested that the whole issue be reexamined "with an eye toward determining whether statutory revision is appropriate.")

After a survey of the present state of the law on review of remand orders, Professor Pfander proposes a new solution: The Supreme Court should "reinvigorate its established powers of supervision" of the district courts by using its authority under the All Writs Act (28 U.S.C. § 1651) to issue an extraordinary writ to a district court that has committed a serious error in remanding a case to a state court. Pfander, *Collateral Review of Remand Orders: Reasserting the Supervisory Role of the Supreme Court*, 159 U.Pa.L.Rev. 493 (2011). At the same time, he suggests, the Court should "return[] to a literal reading of § 1447(d)" and close off all appellate review as of right. Section 1447(d) prohibits review of a remand order "on appeal or otherwise", but Pfander argues that a limited reading of that language is warranted both by the history of the prohibition and by accepted canons of statutory construction. Given the breadth of the statutory language, the argument, as Pfander recognizes, is not an easy one—though it may well be less of a stretch than that adopted in Thermtron and its successors.

### Page 1443.   Add a new Paragraph (1)(e):

(e) In the Clarification Act, p. 157, *supra*, Congress rewrote § 1441(c) to further limit its operation and at the same time (at long last) to resolve the constitutional issue discussed in Paragraph (2) of this Note and in Chapter VIII of the Sixth Edition (at p. 833). As now written, the provision permits removal of a state court action containing both a removable claim falling within the district court's original federal question jurisdiction (within the meaning of § 1331) and a claim *not* within the original or supplemental jurisdiction, but then *requires* severance and remand to the state court of any claim in the latter category. Only those parties to the removable claim are required to agree to the removal.

# CHAPTER XV

# OBLIGATORY AND DISCRETIONARY SUPREME COURT REVIEW

## SECTION 1.   STATUTORY DEVELOPMENT

———

**Page 1451.   Add a new footnote 21 at the end of Paragraph (9):**

**21.**   For an informative analysis of the availability and use of petitions for rehearing of a denial of certiorari, and of the Court's extremely rare willingness to grant a motion for leave to file such a petition after the expiration of the 25–day limit imposed by Sup. Ct. Rule 44.2, see Bruhl, *When is Finality ... Final? Rehearing and Resurrection in the Supreme Court*, 12 J.App.Prac. & Process 1 (2011).

## SECTION 2.   OBLIGATORY REVIEW

———

**Page 1455.   Add a new footnote 2 at the end of Paragraph (4):**

**2.**   Two recent articles have noted, with regret, the virtual disappearance of the exercise of the Court's certified question jurisdiction and have then suggested that its increased use might be preferable to the proposal by Professors Carrington and Crampton (in *Judicial Independence in Excess: Reviving the Judicial Duty of the Supreme Court*, 94 Cornell L.Rev. 587, 632 (2009)) for a "certiorari division" of appellate judges to choose cases for plenary Supreme Court review. *See* Tyler, *Setting the Supreme Court's Agenda: Is There a Place for Certification?*, 78 Geo.Wash.L.Rev. 1310 (2010); Nielson, *The Death of the Supreme Court's Certified Question Jurisdiction*, 59 Cath.U.L.Rev. 483 (2010).

## SECTION 3.   DISCRETIONARY REVIEW

———

## SUBSECTION A: COMMON LAW AND STATUTORY WRITS

———

**Page 1460. Add to footnote 3:**

The United Mine Workers case involved only a transfer to the Supreme Court of an appeal that the losing party had made to a court of appeals and that was pending there. In Camreta v. Greene, 131 S.Ct. 2020 (2011), discussed more fully at pp. 13, 27, 54, 113, 115, *supra*, a divided Court held that it had authority (to be used only rarely) to grant a statutory writ of certiorari to a party that had prevailed on appeal so long as the justiciability requirements of Article III were satisfied.

---

## SUBSECTION B: THE CERTIORARI POLICY

---

**Page 1463. Add to footnote 2:**

See also Owens & Simon, *Explaining the Supreme Court's Shrinking Docket*, 53 Wm. & Mary L.Rev. 1219 (2012), a study based on an examination of the dockets of Supreme Court Terms from 1940 to 2008. The authors conclude that both ideological and "contextual" factors are responsible for the decline in the cases granted plenary review, and go so far as to contend that a Court composed of Justices with a similar world view is "likely" to accept 42 more cases per Term for plenary review than a Court that is ideologically divided, and that Congress' decision to remove most of the Court's mandatory appellate jurisdiction has led to a decline in the plenary hearing of roughly 54 fewer cases per Term. The authors, who are critical of the decline on several grounds, predict that the Court's plenary docket will not increase significantly, at least in the near future.

**Page 1468. Add to footnote 6:**

In Thompson v. McNeil, 129 S.Ct. 1299 (2009), the Court denied certiorari in a capital case, with only Justice Breyer dissenting from the denial. But Justice Stevens, without indicating his vote on the petition, filed a "[s]tatement * * * respecting the denial of the petition", in which he left little if any doubt that he regarded the delay (of 32 years) since the petitioner was first sentenced to death as a violation of the Eighth Amendment, and that he viewed the long delays typical in capital cases as a significant factor contributing to his doubts about the constitutionality of the death penalty. This statement (like similar statements in prior cases, see, *e.g.*, Walker v. Georgia, 129 S.Ct. 453, 481 (2008)) prompted an opinion by Justice Thomas concurring in the denial of certiorari. In that opinion, he emphasized that the delays were due to petitioner's pursuit of every avenue of appellate and collateral review, sought to rebut Justice Stevens' other points, and described the horrifying facts of petitioner's crime in some detail.

Assuming that Justice Stevens did not vote to grant the petition because he knew that a majority of the Court disagreed with his views, can his "statement" be justified on the basis that it raises the visibility of the issue of delay in imposing capital sentences and exposes the disagreement within the Court?

**Page 1473. Add to footnote 6:**

Solimine and Gely continued and expanded their study of dismissals as improvidently granted (DIGs) in *The Supreme Court and the Sophisticated Use of DIGs*, 18. S.Ct.Econ.Rev. 155 (2010). Among their findings from a study of the practice from the 1954 Term through the 2004 Term: (1) Only some 2% of cases decided by the Court were DIGged; (2) The Court was more likely to DIG cases raising constitutional issues; (3) The Court generally DIGged a case only when at least six Justices voted to do so; but in 14 instances (of a total of 155) the vote to DIG was 5–4; (4) T he Burger and Rehnquist Courts were more likely to DIG a case when the ideological position of the decision below was consistent with that of the Court's majority, but the same was not true of the Warren Court. With respect to the third finding, should the

Court ever DIG a case by a 5–4 vote, at least if the four dissenting Justices all initially voted to grant?

## Page 1479.   Add to footnote 9:

In his important essay, *On Avoiding Avoidance, Agenda Control, and Other Matters*, 112 Colum.L.Rev. 665 (2012), Professor Monaghan argues that the Court has been embracing a "law declaration" model (see Sixth Edition pp. 72–80 and p. 4, *supra*), and has been expanding its authority through a range of devices, including injection of new issues into cases heard on the merits and the appointment of amici to defend judgments. At the end of the essay, Monaghan considers the Court's certiorari power and suggests that the Court's Rule 10, relating to the grounds for granting certiorari, does little or nothing to confine "Bickelian-inspired prudential discretion".

## Page 1480.   Add to footnote 13:

For an unusual 5–4 summary reversal on the certiorari papers, see Spears v. United States, 129 S.Ct. 840 (2009). The majority, in a per curiam opinion, reversed the decision below on the ground that, contrary to the view of the appellate court, a prior Supreme Court decision allowed categorical (and not just individualized) departures from the Sentencing Guidelines' 100:1 ratio between offenses involving crack cocaine and powder cocaine. Justice Thomas dissented without opinion. Justice Kennedy would have granted the petition and set the case for briefing and argument. Chief Justice Roberts, joined by Justice Alito, dissented on the grounds that the case was both inappropriate for summary reversal (because of the difficulty of the question presented) and, given the lack of a present division in the circuits, an inappropriate one for a grant of certiorari.

If the majority agreed with the Chief Justice that the case did not warrant a full hearing but also concluded that the court below committed plain error, can the summary reversal be justified on the ground that, in the majority's view, such an error (involving the legal basis for a prison sentence) should not be allowed to persist?

## Page 1481.   Add a new footnote 14a at the end of Paragraph (5):

**14a.**   Disagreements over the proper use of the GVR persist within the Court. Thus in Webster v. Cooper, 130 S.Ct. 456 (2009), Justice Scalia dissented from a GVR asking the court below to reconsider its decision in light of a Supreme Court ruling handed down over two months *before* the lower court's decision. And in Wellons v. Hall, 130 S.Ct. 727 (2010), four Justices, in two opinions dissenting from a GVR, contended that the court below had rested its decision not only on a procedural ground rejected by a later Supreme Court ruling in another case but *also* on its separate conclusion that no relief was warranted on the merits. In one of the dissents, Justice Scalia, joined by Justice Thomas, used the occasion to object to a "systematic degradation of our traditional requirements for a GVR"—a development that, in his view, "disrespects the judges of the Courts of Appeals".

In a comprehensive study of the GVR, Professor Bruhl concludes that the present practice of the Court is problematic across a wide range of cases, in that it is inefficient for litigants and poses too heavy a burden on the Supreme Court. Bruhl, *The Supreme Court's Controversial GVRs—And an Alternative,* 107 Mich.L.Rev. 711 (2009). He urges, *inter alia*, that the lower courts use or (if necessary) be given greater authority to deal with cases in which, *before* the filing of a certiorari petition, there is a relevant Supreme Court decision changing or clarifying the law, or in which the Supreme Court has granted certiorari in a similar case. In such instances, he argues, the Court's use of the GVR is neither necessary nor appropriate.

## Page 1482.   Add at the end of Paragraph (6):

● A study of the dockets for the 1986–94 Terms, including the cert pool memos, that tested two hypotheses: (1) if the Court's concern over a conflict between lower court decisions relates to a question of "policy" or "ideology", the Court is more likely to grant certiorari as the distance between the conflicting policy positions increases, and (2) in such cases, the Court is more likely to grant review "as the distance between the Court [measured by what the authors describe as the ideological position of the 'median' Justice in the prior Term] and one side of the conflict increases." Grant, Hendrickson & Lynch, *The Ideological Divide: Conflict and the Supreme Court's Certiorari Decision*, 60 Clev.St.L.Rev. 559 (2012). The authors conclude that the data are consistent with the first hypothesis but lend only "the weakest of support" to the second.

• A study by Owens and Simon (discussed at p. 162, *supra*) that examined the Court's dockets over almost 70 Terms in an effort to determine the causes of the decline in cases granted plenary review.

### Page 1482.   Add to footnote 18:

In a recent critique of the certiorari practice, Watts, *Constraining Certiorari Using Administrative Law Principles*, 160 U.Pa.L.Rev. 1 (2011), echoes the Provine study in proposing mandatory disclosure of individual votes on certiorari petitions, and suggests that in formulating such a rule, the drafters might want to distinguish between those cases that are not placed on the "discussion" list and those that are (see Sixth Edition pp. 1463–64 for a review of this practice), and between petitions that are denied and those that are granted.

†